WITHDRAWN

MAO TSE-TUNG

The photographs of Mao Tse-tung on the following pages reveal his many-sided personality at several stages of his career. They show him as revolutionary poet and scholar, as leader of the incredibly difficult but victorious Long March, and finally as ruler of communist China.

HENRY SCHUMAN INC   NEW YORK

Mao Tse-tung

Ruler of Red China

Robert Payne

To the memory of **Stephen Simmons**
the first English correspondent to die in the Korean War.

Contents

	Introduction	XV
ONE	The Forerunners	3
TWO	The Young Rebel	24
THREE	The New Youth	52
FOUR	The Years of Warning	75
FIVE	Five Battles	109
SIX	The Long March	138
SEVEN	The Years in the Desert	157
EIGHT	Five Books	171
NINE	The Storm Breaks	200
TEN	The Wind and the Sand	222
ELEVEN	The Conquest of China	241
TWELVE	The Shape of the Future	263
	Chronological Table	281
	Bibliography	291
	Index	295

Illustrations

Five photographs of Mao Tse-tung   iii–vi

MAPS

First Annihilation Campaign   115
Second Annihilation Campaign   118
Third Annihilation Campaign   121
The Long March   142
The Conquest of China 1948–1950   249

Introduction

This book is a study of the mind of Mao Tse-tung from his
birth in a small village in Hunan to his arrival in Peking as
the conqueror of China in 1949. I have been more interested
in the influences which went to form his mind than in a
recital of his day to day activities: so the Taiping rebellion,
the translations of Yen Fu, the commentaries of Kang Yu-wei,
his friendship with Hsiao San, the long period under which
he was under the influence of Chen Tu-hsiu, and his close
attachment to Hu Han-min are studied at some length, and I
have discussed his poetry, his political writings and his theories of guerrilla warfare as though they are, as I believe them
to be, more important than his actions, or even his political
speeches. I have said little about his associates, men like Chou
En-lai, Chu Teh, Lin Piao and Peng Teh-huei, without
whom the victory might never have come about, because
enough is known about them from the writings of Edgar
Snow, Nym Wales, Agnes Smedley and others. Mao Tse-tung
did not, of course, launch the Chinese Communist revolution
single-handed, and in a sense this book is unfair to his friends.

Their successes resulted from the sharp interplay of many minds with many different origins, and almost alone of the leaders Mao Tse-tung possessed no roots abroad, and was therefore untypical. But because all the leaders recognize his primacy and nearly all the important decisions were made by him, it has seemed best to study him alone, even if sometimes he seems to be removed from a proper context.

I am aware that there is a tendency to condemn an interest in the historical origins of Chinese communism. To discuss them at all may seem a betrayal of democratic principles: to those who have decided that the Communist conquest of China is the work of the devil this book will have nothing to offer. But I suggest that an understanding of the origins of Chinese communism has never been more necessary than at the present. The famous Chinese rhyming adage, which reads in English: "Know yourself, know enemy: hundred battles, hundred victories" is one which we should follow with considerable humility if we are to understand the revolutionary movement which has swept over a fifth of the world's population.

We have been fatally ignorant. Catastrophic mistakes have been made because politicians and military commanders were completely unaware of the forces at work. It is almost as though the West had turned its face away from any effort at understanding, secure in the knowledge of its own ignorance, with the result that policies undertaken under one set of circumstances were continued when the circumstances were entirely reversed, only because no one was aware of change. Today we are faced with a threat of unimaginable potential violence; and for the first time we are presented with the possibility that our whole civilization may perish, not because its foundations are invalid, but because we are unaware of the nature of the emerging civilization which confronts us.

Today, Mao Tse-tung could, if he desired, command an army vastly larger than anyone has ever commanded before. A new, vigorous and defiant China has emerged. For the first time in centuries China is ruled by men who are perfectly conscious of having their roots among the people who are most numerous and most representative—the peasants. To underestimate the power of the new China would be dangerous, and there is hardly anything quite so important as the deliberate attempt to understand the new forces at work.

In writing this book I have been helped by long talks with Hsiao San in Kalgan; by visits to Hsiang T'an, Changsha, Peking, and Yenan; and by friends in America who have very kindly put their libraries at my disposal.

Some sentences and phrases in this book are based on material contained in my *China Awake* (Dodd, Mead, 1947) and *The Revolt of Asia* (John Day, 1947), and in articles which have appeared in *Asian Horizon, World Review,* and *United Nations World.* The usual acknowledgments are made to the publishers of these books and periodicals.

ROBERT PAYNE

MAO TSE-TUNG

The Forerunners

The greatest mistake ever made concerning the Chinese was to believe that they were a gentle and scholarly race removed from the temptations of modern civilization. Even now there is a tendency to regard the Chinese as though they were the ectoplasms described by Lin Yu-tang—those ghostly scholars who wave ghostly fans and believe in the importance of living with the utmost tranquillity. We forget the vigor and violence of the Chinese mind at its best, grappling with human problems like naked wrestlers. Worst of all, we forget that China is the hardest and toughest of all countries to live in.

For a hundred years there have been continual revolutions in China: most of them came about as the result of the invasion of Western ideas. After the Opium War of 1840-42 a hurricane began to blow through China. The hurricane was to continue to blow for more than a hundred years. The settled traditions were destroyed; no other traditions came to take their place. Somehow, by some means unknown, it was necessary to destroy the Manchus and replace them with another kind of rule altogether, based upon the experiences of the West, but until recently it was impossible to obtain the assent of the Chinese people. The revolutionaries, many of them trained abroad, were rarely in a position to understand the problems which weighed most heavily on the people; and the successive failures of successive revolts embittered the people against the revolutionaries. Yet four of these revolutionaries are outstanding, and because three of them are almost unknown in the West, and all of them deeply influenced the Chinese Communist revolution, they should be discussed briefly. The first, and perhaps the most important, was a peasant from Kwangtung who ruled over vast areas of central China in the middle years of the last century: a strange genius who believed devoutly in Christianity and called himself "the younger brother of God" and "the Prince of Heaven."

HUNG HSU-CH'UAN

Tall, thin, with a slight stammer, unusually large almond eyes, and delicate small ears, Hung Hsu-ch'uan in his youth was probably the last person anyone would believe to be a future emperor of China and a consummate revolutionary. He was handsome, moody, and intractable. He belonged to the Hakka race, which had come down from the north to the coastal regions of Kwangtung and had never become assimilated to the native population. Born near Canton, in a small village, he had set himself when very young to become a scholar: he would take the imperial examinations and so rise to high position in the Manchu government.

He failed in the examination when he was sixteen. He believed that his failure was at least partly due to his ancestry: seven generations previously there had been members of his family fighting against the Manchus. He brooded over his failure, and attempted the examination again three years later. He failed again. Altogether he failed four times, and each time he suffered a kind of nervous breakdown. The third failure, in 1837, appears to be the one which affected him most. He lay prostrate in bed with a high fever, and during the fever he experienced the visions which were to change the course of Chinese history.

These visions began simply enough. First he saw a dragon, a cock, and a tiger; then there came a great multitude of men playing musical instruments who approached with a beautiful sedan chair, on which he was transported to the neighborhood of a heavenly mansion. For a while he rested among green fields, then an old woman came to bathe him in a stream. Shortly afterward an old man came with a knife: the visionary's heart and entrails were removed, and replaced with new ones. Soon he was led to the heavenly mansion, where he was received by an old man who is described as "most ancient, wearing a gold beard and a long black robe." This was God, who said: "All human beings in the world are produced and sustained by me. They eat my food and wear my clothing, but not a single one among them has the heart to remember and venerate me: they worship demons, they rebel against me, and they arouse my anger." Then God offered him a sword, a gold signet ring, and a yellow fruit. Finally, God took him to a high mountain from which he could look down on all the kingdoms of the world. Here Hung Hsu-ch'uan received the command to destroy utterly all those who opposed God's will, for God could no longer endure the sight of the depravity and sin which existed in the world. When he woke up from the fever, Hung Hsu-ch'uan went running madly round the room in his sickness, shouting in his Hakka dialect: *"Tsan ah! Tsan ah!* Slay the demons! Slay the demons! There is one and there is another. Many cannot withstand one single blow of my sword."

At that moment he was clearly mad; but he recovered quickly. He worried about the meaning of the vision and began to wonder whether, after all, it might not have been a direct message from God. He remembered nine small pamphlets given to him by Liang A-fah, a missionary belonging to the London Missionary Society. These pamphlets, issued under the title *Good Words Exhorting the Age*, comprised an almost incredible olla-podrida. Here were religious discourses, sermons, paraphrases, a fragment of Liang A-fah's autobiography, and translations of some of the more imaginative chapters of the Bible. The whole of the first chapter of Genesis was included; so was the Nineteenth Psalm; so were the first and fifty-eighth chapters of Isaiah and the fifth chapter of Ephesians, and long passages from Revelation. In particular, Revelation seems to have affected Hung Hsu-ch'uan. Had he not seen the demons becoming birds and lions? The apocalypse was at hand, and he was the cherished evangel.

After his fourth failure, Hung Hsu-ch'uan wandered away among the hills of Kwangsi, selling pens. He had wanted to be a scholar. Instead, he was a poor beggar who had suffered a vision. Gradually, he drew about him a small but devoted band of followers who believed in him implicitly. There were famines in Kwangsi, and with these there came a sudden outbreak of idol-destroying. Hung Hsu-ch'uan urged upon his followers the destruction of all Buddhist and Taoist idols. Curiously, he omitted to urge them to destroy the Confucian tablets, perhaps because he remained half a Confucian to the end. Soon, joining forces with the secret society called the White Lotus, which was dedicated to the overthrow of the Manchus, he established himself in the marshy and hilly regions where the three provinces of Kwangtung, Kwangsi, and Hunan meet. Like all rebels against the government, he found safety in the border regions. It was here that he inaugurated the society called the *Shang Ti Hui,* or the "Society of the Highest God."

He was waiting his time. He spoke of his vision to everyone who cared to listen, calling himself already "the younger brother of God." It is probable that he was completely unaware that God had said in the vision what Hung Hsu-ch'uan himself desired to say: had not God worn the black robe of the poor scholars of the time? God demanded vengeance of the world. His words spoke of the vengeance which Hung Hsu-ch'uan himself desired to exact from the world, for his own failure in the examinations; and God's final words, with their nihilist violence, echoed across the centuries the terrible tablet which the mad General Chang

Hsien-chung had ordered to be engraved in Chengtu during the Ming Dynasty, after he had slaughtered 30,000,000 inhabitants of Szechuan—slaughtering so well that eighty years later Father de Mailla declared that in spite of every care and privilege Szechuan had not recovered from the catastrophe. The message on the tablet read:

> *Heaven brings forth innumerable things to support man.*
> *Man has not one thing with which to recompense Heaven.*
> *Kill.   Kill.   Kill.   Kill.   Kill.   Kill.   Kill.*

But, though the movement which Hung Hsu-ch'uan began gave signs, in its origins, of a nihilist violence, its development showed that he possessed a quite extraordinary insight into Chinese politics, and he understood the social problems which weighed upon China.

In the border regions he published his divine commission: "We command the services of all, and we take everything. All who resist us are rebels and idolatrous demons, and we shall kill them without sparing. But whoever acknowledges the Prince of Heaven and exerts himself in our service shall have a full reward." He called himself "the Prince of Heaven," and he published five new gospels, including a *Book of Celestial Decrees* and *The Revelations of the Heavenly Father*. He also produced a *Trimetrical Classic*, which recounts the whole story of the creation of the world to the time when he received his visions, a surprisingly beautiful poem which passes in review all the religions which have ever existed in China and dismisses all except Christianity and Confucianism.

The strange epic had hardly begun. Hung Hsu-ch'uan had assumed a title, but he possessed no empire over which to rule. Now, with the help of an early convert named Feng Yun-shan, who received the title "Prince of the South," Hung set about conquering China. Under his command he had hardly more than 3,000 men and women armed with spears and pitchforks, distinguished by the bright red cloth turbans which held up their long hair.

The war, which was later to lead the rebels almost to the gates of Peking, began in 1848. His peasant columns descended from the hills, seized small villages, converted the villagers, and then withdrew to the hills. There were small, hastily fought battles with imperial garrisons. The guerrillas, who called themselves "the little children of God," already possessed a sense of purpose, and they were ruled by a hard taskmaster, who invoked the Mosaic law to punish them whenever they disobeyed his commands. The small battles were easily won. The popular faith in the Prince of Heaven deepened, for was he not God indeed? And would they not go immediately to Heaven when they were killed in battle? Seeing his small bands of guerrillas at work, the Prince of Heaven could reflect that only a small knife was needed to open China.

A peasant uprising in the winter of 1850 against the tax-gatherers led to a sudden increase in the size of his armies, for though the rebellion in Kwangsi was suppressed, the survivors flocked to his banners. He now felt himself strong enough to attack walled towns. Six months later, on August 27, 1851, the market town of Yunganchow was captured, and there, in the market place, wearing the imperial robe with the five-clawed dragons embroidered upon it, Hung Hsu-ch'uan announced the creation of a new dynasty, to be called *Taiping Tienkuo,* or "the Heavenly Kingdom of Great Peace." [1] He gave himself the dynastic title *Tien Teh,* or "Heavenly Virtue." Here, too, he made an appeal for universal brotherhood and wrote a poem called "The Awakening of the World" in which he announced the social purpose of the revolution. "We are the light, and should fight against darkness," it says. "We desire to build the fallen society so that the world shall become just, the strong shall not oppress

1. The name "Taiping" was not invented by Hung Hsu-ch'uan, but seems to have been derived from the *Taiping Ching,* a Taoist compilation written during the later Han dynasty. It was with this book as their vade mecum that the Taoist sect of the Yellow Turbans arose in the second century A.D., to destroy the remnants of the Han armies. Chang Chio, the leader of the Yellow Turbans, called himself *Tien Shih,* or "Heavenly Teacher." A comparison between the Yellow Turbans and the Taipings reveals many similarities, and a survival of Taoist mysticism within Taiping Christianity can be clearly demonstrated.

the weak, the wise exploit the ignorant, or the brave impose upon the timid." At last he was welding his own visions of kingship with a far more powerful force—the peasant revolt. From this moment there begins the story of the Prince of Heaven who hoped to impose communism on China.

The victory at Yunganchow was followed by reverses. By creating a new dynasty, Hung Hsu-ch'uan had raised the standard of open rebellion. He was openly building up his armies and buying arms. The government in Peking was alarmed and sent the Emperor's chief minister, Saishangah, with thirty thousand imperial troops to reduce the town. Yunganchow was surrounded and an attempt was made to starve it into submission. The imperial armies arrived in December, and it was not until April that a small band of Hung Hsu-ch'uan's followers, numbering no more than three or four thousand, escaped through the enemy lines. They moved westward, in the direction of Hunan, and somewhere along the borders of Hunan the dispirited group of survivors of the new dynasty encountered one of the most mysterious men in Chinese history. His name was Chu Kiu-t'ao, he was a Hunanese and a military genius of the highest order, and almost everything else about him is unknown, except that he too had failed in the provincial examinations and like Hung Hsu-ch'uan was descended from a clan which had fought for the Ming dynasty against the Manchus, and he was consumed with the desire to overthrow the foreigners who ruled in Peking. Unlike Hung Hsu-ch'uan, he was not moved by visionary dreams. For years he had secluded himself in a monastery, where he studied military tactics. He had met Hung Hsu-ch'uan somewhere in Kwangtung in 1844. They had kept up a correspondence, and they seem to have sworn blood brotherhood at some stage in their acquaintance. From this point onward, until he disappeared into obscurity, the Hunanese took command of the Taiping armies, and welded them together into a force so powerful that in time the Prince of Heaven was able to say that he had thirty million soldiers, and could if he desired have conquered the world.

To Chu Kiu-t'ao goes the credit of introducing organization where none existed before. Until this time the army consisted of volunteers; he introduced conscription. He gave the Taipings their military system of squadrons, companies, battalions, and divisions; he made a professional army out of the guerrillas. He introduced the strictest discipline. No one in the army was allowed to requisition food; everything must be paid for. Rape was punished with death. The soldiers were ordered to carry their own cooking utensils, oils, and salt, and they were refused permission to enter any dwelling place unless invited. All must attend morning and evening prayers. The smoking of opium in the army was absolutely forbidden, he gave women a privileged position in the army, and he arranged that the families of soldiers in service should be supported from a common treasury. All these regulations were enforced. He was also responsible for the introduction of a form of communism in the army. He based his entire administrative system on a unit of twenty-five households, the largest unit, comprising 12,500 households, being known as a *chun,* or army. He arranged that each communal unit of twenty-five households should possess its own treasury and its own church. The fields were to be tilled in common. Food, clothing, and money were to be used in common, and the surplus of the harvest reverted to the communal treasury. He advocated that the private ownership of land should be abolished, and he began very early to organize a system of promotion in the army based on the recommendations of soldiers who acted as guarantors of those who were promoted. In the proclamations of the time there can be detected a hard residue, which clearly comes from Chu Kiu-t'ao, embedded in the soft visionary declamations of the Prince of Heaven.

But most of this lay in the future. Chu Kiu-t'ao was busy organizing his army and leading it along the Hsiang River toward Changsha, hammering out of an army equipped with bows and arrows, sabers, and pitchforks, an incredibly hard-hitting force. All the towns and villages along the Hsiang River were occupied, the Taoist and Buddhist idols overthrown. Because his soldiers neither pillaged nor plundered, and because they sided with the peasants against the landlords, the army gained in numbers; and they were fifty thousand when they reached the gates of Changsha on September 18, five months after the escape from Yunganchow. Here they halted. They intended to besiege the city, but the resistance of the garrison was far greater than they had expected, and in November they were compelled to raise the siege.

Though Changsha held out, the Yangtse Valley offered softer material for the Taipings. In January 1853, Hankow, Wuchang, and Hanyang were in their hands. Almost immediately they fitted out war vessels, and sailed down the Yangtse River. In the beginning of March they were outside Nanking, and ten days later they were butchering 20,000 Manchus who had remained in the city. In May a column led by Li Hsin-cheng, a Taiping general who had once been a charcoal seller, came almost in sight of Peking, and they might have conquered the capital if the Mongol general, Sankolinsin, known to British soldiers as "Sam Collinson," had not fought them off. The Taiping armies turned south. They marched through Fukien, Szechuan, and Kwangtung; and Yeh Ming-shen, the fiery Hunanese viceroy who was later to be captured by the British and sent into exile in Calcutta, turned away from the contemplation of a coastal war with the British to observe: "Our whole country swarms with rebels. Our funds are nearly at an end, and our troops are few. The commander of the imperial forces thinks he can put out a bonfire with a thimbleful of water. I fear that we shall have hereafter some serious affairs, and the great body of the people will rise up against us and our own followers will leave us."

Meanwhile, foreign opinion concerning the Taipings was divided. "I hope Tien Teh will be successful," wrote an official of a Shanghai company to Humphrey Marshall, the American commissioner. "We cannot be worse off, and he is said to be a liberal man." Bishop George Smith, speaking in Trinity Church, Shanghai, delighted in the new outbreak of Christianity. "Dynasties and thrones are crumbling in the dust," he said, his eyes on the tottering Peacock Throne in Peking.

Other missionaries deplored the eighty-eight consecrated wives and unnumbered concubines of the Prince of Heaven. All were perhaps secretly afraid of him and the strange power he exerted over the faithful.

The Taipings had spread like wildfire over South China, they had threatened Peking, they were introducing reforms on an unprecedented scale, and to none of them would it have occurred that their fate depended upon the decisions of a Kentucky lawyer, who had been chosen for the post of American commissioner in Shanghai only after it had been formally offered to three others and declined. Humphrey Marshall had graduated from West Point, served two terms in Congress, and at the outbreak of the Civil War he was to become a brigadier general in the Confederate Army. He knew no Chinese, and he was pitifully vain, dictatorial, and ignorant. He arrived in China in January 1853. By April he had come to the conclusion that the Taiping rebels would overthrow the existing dynasty, but in the next month, having heard that Sir George Bonham had attended the Prince of Heaven at his court, he suddenly reversed his position. He became suspicious of the British minister, and especially of the minister's interpreter, and he began to believe that the British desired to exercise a protectorate over the Taipings. When he heard that the Manchus had received an offer of protection from the Czar, he reported to the Secretary of State his fears for the future. The letter is important, for it bears heavily on events which happened a hundred years later. He wrote:

Her [Russia's] assistance would probably end in passing China under a Russian protectorate, and in the extension of Russian limits to the Hoangho, or the mouth of the Yangtse; or, it may be, when circumstances and policy shall favor the scheme, in the partition of China between Great Britain and Russia. The interference of the Czar would readily suppress the rebellion, by driving the rebels from the great highways of commerce, and from the occupation of the towns on the seaboard. Whatever might be the ultimate compensation demanded by Russia for this timely service, China could not resist its collection.

I think that almost any sacrifice should be made by the United

States to keep Russia from spreading her Pacific boundary, and to avoid her coming directly to interference in Chinese domestic affairs; for China is like a lamb before the shearers, as easy a conquest as were the provinces of India. Whenever the avarice or ambition of Russia or Great Britain shall tempt them to make the prizes, the fate of Asia will be sealed, and the future Chinese relations with the United States may be considered as closed for ages, unless *now* the United States shall foil the untoward result by adopting a sound policy.

It is my opinion that the highest interests of the United States are involved in sustaining China—maintaining order here, and gradually engrafting on this worn-out stock the healthy principles which give life and health to governments, rather than to see China become the theatre of widespread anarchy, and ultimately the prey of European ambition.[2]

The letter is illuminating, for Marshall represented a hard core of merchant opinion in Shanghai. The rumor concerning the Czar was false; he never referred to it again, but he never changed his opinion about the necessity of "maintaining order." There was widespread sympathy for the Taipings in America. His government ordered him to make contact with them. He refused. Hardly conscious of the effect of his actions, he was setting down the policy which was to lead eventually to the débacle of 1949.

Meanwhile the Prince of Heaven ruled from the Heavenly City, wielding his imperial powers with considerably more understanding of the problems of the Chinese people than the Manchus in the North. He instituted equality of the sexes, inveighed against slavery and concubinage, and forbade foot-binding and the wearing of the queue. Even more important, in the third year of his assumption of power,

2. The full text of the letter is given in Tyler Dennet, *Americans in Eastern Asia*, New York, 1941, pp. 214-15. Fear of the British was strong at this time. Nikolai Muraviev, the governor general of eastern Siberia, wrote in 1850, when a young and short-lived Chinese emperor was coming to the throne: "The British will use this change to seize control of not only the trade but also the policies of China." But it should be added that Muraviev only rarely represented public Russian opinion, and the anarchist Bakhunin described him as the one Russian in high position "who can and must fully and without the least reservation be considered one of us."

he introduced agrarian reforms, dividing the land into nine classes, graded according to the fertility of the soil, such that one *mou* of the highest class of land was equivalent to three *mou* of the lowest. Land was to be allotted according to the number of mouths in the family, though some preference was given to men above sixteen and under fifty, largely because these were the men who formed the army. He proposed the complete redistribution of the land and stated his program most succinctly when he declared: "All shall eat food, all shall have clothes, money shall be shared, and in all things there shall be equality: no man shall be without food or warmth."

These social and agrarian reforms sprang from the movement he led. They were deeply religious, but they corresponded to the age-old desires of the peasantry. They destroyed the land titles, exactly as the Chinese Communists were to destroy land titles later, and nearly all the reforms first instituted by the Taipings were followed by the Chinese Communists, almost to the letter. There is no evidence that the reforms were instituted as the result of any knowledge of foreign social doctrine, and though the *Communist Manifesto* appeared during the rule of the Taipings, it was not translated into Chinese until thirty years later. And it was not only the peasantry which demanded these reforms: the merchants and the gentry had their own grievances against the Manchus, and so, too, had the educated classes, the scholars who were at the mercy of the Manchu academies.

For more than a decade the Prince of Heaven ruled over the Yangtse Valley. Feng Yun-shan, the Prince of the South, died fighting in 1852. Chu Kiu-t'ao, the Prince of the West, mysteriously disappeared, and his place as the chief military strategist was taken by General Li Hsin-cheng, now elevated to the title of *Chung Wang*, or "Faithful Prince." But not everything went well with the Taipings. Those who had taken part in the long march from Yunganchow to Nanking received preference, and discrimination began to undermine the morale of the army. Discipline began to fail. In the upper hierarchies a strange violence broke out. Yang

Hsiu-ch'ing, the Prince of the East, had claimed to be the holy spirit and on one occasion exercised the privilege of scourging the Prince of Heaven on the strength of a revelation received, but he fell into disfavor and was executed. Worse still, the puritanical laws of the Taipings were being exchanged for licence. The foreigners watched. In 1860 they decided to strike. Curiously, the foreigners did not strike their first blows at the Taipings. They struck at Peking, captured Taku, destroyed the Emperor's Summer Palace, demanded an indemnity of 8,000,000 taels for their trouble in destroying so much splendor, and only later launched a campaign against the Taipings. First an American, Frederick Townsend Ward, and later an Englishman, General Gordon, helped the Manchus to recover their lost territory; and there was formed an Ever-Victorious Army under foreign leadership to fight against the Long-Haired Army of the Taipings. Both sides fought mercilessly; the Manchus fought treacherously.

On December 4, 1863, four surviving Taiping princes under a safe conduct from General Gordon surrendered Soochow. They came with their long hair falling down their backs, in yellow robes and wearing royal crowns. They sued for terms: they proposed that they should receive commissions in the imperial army and that their followers should be enrolled among the imperial troops, and that part of the city should be assigned to them for a *place d'armes*. Instead, they were summarily executed, and some time later General Gordon resigned his commission on the grounds that their execution was an act of unpardonable treachery.

There followed eighteen months of sporadic fighting, but by now the tide was turning. On June 1, 1865, the great Hunanese scholar-soldier Tseng Kuo-fan completed the close investment of Nanking, and within a month the strange genius Hung Hsu-ch'uan had committed suicide by poison, his body being buried behind his palace by one of his wives. On July 19 the city fell. The *Chung Wang* escaped on horseback, carrying in his arms the son of the Taiping Emperor, but both were captured and executed, though the death of the *Chung Wang* was delayed a week to enable him

to complete the writing of his memoirs. All the defenders
of the city were put to death, and all the members of the
Prince of Heaven's family were dismembered. There were
left only the armies of Prince Shih Ta-k'ai, known as the
Helping Prince: they were pursued into the remote gorges
of the Tatu River on the frontiers of Tibet and cut down by
the armies of Tseng Kuo-fan. Eighty years later the Chinese
Communists during their own Long March came upon the
weapons of these rebels against the Manchu Empire. Some
of their spears could still be sharpened: they picked up
these relics of an ancient war and used them in their own
battles.

The Taiping Empire fell, but the causes which brought it
into being remained. The strength of the Taipings lay in the
visions of the Cantonese, Hung Hsu-ch'uan, and the administrative genius of the mysterious Hunanese, Chu Kiu-
t'ao, and their social policy which obeyed a classic canon
derived from the Confucian *Book of Rites*. "All the families in
every place will be equally provided for, while every individual will be well fed and well clothed," wrote the Prince
of Heaven; and the social form attempted by the Taipings
approached a primitive communism. They destroyed private
property. They regarded themselves as people with the mission to share the world's wealth equally among the world's
inhabitants, and they used the phrase, "The wealth must be
shared," a phrase which the Chinese Communists were to
employ later when they came to name their party *Kung-
ch'an-tang*, or "the Sharing Wealth party." The remarkable
similarities between the programs of the Taipings and the
Chinese Communists should not be underestimated: both
drew their strength from the same common cause.

In *China's Destiny*, Chiang Kai-shek dismissed the Taipings as ignorant and stupid men entirely outside the current
of Chinese history. Sun Yat-sen, with more reason, claimed
that the Kuomintang had come into existence to complete
what the Taipings had only begun.

THE REFORMERS: YEN FU AND KANG YU-WEI

Yen Fu and Kang Yu-wei never held guns, but they, too, changed the course of Chinese history. Coming before the revolution—their most imposing work was accomplished under the Manchus—they subtly changed the atmosphere of the time. The defeat of the Taipings had confirmed the Manchu Empress in her contempt for social change, but vast social and intellectual changes were occurring nevertheless.

A young naval cadet called Yen Fu returned from the Naval College at Greenwich with a rough draft of a translation of Darwin's *Origin of Species* in his pocket, completed the translation in Peking, and had it published. The Empress Dowager read the book, admired the classical perfection of his prose, and shook her head uncomprehendingly. Of course, it was nonsense to say that men were descended from apes, but if it was clearly indicated that this was a foreign belief, it only made the foreigners appear more stupid in Chinese eyes.

More and more translations by Yen Fu appeared. He translated Huxley's *Evolution and Ethics*, Adam Smith's *Wealth of Nations*, Herbert Spencer's *The Principles of Sociology*, Montesquieu's *De l'Esprit des Lois*, which became almost a handbook for the young students of Peking at the beginning of the century. More important, he translated John Stuart Mill's *On Liberty*, though necessarily he gave the book a more innocuous title. In all he translated more than 112 books from five languages, even from languages of which he was entirely ignorant. He was still translating vigorously when he died in 1920, having spent the last thirty years of his life translating one book after another. He was not a good translator. He was often inaccurate. He had a habit of adding commentaries, and he delighted in showing similarities between foreign opinion and Confucian doctrine, even when, as often occurred, there were no similarities at all.

His innate Confucianism had important consequences. The philosophy and the social sciences of the West penetrated China in Confucian clothing. A few of his books were banned by imperial edict: most of them were in wide circulation throughout even the most troubled times of the Empress Dowager's reign. Reading these authors in translation, Chinese scholars could feel that they were reading some lost classics which might have appeared at the time of Confucius, so antiquated was the style, so solemn the presentation of the perennial problems of government. Confucius, that vast image which the Chinese have erected as a mirror of themselves, seemed indeed to be leading the West into the Chinese fold.

Yen Fu translated the documents, but Kang Yu-wei, a Cantonese who came like Hung Hsu-ch'uan from a village near Canton, put them to use. Like the Prince of Heaven he too suffered an apocalyptic vision of the whole world at peace. Standing on the Bund in Shanghai, it occurred to him quite suddenly that all the vast resources of modern industry, steamships, the telegraph, the postal service, even the destructiveness of modern weapons, were moving the world toward a stage where a single empire or a single world state became inevitable. He had read Yen Fu's translations. He knew something about the mechanics of Western thought. He also knew Confucius, and he knew the theory, expressed in the Confucian *Book of Rites,* of the three stages of human progress culminating in a final stage of peace and contentment.

He was so impressed with his vision that he returned to Canton and surrounded himself with young students with the express purpose of discovering whether his dream was valid. With a vast knowledge of Confucianism and Buddhism, and deep learning of the Sung and Ming philosophies, he examined the histories of the East and the West, coming to the conclusion that the most dangerous disease of all was nationalism, and that the most dreadful torments awaited the world if this disease was allowed to remain unchecked. He admired the West for its industry, its parliaments, its inventiveness, its unquenchable desire to tame the elements;

he particularly admired the institution of the ballot box. He turned to the chapter called "The Evolution of Rites" in the *Book of Rites*. There you could read that the world would pass through the stage of disorder and confusion, followed by a stage of "small tranquillity," until finally there came the stage of "great unity":

When the great *Tao* was practiced, the world was common to all men: men of talents, virtue, and ability were selected: sincerity was emphasized, and friendship was cultivated. Therefore, men do not love only their own parents, nor did they treat as children only their own sons. Provision was secured for the aged until their death, employment was given to the able bodied, and means were provided for the upbringing of the young. Kindness and compassion were shown to widows, orphans, and childless men, and those who were disabled by disease, so that all had the wherewithal for support. Men had their proper work, women had their homes. They hated to see the wealth of natural resources undeveloped, but when they developed these resources, they did not put them to their own use. They hated not to work, but when they worked, it was for the common profit. This was known as the Great Unity (*Ta Tung*).

It was a dream which was to haunt the Chinese, who stated and restated it in a thousand poems. It was the significance of Kang Yu-wei that he interpreted the dream in modern terms and was the first to envisage Confucius as a social reformer.

For Kang Yu-wei the famous phrase *Ta Tung* had vast social implications, but to the end of his days he remained the dreamer, living in proud isolation in a foreign settlement in Shanghai, annotating the classics, seeing the world still in terms of the fantasy of his dream. It was left to Mao Tse-tung to employ the ancient Confucian phrase for a practical purpose, and he was probably the first to see how the phrase could be harnessed to the Chinese revolution. Years later, when he came to power in Peking, he was to use the phrase again, but this time it meant the dictatorship of the proletariat over the whole earth: so subtly had a Confucian text received a Marxist-Leninist interpretation.

Though Kang Yu-wei was a powerful and imposing figure,

and was the first to claim the authority of Confucius for a world state, Mao Tse-tung was almost certainly right when he said later that Kang Yu-wei did not, and could not under existing conditions discover the road which led to the "Great Unity." Kang Yu-wei's judgment was often confused. He envisaged companionate marriage, the partners being allowed to associate for a year before deciding to marry; he favored a constitutional monarchy, and he believed that the state should own all the means of production; and there were too many contradictions in his plans to make them practicable. He desired a world in which monkeys and parrots were taught to speak, and oxen, chickens, geese, and fish, instead of being killed, would be allowed to multiply.

Under the impulse of Yen Fu's translations and Kang Yu-wei's interpretations, and with the help of the young Emperor Kwang Hsu, who had recently come to the throne, a vast program of reform was instituted. Kang Yu-wei was appointed chief of the *Tsungli Yamen,* or Foreign Office. The young Emperor, handsome, brilliant, delighting in everything that appertained to the West, with a passion for maps and Swiss watches, became the willing prisoner of the Reformers. In the space of a hundred days, from June to September 1898, he issued twenty-seven imperial rescripts, all of them concerned with essential reforms. The whole of society was to be reorganized from top to bottom. The Army, the postal services, the banks, the railroads were to be reorganized; and Kang Yu-wei began to believe that he would see the day of *Ta Tung,* when the state disappears and there occurs a universal equality and both money and private property are abolished, the day when there is no punishment because there is no crime and there is no need for armies any more.

Driven by the vision of *Ta Tung,* he overreached himself and drew up reforms so far-reaching that they attracted the hostility of the noblemen at the court, who recounted the proposed reforms in great detail to the Empress. She was not driven by visions. She was in semi-retirement, and now she suddenly showed her strength by arresting the Emperor, who spent the last ten years of his life on an island in one of the lakes within the high walls of the Forbidden City. The Reformers were publicly cursed, and orders were given for their execution. Some were strangled; others, like Kang Yu-wei and Hsiung Hsi-ling, escaped to Japan. For the second time in fifty years the Manchus had prevented necessary change.

SUN YAT-SEN

Sun Yat-sen bridges the gap between the Taiping rebels and the Chinese Communists, for he was born in the year which saw the defeat of the remnant of the last Taiping armies and he died as the Chinese Communists were slowly mounting into power. This young doctor, who had received his early education under the British in Honolulu, had studied the Taiping rebellion at its source—in the villages of Kwangtung. Inspired by it, he had smashed idols and at one time declared that Christianity was the sole solution for China's problems. Thirteen times he led or ordered revolutionary expeditions against the Manchus from bases in Hong Kong and French Indo-China. All failed. But he fought so bitterly that when, in 1911, the Manchu dynasty tottered under the weight of its own contradictions, he had become for most Chinese south of the Yangtse River the indispensable president of the new republic.

The revolution of October 1911 changed the current of Chinese history, releasing the forces submerged under the dictatorship of the Manchus, but it was a rebellion without deep purpose, having its source in the same contradictions which plagued the Manchus. A thousand disparate elements were involved. The Szechuanese rebelled because a railway was being built between Chengtu and Chungking. The Hunanese revolted against a predatory governor, and the Kwangtungese revolted against land taxes. It was a curiously anarchic rebellion, carried out under the banner of "Down with the Manchus," but without any positive element of social revolution. As soon as he realized that he would be called to the presidency of the new republic, Sun Yat-sen appealed to the Western powers for help; but their replies were unconvincing. Strangely enough—for his sources of information were limited—Lenin alone among Westerners seems to have realized the almost legendary authority which Sun Yat-sen was later to exert. Early in 1912, in an article called *Democracy and Narodism in China,* he wrote:

A militant, sincere spirit of democracy pervades Sun Yat-sen's thoughts. He shows no trace of a non-political spirit or of indifference towards political liberty, or any admission of the idea that Chinese autocracy is compatible with Chinese social reform; and he directly presents the problem of the conditions of the masses, and of the mass struggle, with warm feeling towards the toilers and the exploited, and belief in the justice of their cause and in their strength.

What we have before us is a really great ideology of a really great people, which is able not only to bemoan its age-long slavery, not only to dream of liberty and equality, but is able also to *fight* the age-long oppressors of China.[3]

Lenin's admiration of Sun Yat-sen remained, but by the time the article was printed, Sun Yat-sen no longer possessed the power, the inclination, or the social knowledge to direct a successful revolution.

At his death, in 1925, Sun Yat-sen left behind him a dangerous legacy. The famous *Three Principles of the People,* written hurriedly in 1924 in Canton and constantly interrupted by civil war, elaborated a wholly unreal system of government. The mild-mannered doctor showed, as he grew older, a strangely authoritarian temper. Continual defeats and perpetual frustrations led him to harden his views of the Chinese people. In 1905 the oath of the revolutionary party he led contained the words: "The spirit and the binding principles of our various aims are Liberty, Equality, and Universal Love." Nineteen years later he wrote:

There is one thing of the greatest importance to a political party, that is, that the members of the party should possess spiritual unity. In order that all members may be united spiritually, the first thing is to sacrifice freedom, the second is to offer abilities. If the individ-

3. Lenin, *Selected Works,* IV, 306.

ual will sacrifice freedom, then the whole party will have freedom. If the individual can offer his abilities, then the whole party will possess ability.

It was a strange progress. The wheel had turned full circle: the revolutionary who had once fallen in love with love, with egalitarianism, and with freedom had become transformed into the hardened ruler who desired nothing so much as to be dictator. The freedom of the individual had no place in the *Three Principles of the People*. For him, individual freedom was irrelevant, for were not the Chinese like "shifting sand," too individualistic for the safety of any government? When the Kuomintang came into power under Chiang Kai-shek, it was inevitable that the new government should have all the appearance of a dictatorship. Chiang Kai-shek was merely carrying out the wishes of Sun Yat-sen. One wish, however, he never carried out. The third of the three principles was called simply "livelihood." By this Sun Yat-sen meant that the people should be provided with sufficient food, clothing, and sustenance in exchange for their liberties; and this the Kuomintang dictatorship was incapable of providing.

These four revolutionaries have not been chosen at random. When Mao Tse-tung came to power in 1949 he carefully singled out these forerunners as "the four men who sought the truth from the West," to be regarded with an especial respect. In another age he would have ordered their names to be "honored in the temple halls and worshiped with bowls and censers for ten thousand autumns." They had opened the way. Each had attempted a revolution. Each had failed. Mao studied their failures, and contrived to bring about a fifth revolution, which bore the traces of all the previous ones; and his peculiar achievement was to weld many ideas together, and to make them viable to the social group which previous revolutionaries had rarely taken into account—the peasantry, who are the sources of his own weaknesses and his amazing strength.

TWO The Young Rebel

The Hsiang River cuts through the heart of Hunan like a sword. White-sailed sampans laden with rice float down the deep blue river: ring-necked cormorants fish in midstream; red cliffs hang over the sandy beaches, and silver lakes among forests of reeds lie in the north. The inhabitants of Hunan are generally handsomer than the inhabitants of neighboring provinces, with red cheeks and clean, open faces, broad foreheads and striking dark eyes; many of them show signs of tribal blood derived from the Miaos who live in the shelter of the lakes. The Chinese of other provinces are occasionally inclined to accept the superior virtues of the Hunanese, but they tend to say that the Hunanese are incorrigibly rebellious. "If there is no Emperor," they will tell you, "the Hunanese will invent an Emperor for the pleasure of rebelling against him." They are a hot-tempered people, but their temper generates heat slowly, like the red peppers they are continually chewing, and they are hardly aware of their own capacity to hurl themselves into violent fits of anger. They claim that the best soldiers and the best scholars come from there: and they regard themselves quite dispassionately as a race apart.

Mao was born in the village of Shao Shan, in 1893, not far from Hsiang T'an. At the time of his birth, his father had acquired some wealth by trading in rice. His name was Mao Jen-sheng, which can be translated as "Hair Increase Gentlemanliness." Mao Tse-tung means "Hair Anoint East." The names of his brothers, Tse-hung and Tse-t'an mean "Anoint Red" and "Anoint Dawn." But nothing could have been further from the father's mind than any suggestion of prophecy. He was a hard-bitten peasant with a taste for the Confucian classics, and a friend who knew Mao in his youth remembers the old father grumbling by the stove in winter and hurling Confucian maxims at his unwilling listeners, or poring over his accounts, a sharp-faced, bigoted man who had fought for the Manchus and respected the Empress Dowager and treated his servants and farm laborers with contempt. He had few friends and took little interest in his family. Some secret anxiety gnawed in him; he was always restless, ill at ease, the hot temper never very far from the surface. By contrast, the mother was placid, with a handsome round face, not unlike the faces which are found in the north of China and called "pear-shaped." She was deeply religious, a Buddhist, and therefore averse to any form of killing. For a long period of his childhood and his early youth Mao Tse-tung attended the Buddhist ceremonies with his mother, sang Buddhist hymns, and believed that nothing was more criminal than the killing of living things, and nothing more necessary for salvation than the giving of rice offerings to the poor. The father kept meticulous accounts of the rice, bursting into temper whenever he found that some had been given away; and these inexplicable bursts of temper, arising sometimes from no known cause, threw the whole family into hysterical recriminations. After one of these outbursts, the boy ran away and hid in the woods for three days, returning only because it had occurred to him that his mother would have no one to defend her.

Except for the terrifying presence of the father, whose anger could rarely be placated, life in the village of Shao Shan was pleasant enough. The house was well but sparsely furnished, and kept spotlessly clean by the mother, who employed no servants. It was a house like all the other houses, with a roof of thatched rice straw, with red peppers hanging from the roof beams and a high-walled courtyard.

The boy was physically frail—this may have been the reason for his father's dislike of him—but he grew rapidly: at the age of ten he had his first serious fight and pummeled a boy who was slightly larger, only to receive the plaintive remonstrances of his mother, who still hoped he might enter the Buddhist priesthood, or perhaps, by becoming a merchant, support a monastery. By the age of seven he was already working in the fields, helping to plant rice seeds, or sitting on a wicker platform to frighten the birds away. He was reading avidly. He intensely disliked working in the fields when there were so many books to read, and all the time he was having endless secret discussions with the laborers his father employed, and he would listen to their complaints and advise them on how to deal with his father. In China, where family problems are fought out with an intensity usually unknown in the West, there was nothing in the least extraordinary in Mao's relentless fight against his father from the age of five or six. The fight was fought with all the weapons at the boy's command, and it never ceased while he remained in the village.

Already a hagiography has grown up around Mao's childhood: the story has been told and retold so many times by Chinese writers that it is no longer possible to see him clearly. The small boy, with the shock of black hair, wearing only a pair of blue linen trousers—exactly like all the other small boys of Hunan—recedes: in his place there is the ghostly wraith of a future emperor. Mao himself has done his best to discount the legends, but occasionally he has added to them. He told Edgar Snow that his father was walking down a road one day, intending to collect some money, when he was surprised by a tiger. Reflecting on the incident it occurred to him that he might have offended the gods and that his miraculous escape had been ordained by Buddha as a means of bringing him to the Buddhist religion. It is a good story, but unfortunately there were no tigers in Hunan at that time, though a few existed in Manchuria and the mountains of southeast Kiangsi. Strangely enough, a very similar story is told by the "Christian General" Feng Yu-hsiang in his autobiography, where an enormous yellow snake, twenty feet long, slowly entering the house and quietly coiling up near the wall takes the place of Mao Jen-sheng's tiger.

What is certain is that the father mellowed as he grew older. Though there were sudden flashes of the old temper, a kind of weariness settled on him, and he could be seen burning incense and bowing mechanically before the bronze Buddha which stood on a blackwood table in a place of honor, an old and gaunt man, ready even at such moments to curse the first person who came into his field of vision, but generally quiet, resigned to living in a rebellious household.

By this time a technique for dealing with his tantrums had been elaborated. If necessary, his rage could be brought on deliberately, to forestall the greater rage that might come later; his Confucian texts could be answered with even more pertinent texts, and if he threatened to strike anyone, he would be reminded of the most classical of all Confucian texts: "Not a hair of the head must be touched." Around the old soldier, the boy played with a deliberate cunning. It is as though he had been trained from birth to sabotage quietly and effectively the pretensions of a nineteenth-century soldier with a propensity for Confucian maxims; and the figure of the old father merges imperceptibly into the figure of Mao's future adversary.

In all this Mao was not alone. Though born much later, his two brothers and his sister were useful weapons in the continual struggle with the father. Mao was very close to them. Like most elder brothers in China, he assumed the role of teacher: from the beginning there was the element of the pedagogue in him. As he grew older and more skeptical of the Buddhist religion, his mother began to believe that if he was not made for the priesthood, at least he would become a teacher.

In those days little news came to the villages of Hunan
except by word of mouth. There were no newspapers. The
imperial rescripts were posted in the village and read aloud
by the village schoolmaster, but usually they were concerned only with taxes, conscription, and the special ceremonies to be performed on the birthdays of the Empress
Dowager. When Mao was eleven, on October 10, 1904, the
birthday of the Empress Dowager was celebrated with the
usual offerings of incense, the usual flowery speeches calling
upon heaven to preserve the Empress for ten thousand years.
On the same day, columns of soldiers passed through Hsiang
T'an on the way to Changsha. It was whispered that Hwang
Hsing, a young Hunanese revolutionary, had attacked the yamen in Changsha at the head of some peasant guerrillas. He
had fought his way into the interior of the yamen, had been
captured, thrown into a dungeon, and then by some miracle
he had escaped in disguise—no one knew where. Martial law
was proclaimed. Through all the villages soldiers came in
the hope of discovering Hwang Hsing's hiding-place. It was
learned that a reward of 10,000 silver taels had been placed
on his head. For the first time Mao came in contact with
the thought of insurrection. He was not particularly impressed. Changsha was a long way away. Besides, he possessed something of the peasant contempt for disorder, and
his loyalty to the monarchy was undimmed.

Hwang Hsing escaped to Tokyo, fleeing down the Hsiang
River and then taking boat from Hong Kong to Japan, only
to return the following February. The second insurrection failed. The third was more successful, for by this time
Hwang Hsing possessed the help of the *Tung Men Hui*,
the revolutionary organization he had founded together with
Sun Yat-sen. He had intended to capture the city again on
the anniversary of the previous uprising, but the outbreak
was delayed until October 19 because some of the ammunition failed to arrive in time. This time the insurrection was
more carefully planned. Three columns were formed,
amounting to about 30,000 men, a force which included the
coal miners of Pinghsiang, the garrison at Lilin, and the
secret societies of Liuyang. It was the largest force ever

brought together for the purposes of insurrection since the Taiping rebellion. The Viceroy saw the danger and ordered the combined forces of the four provinces of Hunan, Kiangsi, Hupeh, and Szechuan to put down the rebels. Faced with these overwhelming forces, the revolutionaries were compelled to withdraw; and Sun Yat-sen, from his small rooming-house in Tokyo, observed sadly that the insurrection had been premature, there were no clear communications, and the attack was unauthorized.

Following a pattern which was to be repeated many times during the following years, the rebellion was crushed ruthlessly, and Hwang Hsing fled, joining Sun Yat-sen, Wang Ching-wei, and Hu Han-min later in Annam, where they prepared a fourth insurrection from bases within French Indo-China. With these revolutionary figures Mao was to become intimate in later years, and these three revolutionary centers, Pinghsiang, Lilin, and Liuyang were to supply guerrilla forces for his own revolutionary army.

SCHOOL DAYS

For Mao, the year 1906 was full of strange events. There had been a severe famine during the year, especially affecting Changsha, and now for the first time he was faced with the problems of poverty and insurrection. In the early autumn, peasants had assaulted the yamen and demanded that the rice granaries be opened. They were reprimanded for their audacity and ordered to be punished. The peasant leaders were executed, and the whole province was in ferment. Everything in which Mao believed was now put to the test. His Buddhism, his belief in the monarchical system, his family's comparative wealth based on rice, even his growing delight in learning—all these were assailed by the fact that innocent peasants were executed in broad daylight, officially, with all the sanctions of the monarchy. What could he believe in? He discussed the murders endlessly with the students in the small schoolhouse, and only his position as the elder son of one of the richer rice merchants in the village saved him from being labeled a rebel.

There were insurrections nearer home. The centuries-old secret society called the *Ko Lao Hui,* or "Society of Elder Brothers," had ramifications throughout Hunan, and all the small peasants in the village belonged to it. The society had originally been organized to protect the peasants from the landlords, with elaborate rituals and a mysterious oath of brotherhood, but it had developed anti-Manchu leanings, and in Kwangtung it was sufficiently powerful to threaten an attack on Canton in 1860, "in order to preserve the honor of our country and to prevent our city from falling into the hands of the enemy," at a time when Peking was captured by British, American, French, and Russian forces. In Hunan the society was only less powerful than in Kwangtung. In Shao Shan it was in conflict with the landlords, who called to their assistance their own secret society. The small local rebellion was put down, and the leaders fled to a nearby mountain, where they held out for some months before being caught and publicly executed.

In a single year, at the sensitive age of thirteen, Mao had been brought into contact with two insurrections, a riot of famine-starved peasants, and a small uprising in his own village.

Meanwhile, his studies progressed. He read the Trimetrical Classic, which all children were taught to read in their first school year, and went on to the Confucian Analects and the Four Classics; and these extraordinary books, written with a careful humanism, had a far deeper influence on him than he was ever to admit. If he objected to the Confucian concept of filial piety for good reasons, certain Confucian terms and many of the characteristic Confucian methods remained with him. "I hated Confucius from the age of eight," he told a friend. "There was a Confucian temple in the village, and I wanted nothing more than to burn it to the ground. At first it was because I hated the teacher, and because my father quoted Confucius against me: only much later did I reason out my hatred." He seems to have been protesting too much. He was not alone in his detestation of

Confucius, which was sweeping over the whole of China: Sun Yat-sen at an equally tender age had suffered from the same virus. There remained with him the Confucian concept of political power and political energy, the idea of the Great Unity (*Ta Tung*), and a host of Confucian apothegms, which he employed then, as he does now, with surprising accuracy and wit.

He was friendly with one of the village teachers, who began to lend him books He was under ten when he first began to read the great Chinese novels, *The Dream of the Red Chamber*, *The Journey to the West*, *All Men Are Brothers*, and *The Three Kingdoms*. There was nothing particularly unusual in this. Most sensitive Chinese schoolboys read these books at an early age, sharpening their minds on the fantastic subtlety and complexity of these enormously long books, written in such a way that it is almost impossible not to surrender to the world they create. He was particularly impressed with *All Men Are Brothers* after the insurrection of the *Ko Lao Hui*, for the novel told the story of bandits who took refuge in the hills.

One other writer, the celebrated Han Yu, influenced him deeply at the time when he was growing skeptical of Buddhism. His mother's explanations of Buddhism were subtly satisfying. The Buddhist heaven, to be reached only when the last of the sinners has entered into Buddhahood, possessed an essential theological charm, and he delighted in the incantations and prayers in the evening. Buddhism was almost the official religion of Hunan, but he suspected an error somewhere, something unexplained, some lapse of logic or rhetoric. Where was it? He found it in the essay Han Yu wrote to the Emperor Hsien Tsung on the subject of Buddha's finger bone, which the Emperor, in an imperial rescript, had ordered to be brought ceremoniously to the capital. Han Yu laughed the project to scorn. He pointed out that Buddha had disobeyed two of the cardinal Confucian duties: he had rejected the throne, and he had fled secretly from his father's palace; he possessed neither a sense of duty nor filial piety. The reasonable behavior toward the finger would be to treat it as an honored guest, invite it to a

banquet, let the dancing-girls dance before it, bestow gifts on
it, and then escort it to the frontiers of the empire: it should
be treated as one treats any barbarian visitor from abroad.
Or else it should be destroyed. He wrote:

I request that the proper officials may be entrusted with the relic
and it shall be hurled into water or consumed by fire: that the error
may be destroyed root and branch: that in all the earth the threads
of doubt may be severed, and for all future times difficulties may
be avoided; and that the people under Heaven may rise ten
thousand times ten thousand times above their own mortality. Is
not this excellent? Is not this inspiring!

For his effrontery Han Yu was summarily banished to the
wilds of Kwangtung, at that time considered to be an immense miasmic swamp. His adventures were not over. An
enormous crocodile infested one of the rivers. Han Yu, as a
celebrated scholar, was asked to use his influence with the
crocodile. He obeyed the request, proceeded to the river, recited an ode to the crocodile and threw the ode into the
river together with a propitiatory pig. The crocodile was
never seen again.

Han Yu's furious wit was close to Mao's heart. He modeled his style on the old Confucian who opposed Taoism and
Buddhism and employed magic against the magicians and,
bitterly but in the most rhythmic prose, mocked the most
sacred cults. The soaring innuendoes, the savage humor, the
pomposity which is half mockery and half delight in an exalted poetic prose, the vigor and deliberation of the attack—
all these made Mao confess to being a disciple of Han Yu. It
delighted him that Han Yu should resolve the problem by
simply destroying the finger. He did not, however, approve
of all the writings of Han Yu. In particular, he disapproved
of a famous essay in which Han Yu defends the actions of
Prince Po Yi, who lived at the time of confusion between
the Yin and Chou dynasties a thousand years B.C., and
who decided to live a life of contemplative solitude beside a
white lake, while the wars were fought all around him. "I
decided that such an attitude was essentially non-Marxist,"
Mao said later. But he remembered the story of the croco-

dile when he nicknamed Chiang Kai-shek "the crocodile of the Kwangtung River."

At an age when he was beginning to see himself as a future teacher with years of quiet study in front of him, Mao suddenly discovered that he was expected to spend his whole time either in the fields or poring over the account books of his father. For some time his father had encouraged him to keep the accounts. Mao Jen-sheng had suffered losses owing to his inaccuracy with the abacus. The boy could do better. As the eldest son—there were by now two younger brothers and a sister—Mao was expected to take over the family business; and it is possible that he would have remained a rice-broker all his life if he had not been encouraged by one of his schoolteachers to go to the middle school at Hsiang-hsiang, which lay some fifteen miles upriver.

At first his father refused to let him go. Mao rebelled. He reminded his father that the proper vocation of a Chinese was to follow in the path of Confucius; he would become a scholar, enter the imperial government, and per-haps—for all positions were open to scholars—receive high office and bring fame to his parents and his native village. The parents of great scholars received almost the same ven-eration as the scholars themselves, but Mao Jen-sheng seems to have been concerned only with the possibility that his son might provide a stable income. In September 1907, at the age of fourteen, carrying only some books and a few ragged clothes in two pieces of luggage, which hung from a carry-ing-pole slung over his shoulders, Mao arrived at the school. He was friendless except for some peasant cultivators, rela-tives of his mother, who lived outside the town.

Again and again, in his conversations and in his writings, Mao has spoken of the horror of that first day in school. In Shao Shan he was known, and generally liked; here he was unknown, and despised. His father had given him money for his school fees, but no other money was forthcoming. Most of the other students were comparatively rich; they could afford good clothes, good food, and sometimes good servants. Laughing, one of the students offered Mao em-ployment as a servant. For a few pieces of cash delivered monthly, he would be expected to perform a few menial services. He indignantly refused.

Poverty-stricken, given the worst food and the worst sleeping quarters, hating the other students, who referred to him as "the dirty little peasant from Shao Shan," Mao had only one resource, his excellence at his work. He studied hard, melted down old candles to fashion new ones, hid at night over his books while the other students were asleep, and was soon at the head of his class, only to discover that he was now even more despised for being diligent. He had half-hated the classics at Shao Shan; now he spent nearly all his waking hours in a prolonged study of the Four Classics, egged on by his teacher, who admired the prose style based on Han Yu's essays, and the bitter romanticism of the boy's themes. At the same time he was coming to know more and more about the Reform Movement, and he was a fervent admirer of Kang Yu-wei.

It was during this time that he met a young student called Hsiao Chu-chang, who, though two years younger, fell under his spell and became one of his closest friends, encouraging Mao when he was depressed, listening to him open-mouthed in admiration when he fell into one of those moods in which he found himself thinking aloud—thinking as Han Yu thought, with extraordinary violence for one so young. Hsiao Chu-chang constituted himself Mao's bodyguard, servant, nurse, and confidant. They swore an oath of brotherhood. For the next ten years they were rarely separated.

Hsiao Chu-chang was the son of a rich farmer in Hsiang-hsiang. Thin-boned, elegant, with a high forehead and unusually expressive hands, he looked as though he had stepped out of *The Dream of the Red Chamber*. He was a natural aristocrat, gentle where Mao was impetuous, subtle where Mao was ingenuous. He was older than his age, while Mao gave the impression of being either very much younger or ancient with the wisdom of aged peasants. Mao called him Hsiao San (Hsiao the third), because he was the youngest of three brothers. Years later, when Hsiao Chu-chang went to live in Russia, he received still another name, Emi Siao, and under this name achieved some fame as a translator of Chinese poetry into Russian. He learned French, Spanish, and German, and it was from him that Mao derived most of his knowledge of Europe.

It was the time when the monarchy was gradually crumbling. In 1908 it seemed that the Reform party, proscribed ten years before, was about to assume control of the government. The Empress Dowager was dying. Inevitably, the young Emperor Kwang Hsu would come to the throne and summon Kang Yu-wei to his side. Immediately the famous edicts which were issued at a mounting pace in 1898 would be reissued, and once more China would be able to hold up her head.

Hsiao San and Mao debated the future. They were both Reformists; and they began to look forward to a time when China would become a constitutional monarchy: there would be peace and plenty for all, and there would be no need for them to disturb themselves over politics, for both would become teachers or writers. Then they learned that the young Emperor had died on the same day as, or the day before, the Empress Dowager and that the two-year old Emperor Hsuan T'ung had come to the throne. Power was being wielded by a regent as reactionary as the Empress Dowager.

About this time there occurred an incident which later became famous. Hsiao had found a book relating the lives of great generals and rulers in foreign countries. It was called *Great Heroes of the World.* Translated from an American original, it described the lives of Peter the Great, Wellington, Washington, Lincoln, Rousseau, Montesquieu, Catherine the Great, Gladstone, and Napoleon. Not all the articles came from the American book: the article on Montesquieu, for example, had been inserted because Liang Chih-chao, the disciple of Kang Yu-wei, had made great capital of *De l'Esprit des Lois,* until the youth of China had come to regard Montesquieu as perhaps the fountainhead of all Western knowledge. In this book it was not Montesquieu but Washington who fired Mao's imagination. Given *Great Heroes* one evening, he returned it the next morning. He had read it all. "We need great people like these," he commented. "We ought to study them and find out how we can make China rich and strong, and so avoid becoming like Annam, Korea, and India.[1] You know the old proverb 'If the cart in front turns over, let the cart behind take warning.' China is very weak; she will grow strong, rich, and independent only after many years; but the important thing is that we must learn these things. And it is not impossible. After six years of hard fighting, Washington defeated the British and began to build up America."

There was nothing in the least astonishing in this incident: similar discussions were taking place all over China. What was astonishing was the peculiar expression on Mao's face when he returned the book. "It was all very strange," Hsiao San told me when I met him in Kalgan. "I can remember exactly how he looked, and I can remember his tone as he said, 'We need great people like these.' I had the feeling that he had made his decision. Many years later I read Turgenev's *Fathers and Sons*, and instantly I recognized the authoritative Mao I had known in my youth. He breathed authority, never more than at that moment, and yet he looked just like all the other students, and he differed from them in being a little more handsome than most, and because he had a quick, loping stride, and always carried a load of books under his arm. He was Bazarov, dedicated to scholarship—particularly history—and the peasants."

Though Hsiao San knew Mao better than most people, there were defenses he never penetrated. He says he never came to understand Mao intimately: there were secret springs never disclosed. Mao could read twice or three times as fast as any other man. In libraries he surrounded himself with a wall of books. No one Hsiao San had ever known hungered for such a vast quantity of knowledge on so many different levels. Mao was the first to enter the library and the last to leave. Though he was the most brilliant scholar at the school, he discounted scholarship, saying that it was perfectly easy to read but that something more was necessary—an understanding of the laws of civilization. It was

1. These were the countries which the Hunanese viceroy, Chang Chih-tung, in his book *Five Objects of Knowledge*, described as "warnings."

a chance phrase from a famous essay by Liang Chih-chao. So Mao talked continually about social rights and social duties, from the point of view of one who sees hope of peaceful change.

REVOLUTION AND SOCIAL THEORIES

To understand Mao Tse-tung, it is necessary to understand the social theories advanced in China at the beginning of the century, the peculiar atmosphere of the times. His Marxism was a later accretion; in the most impressionable years of all he was influenced by the Taipings and by the Chinese revolutionary movements of the past, about which he was extraordinarily well informed. He was fundamentally under the influence of Kang Yu-wei and Liang Chih-chao. He was passionately delighted with the Reform party. All that was modern and advanced was represented by these two figures, one the theoretician, the other the popularizer. Both, in a sense, were nineteenth-century mechanists. They drew their inspiration from Darwin and Spencer, and from an obscure book called *Principles of Western Civilisation,* by the Englishman Benjamin Kidd. It was one of the books translated by Yen Fu, and according to Liang Chih-chao it was destined "to influence all the races of the world, to be a great light to the future."

The book, now forgotten, possessed an incalculable influence, for it sought to answer the precise questions which disturbed the Chinese. The evidence of Western civilization they knew: the principles by which Western civilization arose and commanded its own strange progress were unknown. For the reformers, Kidd was the answer to all their problems, for he traced all the forms of society through their stages of evolution, and he did all this more solemnly and at the same time more simply than Herbert Spencer would ever have dared to do. This minor sociologist was readable, and Liang Chih-chao found him more stimulating than Marx, and more entrancing than Huxley. "Kidd stands out

above all the others," he wrote, "and takes a step forward."
He continued:

Kidd maintains that man is like the other animals: without struggle there can be no progress. Whether it be a struggle between
individual and individual or race and race, the outcome is that the
unfit is defeated and perishes while the superior who is the equal
to the situation flourishes. This is an unchanging law, and in this
movement of evolution *there must be the sacrifice of the individual
for society, of the present for the future. Therefore the man who
grasps at his own immediate profit entirely misunderstands the
theory of evolution. He is indeed a criminal to the evolutionist . . .
He is not a help but an injury to the cause of man's survival.*[2]

Marx, too, had been impressed with Spencer's development of the theory of the evolution, and it had confirmed
his authoritarian temper. So it was in China. The elements
which really went to make the principles of the West—the
desire for height, the delight in liberty, the far-ranging ex-
altations of the mind, and the belief in youth—were omitted
in the dry-as-dust theories of the Victorian sociologists, who
saw their categories and advanced their philosophies in terms
of a sterile theory of evolution, in which evolution itself,
rather than man, acquired prime importance. Kidd did
hardly more than popularize Herbert Spencer, but he left
upon the awakening minds of the young Chinese indelible
traces.

At this time Mao was reading the *Hsin Min Chung Pao*
(*The New People's Journal*) once edited by the Reformers in
exile in Yokohama, now clandestinely printed in China.
It was heady wine, full of Liang Chih-chao's theories, his
urgent demands that the "new people" should take their
future in their own hands. Kang Yu-wei had believed that
the great dream of *Ta Tung* could not come about until the
surrender of nationality to the greater sovereignty of a world
state. Liang Chih-chao began to see increasing benefits in
nationalism. Was it not their sense of overriding nationalism
which had brought England, the United States, Germany,

2. The italics are in the original. I owe this quotation to Professor E.
R. Hughes' exceedingly significant book, *The Invasion of China by the
Western World*, New York, 1938, p. 211.

and France into their positions of power? He upheld the virile spirit of nationalism and the domination of other races, and showed that China would perish unless she set out to affirm her own nationalism over her neighbors.

The importance of the *Hsin Min Chung Pao* lay less in the particular philosophy it inherited from the English evolutionists than its insistence on the "new people," the new dedicated students who would change China from top to bottom. Hu Shih in his autobiography has explained the changing atmosphere. First, in the 1850's, the idea of *hsi hsueh*, "Western learning," had been prominent. This was followed by a period in which particular prominence was laid on *pien hua*, "reform," and this in turn was followed by a period in which the students spoke increasingly about *hsin hsueh*, the "new learning," which demonstrated the synthesis between East and West. Finally, there was the period of *hsin min*, the "new people." To be new, to be modern, to be completely informed about the nature of social change, and to create an entirely new people—this was the prospect which faced the young Chinese students in the first decade of the century.

There was, however, nothing essentially revolutionary in this attitude. It, too, had origins in the ancient classics; the opening sentence of the first great classic taught to schoolboys introduced the phrase "making a new people," and Confucius himself in the *Great Learning* had pointed approvingly at the famous bath-tub on which were written the words: "Everything must be made anew." Newness, and a new people, and a vast new horizon, and the whole archaic past thrown overboard—with such thoughts the students faced the future, building a theoretical world possessing greater validity than the world of the Empress Dowager which they saw around them. So Liang Chih-chao wrote passionately, and often inaccurately, about Rousseau, Hobbes, Bentham, Spinoza, and Montesquieu, and he saw the new China emerging as a constitutional monarchy with an independent judiciary and a government responsible to the national assembly, and the laws modeled on the laws of England. Indeed, England provided the model, and he particularly approved of habeas corpus; he wanted gradual change on the English pattern, and wrote that "revolution always retards the progress of a nation." In his admiration of England, however, he was almost alone; and something in the temper of the time demanded more violent solutions. The tragedy of the Chinese civil wars can be foreseen in those passionate pages in which Liang Chih-chao, though demanding moderation, suggested solutions which could only come about by violence.

This is, of course, a digression, but it is vitally necessary to understand the temper of Mao's mind as it was formed by the intellectual atmosphere at the beginning of the century. His mind was formed during the years 1906–9, the years during which Liang Chih-chao's reformist *Hsin Min Chung Pao* fought a continual running battle with another clandestine journal, called the *Min Pao,* edited by Wang Ching-wei and Hu Han-min, both of whom Mao came to know intimately later. Mao's intellectual roots are to be found in the mechanistic philosophy of the nineteenth century, and it is from Spencer, rather than from Marx, that he derived the belief that the individual must be sacrificed to the state. His beginnings lie with English sociology and the English conception of constitutional reform. He had nothing but contempt for the revolutionaries. Surely the monarchy would last forever! Surely the order of the universe demanded the most gentle kind of change! It was only much later that he rejoiced in the thought of revolution. Meanwhile, it was perhaps inevitable that the great debate should grow more heated as the issues of reform and revolution— precisely the same issues were debated in China during the recent civil war—were discussed in the pages of the two journals. It is one of the more subtle ironies of history that Mao began by sympathizing with the Reformers, but by the time he came to know the revolutionaries well he was already planning a far more vigorous revolution than they had ever contemplated.

The portrait that emerges is clear: a tousle-haired boy steeped in the classics and the historical novels of ancient China, uncommonly studious, passionately fond of wandering over the low hills of Hunan, perpetually wondering why it was that in all the histories and all the novels there was no account of the peasants. It came to him, as he wandered from village to village during the holidays, that the peasants were the forgotten heroes, possessing an immemorial wisdom. They were kinder than the people who lived in towns, more resourceful, and they possessed an abundant culture of their own. More particularly, they possessed the quality of "energy" which Mao was beginning to demand of everything he respected. "Everything had to be 'energetical,'" Hsiao San remembered. "It was no good unless it displayed the qualities of energy: he tested everything by what he called his 'secret formula.'" And where was the source of energy? Clearly, it was the sun. So Mao developed a theory of nudism: one could suck up the energy of the sun by walking about naked, or nearly naked. The two friends wandered over the hills, wearing blue drawers, barefoot, till they were both tanned by the sun; and when the peasants laughed at them, Mao said: "The sun is the source of health. Isn't it the sun which makes the rice grow? Then why wear too many clothes?" They learned that they were in danger of arrest, for the Manchu police frowned on the two nearly naked students who walked in the sun. They believed that a new and dangerous cult might emerge.

"I think it was at that time that Mao set his face away from the townspeople," Hsiao San said. "He approved of the peasants; he approved of no one else. What he particularly approved of in the peasants was their courtesy and their loyalty to one another. He said that the townspeople were not really loyal to one another; and they were not courteous by nature, they simply followed accepted customs. In a sense he was split between his admiration for scholarship and scholars, and his admiration for the peasants. He thought he would be a teacher, and he would spend his time teaching peasants."

Meanwhile the wanderings over the hills continued during the holidays. Both Hsiao San and Mao came to know the reaches of the Hsiang River. They walked to Changsha, thirty miles away; they walked to Liuyang and Lilin in the

south. There was hardly a village in the five counties of
Changsha, Hsiang T'an, Hsianghsiang, Lilin, and Hung
Shan which they did not know well. It was in these five
counties that Mao was later to launch his own insurrections.
But in those days the thought of insurrection was far from
his mind, and though he studied the conditions in the villages carefully, he was more interested in theories of government, in history, in the pure physical pleasure of wandering among the Hunanese hills. Above all, he was enjoying
his freedom for the first time, no longer at the beck and call
of his father. He said: "It was good training. I lived very
simply, with almost no money, but it was an amazing period of discovery." He was beginning to think ahead. To
gether with Hsiao San, he decided to enter the Junior College in Changsha.

Early in the spring of 1911, Mao and Hsiao San were accepted as pupils, but they had hardly settled down when
there occurred the fourth Kuomintang uprising under the
command of Hwang Hsing. On April 27, between half-
past-four and six o'clock, Hwang Hsing led 130 of his followers against the Canton yamen. These followers included
the flower of the Kuomintang. For the first time they were
provided with adequate funds and ammunition, and they
were given nine supporting columns, numbering altogether
about eight hundred trained revolutionary troops, with orders to concentrate on the outlying fortifications. They did
their work well, but they failed to reach the interior of the
yamen at the time when Hwang Hsing had entered it, and
the fierce little group of guerrillas supporting Hwang Hsing
was cut down. Forty-three revolutionaries were killed in
battle, and twenty-seven were captured and executed. The
"seventy-two martyrs of the Yellow Flower Mound" became famous all over China. "They have failed, but they
will strike terror in the hearts of our enemies," pronounced
Sun Yat-sen.

In Changsha it was believed that the next uprising would
occur in the Hunanese capital. It was the year of decision,
and like everyone else Mao spent the summer in mingled
exasperation and expectation, for the final revolution which

would throw the Manchus from their thrones could not be longer delayed.

In the excitement of the time, Mao began to write political articles. They were not printed, so he posted them up on the wall, signing them with a pseudonym. He also took part in "queue-chopping expeditions" and claimed that he had ten queues to his credit. He was still feeling his way. If he was now against the Manchus, he had not yet declared his allegiance to the Kuomintang.

In October, when the revolution broke out at Wuhan, he was still at college, still undetermined about the future, and still at the mercy of the minute changes in the political atmosphere at the time. "I was a pure weathercock. I knew nothing. I simply followed the trend," he said of this period later. It was probably impossible to do otherwise.

The revolution broke out as the result of the accidental explosion of some gunpowder belonging to the secret Kuomintang organizations, the casks being hidden in the Russian concession at Hankow. From this moment onward there was to be a strange contact with the Russians throughout the whole of the Kuomintang revolution.

Meanwhile, accident followed accident. Li Yuan-hung, the future leader of the revolutionary army, was a liberal officer who had sworn to defend the Manchu Empire. He had no desire to lead the uprising. On the night when the gunpowder exploded, he was found hiding under his bed, with only his boots visible. Asked to sign a document calling upon the whole country to rise against the Manchus, he explained nervously that he had no authority to sign such a document. Hwang Hsing was away. There was no one to command the revolutionary forces. The times were desperate. The revolutionaries, instead of shooting the officer for disloyalty to the revolution, threatened to shoot themselves in his bedroom if he refused. He finally agreed to sign the document only because he was afraid that the blood of the revolutionaries who shot themselves would spoil his favorite carpet.

In this atmosphere, caught up in a wayward revolutionary tide, hardly knowing what was at stake, trusting that the

Reform party would take over power, with Kang Yu-wei
as prime minister and Sun Yat-sen perhaps as president, Mao
decided to join the revolutionary army at Hankow. The
times were too quick for him. Changsha itself declared its
independence before the end of the year; a student army
was formed; everyone was talking about marching on Peking
and dethroning the Emperor, for the Regent did not immediately resign his functions. In the hothouse atmosphere
of Hunan nothing went according to schedule. Not all the
army sided with the revolutionaries. There were conflicts
within the province, and armies were marching and counter-
marching up and down the Hsiang River. Mao joined the
regular army, in the hope that it would be sent immediately
against Peking, but by the end of the year agreement between Sun Yat-sen and Yuan Shih-kai, the warlord who had
assumed power after the collapse of the Manchus, was in
sight. Thirsting for a military career, and with a desire for
glory, Mao found himself a common soldier in Changsha on
garrison duty. He was paid seven dollars a month, and his
chief occupation was to be the servant of the younger officers.

During the revolution, Mao showed no signs of military
brilliance. He detested the violence of the soldiers among
themselves, the perpetual threats of execution for the slightest misdemeanor, and he suspected that the revolution had
failed in its main purpose. Yuan Shih-kai had assumed the
role of Napoleon, turning the current of revolution back
again toward autocracy; and with Sun Yat-sen's inexplicable
surrender to Yuan Shih-kai, Mao found himself for the
first time leading a completely aimless existence in Changsha.
By the summer of 1912 he had left the Army and he was living in poverty in a lodging-house.

RESTLESS YEARS

There appears very often in the lives of men who later
become revolutionaries periods of intolerable poverty and
indecision. Uprooted, without money, suddenly confronted

with harsh necessity, they withdraw into themselves while at the same time, in order to live at all, they take on the most menial occupations. So Hitler painted his postcards and became a paper-hanger, Chiang Kai-shek became a bartender and Lenin a proofreader.

Mao read the advertisements desperately. He was receiving no funds from home, because his father disapproved of his becoming a soldier, and he was living on money borrowed from his friends. The first advertisement he read concerned a new soap factory. Another concerned a police school. A third concerned a commercial school. He toyed with them all. There were advantages in soap-making. Had not Liang Chih-chao thundered in one of his editorials that the one thing which China needed to learn from the West was the importance of cleanliness and sanitation? The police school pleased him, for he had been in some kind of trouble with the military police in the Army. The school of commerce was a last resort: it would please his father, but he knew he had no aptitude for trade. He answered the advertisements, paid registration fees, interviewed the principals and was interviewed by them, and sooner or later he knew he would be compelled to choose between them. He had no desire to choose. He knew now what he wanted to be: the eternal student, the man who goes to college and never leaves, delaying his graduation from year to year, accepting some small position in the college—a junior librarian or a bursar's assistant—happy in his reading, and in the absence of responsibilities. He entered the Teachers' Training College at Changsha with Hsiao San, and there he stayed for nearly six years.

In those early days following the revolution, the teachers' training colleges were at the mercy of conflicting schedules and conflicting aims. An entirely new system of education, with its emphasis on Western science, had been ordered by the government. But there were few teachers trained in science, and the old "eight-legged essays"—those ancient classical essays devised to torture candidates in the imperial examinations—were still being written. All education was in the melting-pot. Subjects taught one year were mysteriously removed from the curriculum the next, and incompetent professors were numerous. It was possible to become a professor of English while knowing only a smattering of English; there were professors of science who maintained their position only by reading a few pages of the textbook ahead of the students.

Mao had thought of acquiring huge areas of knowledge of Western science and philosophy: the teaching was so inept that he revolted. He had studied ancient Chinese philosophy and history, and learned to write passable classical essays at the middle school in Hsianghsiang. These same studies were continued at the Teachers' Training College. Here, too, he met Professor Yang Chen-chi, who was the first to give him the kind of encouragement he needed, praising his essays, putting them in a prominent place on the notice board, and urging the other students to "follow the example of Mao Tse-tung, who writes elegantly and honestly."

Professor Yang Chen-chi was a short man with a small, narrow face and a dome-shaped forehead, exquisite gestures, and a delusive quietness. More than any other teacher Mao had seen, he represented the moral strength of the classical past. He developed a deep affection for Mao, lent him books, spoke about England—which he had visited, though without much profit and with something of a Chinese scholar's disdain—and he habitually gave 100 points to Mao's essays, though always warning Mao of his facility. Mao in turn never failed to show him profound respect.

It was during this time that Mao for the first time came face to face with socialism. As Hsiao San related it, he came quite accidentally upon a book written by Chiang Kan-fu, which gave an inaccurate account of the development of socialism in England and on the Continent. "If you read the book now, you would think it was ridiculous, it was so muddleheaded; but it contained some good quotations and mentioned the names of Owen and Marx. It was the first time Mao had ever heard of socialism, and he was wildly excited. All his sympathies, all his scholarship, all his memories of life on the farm and in the Army seemed to lead to one conclusion: he would become a Socialist. He looked around, and saw no Socialist party in China, and thought the time had come to bring one into existence, with himself perhaps as the founder. Later he read three books: the *Communist Manifesto*, Kautsky's *The Class-War*, and a history of socialism by someone whose name I've forgotten. He was completely thunderstruck by these books."

A JOURNEY TO THE NORTH

By the time the First World War had come, Mao was a convinced and erratic Socialist. He no longer took his lessons at the college seriously. Except for a few professors whose courses he attended, he was spending most of his time studying newspapers or buried among the books of the public library, which had been founded by Hsiung Hsi-ling. The library was excellently equipped, and its discovery represented one of Mao's happiest days. He immersed himself in it, sometimes spending ten hours· at his desk without moving, going without food, continually taking notes; and a prodigious memory allowed him to regard the day as time spent in absorbing knowledge, which could then be conveniently reinterpreted at night. Hsiao San says that he did not merely turn his attention to what he read, but seemed to turn his whole body to the work in hand, and he would come out of the library with a high fever, his eyes like black smudges on the pale face, and immediately launch into an excited description of the things he had read. In the libraries, too, he was able to read the newspapers from all parts of China, and it was at this time that he developed almost a mania for reading newspapers, checking the accounts of events as they were reported in different cities. Sun Yat-sen, though powerless, was beginning to come into prominence in 1915, for Yuan Shih-kai was at last overreaching himself, and under Tsai Ao in Yunnan a formidable army was being raised against the dictator. Mao had paid little attention to the evolution of the Kuomintang. He reread, or read for the first time, old copies of the *Min Pao*, which had ceased publication in 1909, and made a careful comparison between the

strategy of the Reformers and the strategy of the Kuomintang. The Reformers were regarded as far superior to the
Kuomintang, which had failed in its revolutionary attempts
because it was lacking in any carefully thought-out plans:
the Reformers, on the contrary, had numerous and excellent
plans, though it was observed that Liang Chih-chao invented
a new kind of state every spring, only to demolish it by the
autumn; the winters were spent in preparing the foundations for the new, imaginary state to be constructed the
following year. Mao admired them, if only for their inventiveness, and when he came to found his first political society,
it was a society of students gathered together to study the
works of the Reformers and bearing the name long associated
with the Reform party. The society, called the *Hsin Min
Hsueh Hui* ("New People's Study Organization") was subversive only in the limited sense that it disapproved of Yuan
Shih-kai's dictatorship. It was, as Mao came to admit rather
ruefully later, considerably less subversive than many of the
radical societies then coming to birth in the large cities.

With the death of Yuan Shih-kai, in 1915, the civil wars,
which were to plague China for thirty-five years, began in
earnest. Mao was not particularly interested in them. He was
antimilitarist as a result of his own brief experience in the
Army, and he realized that the Chinese wars were being
fought according to obsolete patterns. He read avidly everything he could lay his hands on concerning the World War.
He gave elementary lectures on strategy. He had been particularly delighted with Galliéni's effort to prevent von Kluck's
encirclement of Paris in September 1914 by commandeering
all the taxicabs, and he followed Hindenburg's campaigns in
Russia with interest; the influence of Hindenburg's use of
massive driving wedges in the battle of the Masurian Lakes,
leading to the destruction of a quarter of a million Russians,
delighted him and was to remain with him. These two events
were the only European examples he remembered when he
later came to write *Strategic Problems of China's Revolutionary Wars*.

Mao was now the leader of a progressive movement in
Hunan which made no claim to being revolutionary. Sur-

rounded by a crowd of earnest young men, who included Hsiao San and a youth called Lo Man, who was to become a high official in the Chinese Communist party, Mao was beginning to put his mind to the practical affairs of organization. The *Hsin Min Hsueh Hui* was not a political association; it was simply a society of young students earnestly debating the problems of the day and contemptuous of officialdom. They regarded themselves as the "new people," exchanged newspapers, thought of and discarded ideas of revolutionary action, gave lectures, and enjoyed debate. Mao dominated the small group, which never amounted to more than a hundred. He was slowly testing himself, discovering the sources of his power and enjoying the role of chairman; he was older than most of the other members and considerably more widely read.

But if his age gave him authority, it was also a sign of his inability to find himself: he was developing slowly. Handsome, brilliant, restless, and always poor, with a genius for discovering intelligence among young Hunanese students, already the pedagogue saturated with knowledge on a diversity of subjects, he might have become in time one of those erratic, charming, and aimless teachers who are occasionally to be found in Chinese colleges—men with exceptionally fine minds who write one or two short books during their lifetime and have no influence outside a small circle. "At that time," said Hsiao San, "there were two things he might have become, or rather three. He could become an editor or a teacher, or a combination of both, or he could become a great general. I was firmly convinced that he would make a good general because he talked so brilliantly about war. Also, he had already fought a campaign. This happened quite early during our life at the college. It often happens that soldiers will receive orders to take over colleges for barracks. Our own college received an ultimatum. Mao immediately sprang to its defense. He took charge as though he had received the sanction of the Ministry of War. He drilled the students and professors. His orders, even to the senior professors, were instantly obeyed. He sent out students to buy arms and medical supplies. We kept the soldiers out, and

Mao remarked: 'This is the first time I have taken military command.' He seemed to know it wouldn't be the last."

In the summer of 1918 Mao graduated, and shortly before the graduation his mother died, so breaking the last tie which bound him to Shao Shan. For a long while he had been on bad terms with his father. Peking beckoned. China had declared war against Germany and Austria in August 1917. Shortly afterward, Lloyd George, surveying the loss of manpower on the western front, requested the Chinese government to send laborers to France, and now at last from Tientsin, Shanghai, and Hong Kong, flotillas of laborers were being sent, though Sun Yat-sen thundered against the agreement, saying that imperialism had claimed these men and imperialism would ruin them. Some young Hunanese laborers had decided to make the journey. The *Hsin Min Hsueh Hui,* which had once followed the Reform party, had flirted with Sun Yat-sen, and was coming gradually to accept the ideas of some intellectual leaders in Peking, helped to finance their journey to the coast, and then turned its attention to its own lack of knowledge of Europe. Should not these young students also make the pilgrimage?

In 1915 Dr. Tsai Yuan-pei had formed a society with the strange name of the Diligence-Labor-Simplicity-Educational-Society to encourage students to obtain their higher education in France while performing manual labor. Inquiries were made. Costs were carefully worked out. By borrowing, and by selling some of their possessions, about ten students, including Mao and Hsiao San, set out for Peking with the intention of making their way to France. Among the travelers was one of Mao's teachers, Hsu Teh-li, who was the exact opposite of Yang Chen-chi. This old scholar, born in 1876, who never wore an overcoat and who propounded theories of vegetarianism and had a fondness for swimming in rivers, delighted Mao, who later appointed him director of education at Yenan. He was always laughing, and the journey to the North was made to the accompaniment of his almost superhuman talent for finding amusement in everything.

Mao was appointed commander-in-chief of the expedition,

though he had no desire to go abroad and was content to supervise the operation, delighting in the complexities of travel and happy to leave Hunan and see the world outside for the first time in his life. He had everything to gain. The life in the provincial capital was like life in provinces everywhere: the glory had departed. For a brief moment the white flag with the character for Han[3] written on it in blood-red letters had flown over Changsha as a sign of its conquest by the revolutionaries; then the flag had been hauled down, to be replaced by the five-striped flag, each stripe representing one of the five races inhabiting China: Chinese, Manchu, Mongol, Mohammedan, and Tibetan, and then for a brief while Yuan Shih-kai had resurrected the flag showing the imperial dragon. There were to be other flags later: in less than ten years there was to appear in Hankow a red flag with a small hammer and sickle in a blue center. All this lay in the future. As they tramped round the Tung Ting Lake and took ship down the Yangtse, none of these students could have dreamed what lay before them.

3. Han was the name of an ancient, warlike dynasty. The Kuomintang revolutionaries seriously modeled themselves on its leaders.

The New Youth

In the summer of 1918 Peking was passing through a period of desultory peace. Ruled by warlords, who formed uneasy combinations of power, the city slumbered through the last months of the First World War, a rich city, and now richer than it had ever been, for silver was not yet devalued currency and the Maria Theresa dollar was worth more than one and a half American dollars. The casual observer saw prosperity everywhere, and even when Sun Yat-sen thundered from the small government chamber in Canton against the *tuchuns* of the North, hardly a ripple was perceptible in the dusty streets of Peking. Far away, on the other side of the continent, the Russian revolution was stirring up a convulsive war against the remnants of czarism; huge armies were wandering across Siberia; Lenin was proclaiming the dissolution of the state; but in Peking the state remained, represented by the strange feudal monsters, resplendent in their gaudy uniforms modeled on those worn by obscure princelings of Germany. Meanwhile, from Peking there was being organized the immense army of Chinese coolies who were to be sent, usually too late, to dig trenches on the western front. No one was ever to know exactly how many coolies were shipped to Europe: the figures run from 100,000 to 200,000. Unknown to the *tuchuns*, the mass export of coolies from Tientsin, Shanghai, and Canton was to seal the fate of the Chinese Empire.

In later years Mao was to say that he came to Peking in order to organize the Hunanese students who were planning to go to France on the "work and learn" scheme invented by the French to bolster their dwindling man power. There were other reasons. He had long desired to study at Peking University. He had made sporadic attempts to learn French and English, and at one time, according to Hsiao San, he had contemplated writing a study of the French and American revolutions. But there were no good foreign-language teachers in Hunan outside the missionaries, and he had long ago set his face against missionaries of any kind. He was perfectly prepared to spend his days reading quietly in the great Peking libraries. He would learn languages. He would travel, like Yang Chen-chi, abroad. In the end he would take some minor position in the government. He still regarded himself as the dedicated student, a young Bazarov perfectly content to occupy a small place in the provincial history of Hunan. He helped to organize the Hunanese students, saw that they went through a short training period at Chung-Fa, the Chinese-French university, and then saw them off on the boat at Tientsin. By the time they sailed, the World War was already coming to an inevitable conclusion.

Autumn came early in 1918. With almost no money left, and most of his friends on their way to Europe, Mao found himself alone in Peking without a job and with a desperate desire to bury himself in libraries through the long winter ahead. He was twenty-five, of an age when most men have already settled upon their profession or occupation; and he was farther away than ever from having made up his mind what he wanted to accomplish.

In all this Mao was not alone. Peking was filled with uprooted intellectuals who flocked to the capital, stayed there for a few years, and then retired, defeated, to their ancestral villages. The imperial examinations open to poor students from all over the empire had come to an end, though for a brief period they had been revived by Yuan Shih-kai. Peking University was still the intellectual center of China, and it was at this university that Mao had wanted to study, for here at least he could have the illusion for a few years that he was not uprooted, that he belonged to the classical tradition of the Chinese scholar. Someone reminded him that Yang Chen-chi was then lecturing at the college on Chinese philosophy. Mao went to him, explained his situation, and was immediately whisked off to meet Li Ta-chao, then the librarian and later to become the real founder of the Chinese Communist party.

Mao received a minor position in the library. It was his duty to fetch the newspapers requested by the students, place them on the tables, and then collect them together and return them to the files. In the whole university it was hardly possible to conceive of a more menial position: he was a little above the coolies and the sweepers, but he received the same salary as the coolies, and the students poring over the newspapers treated him as though he possessed only a mechanical existence. The great professors came, demanded their newspapers, and went away; and if Mao so much as paused to ask them a question, he was treated with the indifference with which scholars at that time treated the poor. Years later, when he came to discuss the relationship between scholarship and the people, Mao openly confessed that he came to detest these highhanded professors who spoke to him, when they spoke to him at all, with such evident contempt. "I knew then," he said, "that there was something wrong. For hundreds of years the scholars had moved away from the people, and I began to dream of a time when the scholars would teach the coolies, for surely the coolies deserve teaching as much as the rest."

The story of Mao's first few months in the library is one of baffled retreat before the conventions of Chinese scholarship. He saw little of Yang Chen-chi, not daring to show himself in his worn black gown. Rebuffed after a serious effort to engage the young radical Fu Ssu-nien in conver-

sation—the young radical was later to become a pontifical reactionary president of the university in its exile in Kunming
—he kept very much to himself, nervous and ill at ease in
the huge capital, where nearly everyone disappears into a
quiet anonymity, and where it is possible to die without
anyone paying the slightest attention. He found a translation
of one of Bakhunin's pamphlets, and announced to his rare
friends that he was an anarchist. There were similarities
between Bakhunin's anarchism and traditional Taoism. He
began to think that the only solution for China's problems
was a complete decentralization of government and that the
government itself must be violently overthrown, forgetting
that decentralization would only make China still more powerless to resist the demands of Japan and the Western
powers. He corresponded with other anarchists. He even
thought for a while of founding an anarchist society. Anarchism was in the air, and in Hunan especially there were
small anarchist groups among the industrial workers. But as
winter came on, the rage for an anarchist China gave way to
more simple pleasures. He saw more and more of Yang Chen-
chi, and he began to forget the loneliness and misery of his
life in the contemplation of Peking in a calm, snow-bound
winter.

In his youth, Mao had walked barefoot and bare-chested
across the desolate fields of Hunan, where there are few
trees and almost no palaces. Here there were more trees and
palaces than he could ever count, all of them shining in the
frosty sunlight. Most of the Forbidden City was now thrown
open to the public. He could wander at leisure over marble
bridges and painted colonnades; and around the North Lake
stood the sloping yellow roofs of the palaces emerging among
the bare branches of the willows; and he could pace the borders of the lake, where all the lotuses were frozen, remembering that only a few years previously it would have been a
capital offense to enter these immense parks reserved for the
Emperor's family and attendants. In summer Peking is hidden
in a green carpet of trees; in winter the city shines clear, but the
trees themselves form a kind of silvery frame for the magnificence of blood-red walls and gleaming yellow roofs. Mao

was perfectly aware of the imperial magnificence, and he took careful inventory of the trees. Nearly twenty years later the memory was still vivid. "I saw the white plum-blossom flower while the ice still held over the North Lake. I saw the willows over the lake with the ice crystals hanging from them and remembered the description of the scene by the T'ang poet Ts'en Ts'an, who wrote about Pei Hai's winter-jeweled trees, looking like 'ten thousand peach trees blossoming.'"[1] It was characteristic of Mao that he should have chosen to remember the most vigorous and most pellucid of the T'ang poets; and in fact his own poetry borrows as deeply from Ts'en Ts'an as his prose borrows from Han Yu.

Though he was living in great poverty, this winter was probably the happiest in Mao's life. He fell in love with Yang K'ai-hui, the daughter of his professor of philosophy; he rode over the western hills on pony-back; he attended lectures at the university and immersed himself in poetry. More important, he found himself turning away from anarchism to socialism, and he discovered that the indifference with which he was treated in the library had been due partly to his own nervousness. He was gradually finding himself. He made friends and found himself caught up in all the social and literary movements which centered around the university. Hu Shih had returned the previous year from America with a bold program for substituting *pei hua,* the language of the common people, for the traditional literary language of the classics. Tsai Yuan-pei, the "great innovator", had become president and chancellor of the university and was dedicating himself to renewing the springs of Chinese youth.

CHEN TU-HSIU

More influential than any of these was the dean of the faculty of Chinese letters, Chen Tu-hsiu, who had been editing the magazine *New Youth (Hsin Ch'ing Nien)* ever since the famous day in September 1915 when the students of Pe-

1. Edgar Snow, *Red Star over China,* New York, 1938, p. 151.

king were suddenly made aware from his first editorial that a
new, iconoclastic force had arisen, urging them all to sweep
away the corrupt Confucian past. "The task of the new generation," he proclaimed, "is to fight Confucianism to the
death, all the old traditions of virtue and ritual, all the old
philosophies and all the old political subtleties: and the old
learning must go altogether. We must break down ancient
prejudices and build a new society based on democracy and
science."

It was heady wine, but though the students of Peking hung
on his words and repeated them endlessly, Mao was not
wholly impressed. He was making his way slowly. There
were other reviews besides *New Youth*. In the four years
between 1917 and 1921, nearly four hundred student reviews appeared in China, most of them short-lived, many
of them containing the character for "new" in the title. There
were reviews called *New Woman, New Light, New World,*
and even *New Air*. Mao read them avidly in the library, delighted that he no longer had to starve himself in order to buy
magazines, surrendering to the intellectual ferment of the
time, but wary of making decisions.

He met Chen Tu-hsiu briefly. At their first meeting neither
seems to have made any impact on the other. Intellectually,
Mao was more impressed with some of the young students in
the classes he attended, men like Cheng Kung-po and Chang
Kuo-t'ao, both of whom were to hold high office—the first as
puppet prime minister under the Japanese, until his execution by Chiang Kai-shek in the summer of 1946, and the
second as Mao's own superior within the Communist party,
until his desertion to the Kuomintang. Nearly all of his friends
of this period came to violent deaths. Intellectual violence
was in the air. It was at this time that there were sown the
seeds of the conflicts which came later.

Though Mao failed to come under the direct influence of
Chen Tu-hsiu at their first meeting, he could not escape the
pervading influence of the professor who almost single-
handedly had changed the intellectual atmosphere of his
time. Not until Wen Yi-tuo subtly exercised an intellectual
mastery over the exiled universities of China during the

Second World War did any professor exert so vast an influence on young Chinese students. Short and wiry, with a fine forehead and very large, questioning eyes, nearly always wearing a simple black scholar's gown, with an eye for women and a fine taste in food, Chen Tu-hsiu at the age of forty could already be counted as among the first four who were influencing the course of China, ranking with Sun Yat-sen, Liang Chih-chao and Kang Yu-wei, and in opposition to all of them. His influence was prodigious. It seeped down among the poverty-stricken coolies, if for no other reason than that the students themselves often became coolies. He had the habit of writing in short epigrammatic phrases. "The universal laws of science must take the place of the Chinese heaven," he wrote, and with this single phrase he swept Buddhism, Confucianism, and Taoism, which all concerned themselves in different ways with the interpretation of heaven (*tien*), into limbo. He approved and rejoiced in the Russian revolution, insisting that the Chinese should find comfort in a revolution directed not only against the Czar but against monarchism and imperialism; and at the same time he wrote superbly on the character of Jesus, insisting on the heroism of the Crucifixion, and he gave his blessing to the missionaries, who had, whatever their faults, brought Western culture to China. He flirted with Comte's positivism, and he was the first to comment intelligently on Marxism, devoting a whole issue of the review to a series of interpretations of Marxist philosophy. He was also in a very real sense a historical figure, for *New Youth* had come into being not long after Yuan Shih-kai had accepted the infamous Twenty-One Demands imposed upon China by Japan, and his review represented the only effective response to Japanese hostility.

Of all those Chinese who influenced Mao, Chen Tu-hsiu's influence was the greatest. Though the brief meeting in the winter of 1918 counted for little, there were to be endless meetings later. Chen Tu-hsiu not only influenced Mao's mind, but he influenced his style: and even the famous phrase "New Democracy" derives directly from Chen Tu-hsiu. Whole phrases, first written by this dean of the department of Chinese letters, are echoed and sometimes copied verbatim by Mao in the books he wrote years later in Yenan. It was a style which mingled exhortation with a vast hope, a concise, brutal, and entirely new style, deliberately denuded of the graces which previously informed Chinese apologetics. No one before had addressed the Chinese students in this way:

What I want to say, and to say with tears, is that I hope those of you who are young will be self-conscious and that you will struggle. By self-consciousness I mean that you are to be conscious of the power and responsibility of your youth, and that you are to respect it. Why do I think you should struggle? Because it is necessary for you to use all the intelligence you have to get rid of those who are decaying, who have lost their youth. Regard them as enemies and beasts: do not be influenced by them, do not associate with them.

O young men of China! Will you be able to understand me? Five out of every ten whom I see are young in age, but old in spirit; nine out of every ten are young in health, but they are also old in spirit. When this happens to a body, the body is dying. When it happens to a society, the society is perishing. Such a sickness cannot be cured by sighing; it can only be cured by those who are young, and in addition to being young are courageous. We must have youth if we are to survive, we must have youth if we are to get rid of corruption. Here lies the only hope for our society.[2]

To those who were brought up on classical Chinese, the new trumpet notes, deriving from Chen Tu-hsiu's reading of Nietzsche, were demonstrable evidence that China had come to the turning of the ways. Famous old scholars approached Tsai Yuan-pei and begged that Chen Tu-hsiu be removed from his post. Tsai Yuan-pei refused. He could hardly do anything else, for Chen Tu-hsiu was an excellent administrator, a scholar in his own right—he published voluminous surveys of T'ang Dynasty poetry—and he had also taken part in the revolution of 1911. In himself he represented the new youthful China, and at the same time he was a bridge between the past and the future, for his ancestral roots lay deep in the mandarinate, and for centuries his family had been powerful

2. Tsi C. Wang, *The Youth Movement in China*, New York, 1927, p. 98.

in Anhwei. He had one further advantage: he had traveled in France and Japan and knew the languages of both perfectly. Finally, he was well liked by the students and the faculty.

The Peking over which Chen Tu-hsiu ruled with invisible power resembled Moscow or St. Petersburg in the seventies of the last century. There were the same dedicated youths living in poverty and desperately attempting to work out solutions for the crisis in which China found herself. But while the young nihilists and anarchists of the seventies envisaged a single enemy solidly entrenched on the throne, the students saw countless *tuchuns* parading over China and maintaining a precarious balance of power. The task seemed almost hopeless. Before a new social state could come into being, they would have to be removed one by one; and every time a *tuchun* was removed, another might take his place.

A JOURNEY TO THE TOMBS

For Mao the long winter in Peking was also a period of withdrawal. He took almost no part in political activity. He learned some French and some English, courted Yang K'ai-hui —whom he married a year later in Shanghai—visited all the imperial monuments, walked round the walls of Peking, and attended to his duties in the library. And since the library was open from seven o'clock in the morning to nine o'clock at night, he had little leisure. He saved no money. He wore a threadbare gown and allowed his hair to grow long. He had very bright eyes, and he was almost excruciatingly thin. Before the winter was over, he had absorbed almost all that he wanted of Peking, and when another detachment of students bound for France left for Shanghai, he accompanied them as far as Tientsin, and there, finding himself penniless, he stayed for a few days until a chance encounter with a friend allowed him to borrow some money to continue the journey to Shanghai.

As usual, he made most of the journey on foot. Wandering was by now in his blood, and he was determined to wander over all the historic places, walk round all the historic walls, and make his way down all the historic roads. Yen Huei, one of the favorite disciples of Confucius—the only one of whom it was said that at his death Confucius mourned for him bitterly —had lived, according to tradition, in a village along the Huai River. Mao visited the place as an act of homage. He held Yen Huei in great honor. It was not only that Yen Huei was the most humble and the most devoted of the disciples, but he was also the one who had received more traditional respect than any of the others. Of him it was said that he was able to preserve an attitude of "perfect virtue" for three months, while others were unable to attain that level for more than a month or a few days. Some particular virtue lived in him, and since nearly a half of the Confucian *Analects* is concerned precisely with the problem of "perfect virtue" and the characteristics of the sage, which were never defined, except obliquely, Yen Huei has become a symbol of all that Confucian tradition meant by the superior person.

In all this Mao was perfectly at home. Like Bazarov, he had long ago decided to become a superior person, and the visit to Yen Huei's birthplace was more than an act of desultory homage.

Mao's wanderings led him to the tomb of Confucius at Chufu, and from there he went on to ascend the T'ai Shan, the Great Eastern Mountain, the highest in all China and the most sacred—a strange enough journey for one who confessed to be an anarchist, vowed to combat Confucianism. In fact, he had never wholly departed from Confucianism, and a hard Confucian core remained, to torment his enemies, who were neither so learned as he was nor so conscious of the role to be played by the superior person. There had been a famous sacrifice at the tomb of Confucius by Liu Pang, the first emperor of the Han dynasty. Liu Pang rose from obscurity to the conquest of an empire, raising the standard of revolt when he was still a shepherd, and creating his capital in Sian, a few miles south of Yenan. Mao was saturated in history and followed in nearly all their details the famous travels of the historian Ssu-ma Chien in this territory—as though he were attempting to see through the historian's eyes the past grandeur and the

present decadence of the empire. When he climbed the T'ai
Shan, he must have been perfectly aware that the Han
emperors had performed their sacrifices there and that it was
on the topmost summit that they received the secret utterances
of Heaven as they waved their jade batons.

It is possible, of course, to see too much in this journey. Mao
was marking time. He had not yet decided upon a course of
action. He was escaping from his librarian's job in Peking. He
had neither duties nor responsibilities. It is at such times that
ultimate decisions are made: at such moments of weariness
and wandering the mind plunges forward and scoops out its
own pathways. Later, he was to destroy Confucianism root
and branch; it is inconceivable that he would have been able
to destroy it without having submitted to its power, without,
in fact, being a Confucian himself.

Meanwhile he was the wandering scholar, continually on
the move, hardly to be distinguished from the hundreds of
other wandering scholars who were conscious of the power to
be derived from attending upon the holy shrines. Mao went
everywhere. He walked in the dead of winter on the ice in the
Gulf of Pei Hai, he visited the tomb of Mencius, and he continued to walk round the walls of historic cities, as though
already he was possessed with the desire of conquering them:
in ancient China the ceremonial march round the walls by
the conquering general was a mark of his triumph. Finally,
still nearly penniless, he returned to Changsha, but not before
he had spent a week wandering around the Tung Ting
lakes. He was fit and well. He had even managed to borrow a
little money in Shanghai. He knew more than he had ever
known before about the world outside Hunan, and he was
prepared to "exert himself to the utmost" on whatever political
issues confronted him, for at some time during his wanderings
he had determined to enter politics, and if possible overthrow
the men in power.

In Hunan, the times were ripe for change. While Mao was
away in the North, an expedition was sent against the Hunanese, then in one of their customary rebellions, by Tuan
Chih-jui, the prime minister. The generals in command of the

expedition were Wu Pei-fu and Chang Chin-yao. Wu Pei-fu was a Buddhist, a scholar, and a poet, possessing many of the graces usually absent among Chinese warlords. Chang Chin-yao was the pure type of the corrupt *tuchun*. When Chang Chin-yao was appointed governor of Hunan, and Wu Pei-fu was relegated to the subordinate position of vice-inspector of the military forces in Chihli, Shantung, and Honan, all Hunan was in ferment. Wu Pei-fu had recently written a bitter epigram describing his rival as "one whose fatty remains will serve to fertilize only a few yards of Chinese soil."

Mao, who had become editor of the *Hsiang River Monthly Review*, threw himself into the conflict, organized a student strike, and prepared to use the forces of the *Hsin Min Hsueh Hui,* which had continued in his absence, to attempt to over-throw not only Chang Chin-yao, but all the military governors who followed; and under the banner of the League to Renovate Hunan he proposed some kind of wide-scale anti-militarist revolt. Chen Tu-hsiu had proposed such leagues in the past. Mao thought the time had come to put the revolt into operation, for it was clear that the Kuomintang revolution of 1911 had abundantly failed. He sent himself on a mission to Chen Tu-hsiu, received the professor's benediction, and returned with the necessary blueprints of revolt. Chen Tu-hsiu had insisted upon some dramatic action, though he never made clear what kind of dramatic action was appropriate to the occasion.

Events were moving fast. Mao was continually on the move. Previously he had attended an anti-militarist conference, organized by students, in Peking in January 1919. This followed a mass meeting held during the previous November in the National Central Park, attended by nearly all the students of Peking National University. At the second meeting it was agreed that "if the world refuses to give up militarism, China should lead the way," and with this avowal of nonviolent resistance Mao was perfectly in agreement. The problem of the *tuchuns,* however, remained.

There were, of course, innumerable other problems. There was the deep restlessness of the student body, now replenished by many students returning from abroad; there was growing industrial arrest, a growing feeling of insecurity. China felt herself defenseless in a world at arms. Then, in the spring, came the explosion.

THE MAY FOURTH INCIDENT

On May 4, 1919, there occurred one of those rare critical events which completely alter the course of history. Revolutionary action had been employed by peasants and by guerrillas; it was now to be employed by students, and out of the student revolution, which canalized all the intellectual and moral frustrations of generations of Chinese, there was to emerge the pattern of a new, revolutionary China. With this movement, according to Mao, the Chinese Communist party had its beginnings.

Outwardly, it did not give the impression of being a Communist revolt. What had happened had little enough to do with social change. May 4, 1919 was the fourth anniversary of the presentation of the Twenty-One Demands on China by Japan, a day of national mourning. It happened that on this day there came news that the peacemakers at Versailles had granted the former German concessions at Shantung to Japan. It was an affront to Chinese dignity. It was also an indication of Japan's further designs. Immediately, a violent excitement swept over Peking. There was a sense of furious protest and at the same time a sense of relief. The time for direct action had come. What kind of direct action? Against whom? With what weapons? Chen Tu-hsiu had for some time been awaiting an explosion of this kind. His plans were prepared, and he carried them out with a masterly sense of order. He addressed the 5,000 students of Peking University, told them to elect committees to tour the neighboring colleges, and urged them to elect by ballot a supreme committee to be devoted to direct action. There was to be a student cabinet and a council of wardens to carry out the decisions of the supreme committee. There was to be nothing casual: everything must be done quietly and systematically. The purpose of the new political movement was to overthrow the government, which contained the three cabinet members who had signed and accepted the Twenty-One Demands.

At ten o'clock in the morning of May 4, the students assembled in the Law School of Peking University. In the afternoon they held a mass meeting outside the Tien An Men, the "Gate of Heavenly Peace," at the entrance of the Forbidden City. They were more than 10,000 strong, and they were armed with wooden clubs, iron bars, and cans of gasoline removed from the laboratories. Afterward they marched to the Legation Quarter, to ask the Allied ministers to help in securing justice for China. The American Minister, the first to be approached, refused to see them, though four students were allowed inside the Legation compound. It was a Sunday, and he was perhaps perfectly reasonable when he declared afterward that important business should not be contracted on a Sunday. The students, however, were angry. They had hoped to receive at least some sympathetic advice, perhaps even their recommendations might be transmitted to the Allied governments. Furious at what they considered the treachery of the Allies, they then marched to the house of Tsao Ju-lin, the minister of communications. The house was guarded by soldiers and policemen. They threw small paper flags over the high walls. Their intelligence system was excellent. They learned that all three of the hated pro-Japanese ministers were in the house. Thereupon they forced their way in, found the Ministers in consultation with some Japanese officials, and would have attacked them if the police had not suddenly fired over their heads. The house caught on fire, whether from a police bullet or from a match laid by a student, no one knows, and eventually the students were thrown out. They marched back to the university.

Except for the incident in the house, the procession had been orderly. So it was to remain. Every move which followed was calculated and deliberate: it was as though the students were working coldly and scientifically against the government. They called a roll call and discovered that thirty-two students were missing. They then called upon the chancellor, Tsai Yuan-pei, for advice. They wanted to march in procession to the police station, but Tsai Yuan-pei dissuaded them. He went alone. He was told that the students had been arrested for disturbing the peace.

The students now possessed a weapon with which they could cajole the government. On the next day they called another mass meeting and decided upon a provisional strike. Two days later the thirty-two students were freed, but arrests continued, and on May 14, while the strike was spreading to Shanghai and Nanking, the government issued two special rescripts which exasperated the students still further. The government ordered that the student activities should be suppressed by military force, and they announced that the decisions of the students would have no effect on a responsible government. The students then employed their strongest weapon: they declared a general strike. They had absolutely no warrant for the declaration, and were not empowered to make the declaration; but for a long time there had been an absence of any leadership, and the declaration was obeyed. The shops closed in Peking. The railwaymen on the Peking-Tientsin railway refused to allow trains to pass. Shortly afterward the industrial and craft workers in Peking went on strike, to be followed by those of Tientsin, Shanghai, Nanking, and Hankow. The government gave way. The "three national traitors" escaped to Japan without even the formality of resigning from the cabinet.

The success of the student movement surprised the students. For the first time they became aware of their power. The movement did not end with the defeat of the three ministers. The supreme committee of the Chinese students ordered an embargo on Japanese goods, and throughout the rest of the year there were continual clashes between students and Japanese. Not only Japan was blamed. Bitterness was deep: it was especially deep against America, because the Chinese felt that the Americans possessed a privileged position at Versailles and were ultimately responsible for the offer to Japan.

America's inexplicable disinterest in China's recovery was commented upon at length in the magazines and broadsides which began to be issued in increasing numbers with the words, "Remember May 4th," on their covers. The movement had arisen entirely from within the intelligentsia, who had never until this moment known that they could have such a prodigious influence over the shopkeepers and the workers. The peasants were unaffected; it was a purely urban movement, and it marked the beginning of student influence in politics.[3]

Mao must have known from his talks with Li Ta-chao that something of this kind was in the air. In so far as the movement could be planned, it was planned by Chen Tu-hsiu with the assistance of Li Ta-chao, both of whom regarded themselves by this time as at least under the influence of Marxism. It was no accident that in the same month *New Youth* issued a special edition consecrated to a lengthy study of Marxism by Li Ta-chao. The impact of Marxism and Leninism was now being felt on an increasing scale, and clandestine printing presses began to produce more and more translations of the writings of Marx and the speeches of Lenin. Among these speeches the most important was one delivered by Lenin early in 1918 calling upon the whole of the Orient to rise against the imperialists.

Actually, it was not a speech but a manifesto; yet it was couched in the phrases employed by oriental monarchs, with a strange mingling of revolutionary fervor and monarchical trumpeting. The more famous Manifesto to the Orient, issued two weeks after the Bolshevik revolution, had set the keynote. In it, together with a proclamation renouncing all czarist possessions in the Far East and pledges of support in the struggle for emancipation, there were apocalyptic references to "the empires of the unrighteous that are breaking down" and "the earth that is trembling under their feet." These references,

3. An extremely similar student movement occurred in October 1945 in Kunming, where the students struck in protest against the civil war. The students belonged to Peking, Nankai, and Tsinghua Universities, then in their long exile. They tried to enforce a general strike and very nearly succeeded, though they were finally beaten down by a Kuomintang reign of terror. Three students and one teacher were killed. The place assumed by Chen Tu-hsiu was taken by the poet Wen Yi-tuo, whose sympathies lay more with British socialism than with Marxism.

which show demonstrable signs of having been written by Bukharin, showed the temper of the times, the belief that the fire of revolution was about to sweep the whole world. Years later, with something of the same fervor, and at a comparable stage in the progress of a revolution, Mao Tse-tung, in the great palace at Peking, was to remember some of these phrases when, having declared the beginning of the dictatorship, he thundered: "Let the world tremble!"

With a more skillful administration, Li Ta-chao and Chen Tu-hsiu might have brought about a revolution in 1919. The students, the shopkeepers, the merchants, and the workers were on their side. Japan had been singled out as the main enemy, but all imperialists were included in a general denunciation. Inevitably, mistakes were made. It was one thing to accuse the foreigners of all the evils in China; it was altogether another thing to discover that many of the evils were the result of ancient Chinese traditions and a corrupt social system; and by directing the revolt outward, the leaders of what came to be known as the "May Fourth Movement" failed in their main purpose. Feudalism and the rule of the *tuchuns* remained unaffected; political cliques and warlords retained their power; and nothing was done to heal the breach between the Kuomintang in the South and the warlords in the North. Even more important was the fact that the soldiers and the peasants took no part in the movement.

Mao was swept up in the movement, and some of his original excitement appears in his account of it in *New Democracy*. He saw it as "a Communist revolt without Communists," and with some exaggeration acclaimed it as "the greatest and most thorough cultural revolution in Chinese history." He wrote:

The May Fourth Movement was an anti-imperialist as well as an anti-feudal movement. The outstanding historical significance of the May Fourth Movement lies in the fact that it possessed a feature not present in the 1911 revolution—it opposed imperialism and feudalism in the most thorough and uncompromising way. The reason why the May Fourth Movement possessed this characteristic is that the capitalist economy of China had made a new step in its development at that time. At the same time the revolutionary intelligentsia was witnessing the disintegration of the three great imperialist countries, Russia, Germany, and Austria, the weakening of Great Britain and France, and the construction of a socialist state by the Russian proletariat. Also, Germany, Austro-Hungary, and Italy were in the grip of proletarian revolutions. All these things gave new hope for the liberation of the Chinese nation.

It must be understood that the May Fourth Movement broke out at the call of the world revolution, of the Russian revolution led by Lenin, and formed a part of the world proletarian revolution of the time. Although we did not have a Chinese Communist party during the May Fourth Movement, many intellectuals did accept the primary Communist ideas, and they approved of the Russian revolution. In its beginnings the May Fourth Movement was a united-front revolutionary movement absorbing the energies of three kinds of people: the Communist-inclined intelligentsia, the revolutionary petty-bourgeois intelligentsia, and the bourgeois intelligentsia, who formed the right wing. The cultural revolution of the May Fourth Movement opposed feudal culture in a thoroughgoing way, and there was never such a great and thorough cultural revolution in the history of China. It achieved success in two ways: it opposed the old morality and promoted the new morality, and it opposed the old literature and promoted the new literature.

When Mao speaks of the "outstanding historical significance" of the movement, he is not essentially exaggerating. Professor John Dewey, then in Peking, visited the university at a time when it had been transformed into a vast student prison surrounded with the tents of soldiers, and wrote: "To say that life in China is exciting is to put it mildly. We are witnessing the birth of a nation, and birth always comes hard." When the thirty-two arrested students were released, marching down the streets of Peking to the sound of brass bands, while flowers rained on them, he wrote that "it was a victory for public opinion, and all set going by these little schoolboys and girls." They were not for the most part schoolboys or schoolgirls, but the implications were clear. Tsai Yuan-pei, resigning shortly after the incident because he feared assassination by the police, described it more accurately. He said simply: "It is war between the deluge and the wild beast." But the wild beasts were to remain, and the flood was not to roll over China for many years.

Mao's insistence on the importance of the victory should not surprise us. It was a small war, in which no one was killed. The casualties amounted to a solitary student, who committed suicide. A foreign minister was thrashed, and a young lecturer cut off the tip of one finger in order to write on the palace walls in his own blood, and without using a pen: "Tsingtao must be given back to us." Except for the abrupt flight of three ministers, almost nothing was gained. Yet in another sense everything was gained. Never before had the political power of the students shown itself so successfully. Nor was Mao exaggerating when he wrote that "the May Fourth Movement broke out at the call of the world revolution," for Chen Tu-hsiu and Li Ta-chao both regarded themselves as Communists.

During all this time Mao was in Hunan, armed with his blueprint from Chen Tu-hsiu and attempting to formulate a policy of revolt, obsessed with the idea that the policy must be "correct" and must be calculated to follow the complex laws of revolution he had learned from his study of Marxism; for after the May Fourth Movement he had come to regard himself, too, as essentially a Marxist. But the situation in Hunan demanded characteristically non-Marxist solutions. The *Hsiang River Monthly Review* was suppressed by Chang Chin-yao, but the May Fourth Movement was already in full stride, and the *tuchun* was confronted with interminable waves of protest coming from the students. He threatened to close the colleges; the students went on strike, following the pattern already carefully worked out in Peking; and all the time the *Hsin Min Hsueh Hui,* which was coming to assume something of the character of a revolutionary secret society, grew increasingly powerful. Eventually, Chang Chin-yao was overthrown by Tang Yen-kai, who had held power in the early days of the 1911 revolution. There was no peace. A new army under Chao Heng-ti launched an attack on the new governor. It was as though Hunan was dedicated to perpetual unrest.

Mao was now finding himself. During one of these wars he led an anti-militarist attack on the provincial parliament.

There were scuffles. Blood flowed. But no one was seriously hurt, and the attack altered nothing whatsoever. In the winter some anarchists working in a cotton mill at Changsha came out on a strike. The success of the strike suggested to Mao that anti-militarism and demands for a democratic government led nowhere, and confirmed him in his belief in Marxism, so much so that on the anniversary of the Russian revolution he organized a parade through the streets of Changsha. This, too, was foiled by the police. Thereafter, he saw no hope except in mass action and the formation of a Communist party.

THE FOUNDING OF THE CHINESE COMMUNIST PARTY

The First Congress of the Communist Party of China was held in Shanghai at some time toward the end of June or the beginning of July 1921. No one now remembers the exact date, but Mao has recently selected the date June 30, rather arbitrarily, so that the founding of the party can be celebrated annually. This was not the first attempt to inaugurate the party, for in the Petrograd edition of *Pravda* for July 30, 1920, there appears a short paragraph saying that an organization of the Chinese Communist party then existed in Shanghai, but giving no further details. Pavel Miff, a delegate of the Far Eastern Bureau of the Comintern, who was on the scene shortly afterward, made inquiries and says that about thirteen delegates were present at the original conference, but they included "anarchists, biblical socialists, legal Marxists and camp-followers," and that the anarchists broke away and the conference ended in a fiasco. The meeting which followed a year later was carefully arranged by Chen Tu-hsiu and Li Ta-chao, both of whom had by now resigned their posts at Peking University. They established themselves in Shanghai and began sending out invitations to the conference in May. Among the first arrivals was Mao Tse-tung, who helped to arrange the conference and whose friendship with the two leaders gave him a predominant position.

A complete list of the members of the original congress is

difficult to put together. Mao says there were twelve members, while others have spoken of seven, eleven, and fifteen. Among them certainly were the following twelve:

Chen Tu-hsiu, who was deposed from the Chinese Communist party in August 1927, and died in 1942.
Li Ta-chao, who was executed by Chang Tso-lin in 1927.
Chang Kuo-t'ao, expelled from the Chinese Communist party in April 1938.
Chou Fu-hai, who later became the secretary of Chiang Kai-shek, and still later went over to the Japanese.
Cheng Kung-po, who was executed by Chiang Kai-shek in 1946.
Shih Tseng-tung, who went over to the Kuomintang.
Pao Hui-sheng, who also went over to the Kuomintang.
Tai Chi-tao, who obtained high position under the Kuomintang.
Li Han-ching, who was executed in Wuhan in 1927.
Li Ta, who became a professor of social sciences at Peking University and dropped out of politics.
Shao Li-tse, who became Kuomintang ambassador to the Soviet Union and was governor of Shensi during the time of the Sian incident.
Mao Tse-tung.

Of the original members only three survived to become members of the Presidium, which assumed the governing powers of China in September, 1949. Three were executed, six went over to the Kuomintang, and two were expelled from the party. The survivors were Li Ta,[4] who continued his work as a professor of social sciences in the Kuomintang areas under another name while remaining in close touch with the Communists, Shao Li-tse, whose extraordinary career embraced many of the highest offices of the Kuomintang, and who came to Peking to discuss surrender terms on a mission from Chiang Kai-shek, and Mao Tse-tung himself. Except for the two founders, all of them were young men under thirty, and the greater number of them were students from Peking University.

4. *In Red Star over China*, Edgar Snow says that he was told by Mao that Li Ta had been executed. It is probable that Mao simply did not know what had happened to him, and execution was the probable fate of all those who had disappeared from the scene.

Mao seems to have been conscious from the beginning that the party as it was constituted was unwieldy. Because they were mostly students from upper-class families, with no roots among the people, they were far from being the revolutionary material which, according to Mao, the times demanded. Their speeches were elegant, but determination was lacking. They were in contact with Malin, who had been dispatched by Lenin to confer with Wu Pei-fu and Sun Yat-sen, but Malin had only suggested that they should establish study groups, though he also made promises of support. Malin, who had been Lenin's secretary, was himself confused by the extremely complex situation. A far more capable Comintern emissary was Grigori Voitinsky, who had reached China the previous year. Older than Malin, with a talent for seeing political shapes in broad outlines, he was the first to suggest that the final power would reside neither with Sun Yat-sen in the South nor with the warlords in the North, and he violently disagreed with Malin's contention that the Communists should work through Sun Yat-sen's Kuomintang party based on Canton. There were to be innumerable consequences of Voitinsky's disagreement. For years the official Communist thesis remained: Work within the Kuomintang, assume power through the Kuomintang, make the Kuomintang the servant of the Communists. Of all the Communists who worked on the problem, Voitinsky seems to have been the only one in 1921 who foresaw the future.

The work of the First Congress consisted in passing resolutions, forming various secretariats, and devising a blueprint for political action. It was decided to create a secretariat in charge of labor, but no one suggested a secretariat to deal with the problems of the peasantry; and there was no labor movement behind the labor bureau. Resolutions were passed condemning anarchism, which had now extended over Hunan and Szechuan as a result of the strikes in the cotton mills. An even more significant resolution was passed: the Chinese Communist party rejected affiliation with the Comintern, apparently on the advice of Malin, who saw the danger of adding fuel to the "anti-foreign feeling" always present in China.

While the First Congress of the Chinese Communist Party was meeting in Shanghai, other Chinese Communists, unknown to them, were meeting thousands of miles away. In Paris, Berlin, Tokyo, and Moscow, Chinese gathered, deliberated, passed resolutions, and quietly determined that China would become a Communist state. Chu Teh, studying philosophy at Marburg in a desperate attempt to understand the motivations of the West, turned toward communism with a passionate single-mindedness, seeing it as the last recourse of the underprivileged; the simplicities of communism delighted his fundamentally complex mind. So with Chou Enlai, Lo Man, and Li Li-san, who founded a Chinese Communist party in France. Even in America there were small Chinese Communist parties. Hardly any of these parties knew of the existence of the others. It was dangerous to admit to an interest in communism, still more dangerous to say that one was a Communist, for postal censorship existed throughout all that part of China controlled by the warlords. Chu Teh, for example, wandered aimlessly over half China before he journeyed to Germany, hoping to discover Communists, but finding none.

In this haphazard way, slowly and secretly, continually making mistakes, a handful of people were hoping to make China understand that communism supplied the answer to all political problems: and very few of them knew what communism was, or what its Chinese equivalent would be. They spoke in terms of the dictatorship of the proletariat, which is inconceivable in China. They translated Marxist and Hegelian terms into characters which had little enough meaning in Chinese. But gradually the trap was being sprung.

The Years of Warning

China during the first half of the nineteen-twenties was divided into six large areas, each controlled by a warlord. The survivors of the warlords who inherited Yuan Shih-kai's empire were in the north, but most of the provinces were ruled by independent satraps. The country seemed, indeed, about to split into its provincial elements, and an observer might be excused if he thought, as Lord Henry Beresford thought at the end of the nineteenth century, that the only remaining question was: Which of the foreign powers will pick up the pieces? Yet, though a fatal instability seemed to be increasingly accepted as a permanent condition, there were nevertheless forces at work tending to weld the pieces more tightly together.

What were these forces? First, there was the remarkable growth in national consciousness, arising as a result of the May Fourth Movement among the students. Then, like water perpetually falling on rock, there were the actions of the Kuomintang in Kwangtung—a small party, with little financial power, dependent upon the whims of merchants whose profits derived from Hong Kong, but devoted to the task of breaking the power of the northern warlords.

Mao was now working on one of the few tasks which showed promise of affecting the political structure of the country, and which lay outside the orbit of the political parties. He delegated himself to Hunan, where he organized trade unions among the miners and the railway workers. He also organized trade unions among the printers and the workers in the government mint, as though deliberately attempting to influence people who would be most useful to the Communist party, if it ever emerged and acquired power. The Marxist theory demanded that the "vanguard of the revolution" should consist of the "awakened proletariat"; and now for the first time he came to know the small factory towns of Hunan. The peasants were temporarily abandoned, not because he no longer had any interest in them—he still spent a considerable part of his time at Shao Shan—but because they had no place in Marxist theory.

1922 was a year of Kuomintang failure. When in the early summer Sun Yat-sen gave orders for the punitive expedition to the North, his armies failed even to reach the borders of Hunan. There were uprisings in the rear of his army. Yet the center of Chinese revolutionary activity was now Canton rather than Shanghai. Here, in May, there was held the First All-China Labor Congress and the First Congress of the China Socialist Youth League, both Communist-inspired organizations. But Mao attended neither of these meetings. On May Day a general strike was called in Hunan, and he was too busy attempting to organize it to leave for Canton. The Second Congress of the Chinese Communist Party was held in Hangchow in July, and this, too, Mao failed to attend, though he made the journey to Shanghai—someone having misinformed him about where the Congress was being held.

Mao was still feeling his way. Separation from Chen Tu-hsiu, the decision to remain in Hunan, the extraordinary success of the general strike on May Day—all these things tended to make him a purely provincial leader. During the following year, too, except for a brief visit to Shanghai, he re-

mained in Hunan; and the Third Congress of the Chinese
Communist Party, held at Canton in June, was held without
him, though some of the preliminary work for it was done by
him in Shanghai, where he worked with the Central Com-
mittee of the party. He was already one of the members of the
Central Committee, with the title of "delegate representing
Hunan," but his influence was still peripheral. The Third
Congress was one of the most important of all, for here it was
resolved to allow the Communists to co-operate with the
Kuomintang, a decision brought about by the arrival of
Borodin and the gradual Russian orientation of the Kuomintang itself. During the same summer Sun Yat-sen sent Chiang
Kai-shek on a mission to Moscow, with a letter of introduction to Lenin. By November the Kuomintang party itself was
being recognized, with Borodin's assistance, on the model of
the Communist party in the Soviet Union. The Chinese
Communist party, therefore, had reason to believe that it
would inevitably be able to influence the Kuomintang, and
during November and December the gates of the Kuomintang were thrown wide open to Communist members.

THE BEGINNINGS OF POWER

This time Mao did not fail to seize the opportunity. He attended the First National Congress of the Kuomintang Party
in Canton, which was held during the last ten days of January, as a member of the Kuomintang. At the same time he was
a member of the Central Committee of the Communist
Party. There was nothing particularly reprehensible in being
a member of both parties. Borodin had become Sun Yat-sen's
conscience, and this heavy man with the drooping mustache
and the puffed cheeks dictated the policies of the Kuomintang just as he dictated the policies of the Communists. It
was an enviable position. He knew no Chinese and had made
only a cursory study of Chinese history; but he had the sense
to make a profound study of the Taiping Rebellion, and with
this to guide him he attempted to work out a policy acceptable
to both wings of the combined Kuomintang-Communist

party. But from the first it was the Communists who were most suspicious of him.

The orientation toward Russia had been gathering momentum ever since Sun Yat-sen signed the famous agreement with Adolf Yoffe in January 1923. The agreement encouraged Sun Yat-sen to believe that Soviet communism was preparing to make no claims on the Chinese revolutionary movement. By the end of the year, with Borodin in command, the Comintern was already in the position where it could dictate Kuomintang policy. Canton began to be filled with those strange international adventurers who, knowing little of China, and with no loyalty to the Chinese, argued among themselves, passed resolutions, and considered themselves authorities on "the broad currents of Chinese history" in the name of international communism. There is no evidence to suggest that they ever served the cause of the Chinese revolution, and Mao, who knew no foreign language well and possessed a considerable contempt for foreigners in general, mentions them rarely, and then with scorn.

Now for the first time he was arriving at the stage where he could influence policy. He met Chiang Kai-shek, who had returned from Russia with glowing accounts of Russian industrialization. He was introduced to Sun Yat-sen and the other leaders of the Kuomintang party. When the Communists insisted that their own members should be included within the Central Committee of the Kuomintang, Mao's name was put forward. He was not a good speaker, but he was an excellent manager of debates: he would corner speakers and urge them to discuss certain topics and give them a desired "slant." He was beginning to be a power behind the scenes.

It was during this period that Mao became the secretary of one of the most powerful people thrown up by the 1911 revolution. Hu Han-min is hardly known outside China, yet he played a dominant role in the early days of the Kuomintang revolution. Complex, sometimes mischievous, a reactionary by instinct and a revolutionary by choice, he was second only to Sun Yat-sen at the time when Mao became his secretary. Because the secretaryship to a minister often involves assuming many of his tasks, Mao possessed at this time quite extraordinary powers. He was taken into Hu Han-min's confidence, and the documents that the aging minister was expected to see and approve were chosen by the secretary who four years before had been wandering in rags over the province of Shantung. For the first time Mao was presented with the opportunities of power.

Hu Han-min professed a deep interest in communism. He, too, had been born a peasant—he was one more of those peasants who came to high positions, and who were born in obscure villages near Canton. He had passed the imperial examination and received the title of *chu jen,* been a schoolteacher, studied in Japan, and taken part in the abortive risings led by Sun Yat-sen in 1910. Immediately after the revolution of 1911 he had become governor of Kwangtung, and afterward, during Sun Yat-sen's brief presidency, he was appointed secretary to the president. He was one of the editors of the *Min Pao,* and all of Sun Yat-sen's writings had passed through his hands, to be edited by him. Sun Yat-sen did not entirely trust him. Nepotism, a tone of casualness in his voice, the suspicion that he desired power over all things—all these reflected on the character of the dark-skinned man, whose large, heavy head and cruel mouth and intelligent eyes gave him the appearance of the pure revolutionary.

Mao was his secretary for about three months. He seems to have gained considerable power over the Minister, who increasingly came to favor the Soviet Union—in the following year he made a pilgrimage to Moscow, where he was greeted as the "hope of the Chinese revolution" and addressed continually as Generalissimo. Mao possessed a real admiration for him, if only because he had edited the *Min Pao* at a peculiarly receptive period of his own adolescence. Hu Han-min had supported the Russian orientation in a number of speeches at the First National Congress of the Kuomintang, and like Mao he had risen from poverty. It was Hu Han-min who appointed Mao as a delegate of Hunan to the Central Committee of the Kuomintang.

The Manifesto of the First National Congress of the Kuomintang—the most important of the documents to be issued

during the historic meeting—was not written by Sun Yat-sen,
but by the strange, mercurial and faintly sinister Wang Ching-
wei. He, too, supported the Russian orientation. He had a
simple, handsome face, which rarely revealed what was going on in his mind, and he looked twenty years younger than
he was. Bland, polished, a delightful host, he regarded himself as the historian of the movement. He wrote nearly all
the Kuomintang manifestoes, rewrote sections of the *Three
Principles of the People,* and he rewrote, emended, or entirely revised, where he did not entirely invent, the last
speeches and testaments of Sun Yat-sen made on his death-
bed. He modeled himself on Julius Caesar, whose *Commentaries* he admired; and though incapable of generalship, he
thirsted to be generalissimo. He was a senior member of the
Kuomintang Executive Committee, and when the Whampoa
Military Academy for the training of officers to lead a punitive expedition to the North was opened, he appointed himself "chief professor of the history of the Kuomintang party."
Hu Han-min introduced Wang Ching-wei to Mao, who for a
short period fell under his spell. Wang Ching-wei had taken
part in the movement to send young Chinese students to
France, and for Mao this was also a recommendation. But it
was from Hu Han-min that Mao derived the close knowledge
of the workings of the Kuomintang, and from him too that he
came to understand the ineradicable weaknesses of the party.
In later years Mao suggested that the Kuomintang destroyed
itself through pride. In Hu Han-min the flame of pride burned
very brightly indeed, so brightly that he was hardly able to see
the party without seeing himself as its most glorious defender
and most potent organizer.

There follows in the life of Mao a period of extraordinary
tightrope-walking. A member of both the Communist Party
and the Kuomintang, devoted to the conspiratorial overthrow
of one to the benefit of the other, working in close touch
with the leaders of both, curiously anonymous and detached,
appearing rarely in public, he was beginning to exert a subtle,
invisible influence. He was constantly traveling between
Shanghai and Canton. He inspired trust, and the most important missions were given to him, but his whole existence

was lived on the borderline of history, and his name appears in none of the registers of membership of the Kuomintang party.

In the winter of 1924 the affairs of the Kuomintang were moving toward a crisis. Sun Yat-sen launched another unsuccessful punitive expedition to the North, and once more he was compelled to withdraw as a result of treachery in his own ranks. When the "Christian General" Feng Yu-hsiang invited Sun Yat-sen to Peking to discuss a situation which was getting out of hand, Sun Yat-sen believed the heaven-sent opportunity had at last arrived: with the help of Feng Yu-hsiang he would call for a National Assembly, and all China's problems would immediately be solved. For a few months an astonishing hopefulness reigned in China, and Wang Ching-wei became dithyrambic in his utterances, pronouncing a blessed state of harmony as the inevitable result of Sun Yat-sen's journey to the North. There was to be no harmony. Sun Yat-sen fell ill on the journey, to die of cancer in the spring. That winter, working at the headquarters of the Communist bureau in Shanghai, Mao had fallen ill from overwork, and as a hopeless state of chaos began to descend upon China, he removed himself from the scene, retiring to Shao Shan, leaving his brother to represent him in Shanghai.

This retirement was to have prodigious consequences. The Chinese Communist party under Chen Tu-hsiu was dedicated to the overthrow of the existing government by the methods Lenin had introduced: the proletariat, as the advance guard of the revolution, would take over the functions of the government through its elected representatives. It was the classical thesis classically understood. Now for the first time, as he lay in bed in his small village, Mao began to question the validity of the Communist thesis. Accustomed to compromise through his work in merging the Communist and Kuomintang parties, he began to see that the evolution of Chinese communism could come only through a period of compromise. The theory of proletarian uprisings was dubious; the force of China lay in the peasantry. Not in Canton or Shanghai, but in the millions of small villages like Shao Shan lay the seeds of the revolution.

When spring came, Mao was out in the fields, organizing the peasants. Previously he had attempted to organize miners, railway workers, even the small tradespeople. Now he abandoned them completely. Traveling mostly at night, hiding in the villages by day, talking to the farmers, who remembered him from the days when he walked barefoot over the Hunanese hills, he formed in the spring of 1925 the nucleus of the peasant armies he was to unleash in the spring of 1927. The adventure lasted three months. There was a price on his head, for his activities were becoming known to the landlords and the militarists who ruled over Hunan. He became a legend, for legends grow rapidly in the countryside, only to die in the towns. A tall, thin, sunburned man in a sun helmet, traveling under many names, looking like a land agent, he was beginning to set the spark to the peasant kindling.

The mission he had given himself—he was alone throughout this period—was dangerous. The price on his head increased, and from various directions small groups of soldiers were sent out after him, examining the villagers and demanding knowledge of his movements. Mao could trust the smaller peasants; the middle peasants, he knew, could be bribed; and his horror and fear of them dates from this time. By the late summer he was fleeing for his life over the Hunan border and making his way to Canton, where his activities in Hunan were unknown, or only guessed at.

In Canton the whole political atmosphere had changed. The battle of the satraps, following the death of Sun Yat-sen, ended with the victory of Wang Ching-wei, who now exerted the real political power. Hu Han-min was sent to Moscow, the possesser of wide ambassadorial powers, an aging man who babbled polite irrelevancies to Stalin, promised the unyielding support of the Kuomintang to the Comintern, and drank more vodka than was good for him. But though the real political power lay in Wang Ching-wei's hands, another power was slowly emerging in the shape of a handsome young Chekiangese officer, who wore gold earrings and held himself with the stiffness of a Prussian parade-ground sergeant. His name, in the Cantonese dialect, which he never learned to speak, was Chiang Kai-shek.

Wang Ching-wei had not forgotten Mao. The young, resourceful Hunanese had performed admirably in Canton and Shanghai the duty of forging co-operation between the Communists and the Kuomintang. Now, as the plans for a final punitive expedition against the North took shape, this co-operation became all the more necessary; and Mao's genius for tightrope-walking was given full play. A host of duties were given to him. He became editor of the *Political Daily*, the informative and secret newspaper placed before all the highest government officials every day; he lectured or supervised lectures at Whampoa Academy; he continued to supervise the co-operation of the two parties in Canton, assuming the position of chief spokesman for Communist affairs, since the greater number of the Communist leaders remained in the comparative safety of Shanghai. Chen Tu-hsiu was still the Communist power in the country, but he was almost permanently resident in the French quarter of Shanghai. It was the year that Chen was elected a delegate of the Chinese Communists to the Third International, and in the same year he was also elected a member of the Central Executive Committee of the Kuomintang. Never had the two parties collaborated so closely; nor were they ever to collaborate very closely again.

Mao had become the symbol of the collaboration. Given his talents, it was an ironical situation. Though, outwardly, he performed his Kuomintang functions well, he was essentially a Communist by the conviction, now completely formed in him, that the peasants could lead the revolt. The Kuomintang at this time was prepared to recognize the privileged position of the peasantry. Laws were passed concerning land tenure, and the expropriation of the large landlords was debated at length in the Kuomintang headquarters. It was recognized that the northward march would be completely impossible without the aid of the peasants. Mao could, and did, exert pressure in favor of the peasants. He organized a seminar where men were trained in the organization of peasant movements; and here, for the first time, safeguarded by the whole Kuomintang apparatus, he worked out methods of arming the peasants and made blueprints for peasant revolts, revolts which would break out during the northern punitive expedition. Wang Ching-wei was credited with the belief that an inevitable revolutionary era would be brought in by this northern march. Borodin approved of it. Hu Han-min had given it his blessing shortly before leaving for Russia. It was assumed that Chiang Kai-shek, the commander of the First Army, would obey the government which had assumed the mantle of Sun Yat-sen.

No assumption could have been more incorrect. Chiang Kai-shek had many virtues, including a belief in his own star, but he resolutely opposed revolutionary uprisings among the peasants. "The task of the peasant," he wrote, "is to provide us with information concerning the enemy, food and comforts in our encampments, and soldiers for our armies." He said nothing about the duties of the Army toward the peasants.

By the end of the year, Mao was assuming even wider functions. He became a candidate for membership in the Central Executive Committee, he broadened out the whole scheme of seminars for training peasant leaders, and he became head of the Propaganda Bureau of the Kuomintang. Communists were now taking increasingly high positions within the Kuomintang. Tang Ping-shan was head of the Peasant Bureau, and other Communists were to be found in the Bureau of Finance, the Bureau of Supplies, and the Bureau of Foreign Affairs. They were prominent at the Whampoa Academy and, because they were a cohesive group, they exerted an influence out of all proportion to their numbers. Whatever else happened, they were determined that the success of the northern march would be followed by a greater Communist influence within the Kuomintang; and since they, and particularly Mao, were in charge of bringing the peasants on the side of the punitive expedition against the warlords, the chances of success increased.

Mao wrote some articles on the peasant situation in relation to the forthcoming expedition; and though Chen Tu-hsiu opposed the more radical policies advocated by Mao, he could do nothing to prevent him from exerting his radical influence. When, on July 9, 1926, the northern expedition set out, its success in occupying Hunan, Hupeh, Kiangsi, Anhwei, and Kiangsu within the space of three months could be set down to the co-operation of the peasants, and the Communists could claim with some justice that they had prepared the ground.

Whenever events of dramatic importance occurred, Mao usually found himself in Hunan. It was almost as though he was deliberately placing himself as far away from the scene of major operations as possible. During the May Fourth Movement he was in Hunan; he was again in Hunan during the May Thirtieth Movement of 1925, when a vast anti-British campaign was launched after the shooting of some demonstrators in Shanghai's Nanking Road by Sikhs under British command; and he was in Hunan at the time of Sun Yat-sen's death. When the northern expedition marched out of Kwangtung, he was once more in Hunan, this time as an inspector of peasant unions, preparing the collaboration of the peasants with the revolutionary army which came marching up the Hsiang River.

THE GREAT REVOLUTION

The period 1925–27 has come to be called the Great Revolution. It is difficult to understand why. Chiang Kai-shek's army reached the Yangtse, and then turned east. By the following spring his Cantonese soldiers were outside the walls of Shanghai. The government, meanwhile, remained in Wuhan. It was a government predominantly under the control of left-wing members of the Kuomintang. Chiang Kai-shek had treated it with contempt throughout. There had been quarrels on the march, strange silences, curious pauses while the armies reformed.

Suddenly, on April 12, 1927, Chiang Kai-shek gave the orders for the occupation of Shanghai and, at the same time, commanded the complete extermination of the Communists

and Socialists in the city. This entirely unexpected development—neither the order for the occupation nor the order for
the extermination of the left-wing workers had the sanction of
the government in Wuhan—revealed that entirely new forces
were at work. In March 1926, Chiang Kai-shek had attempted a *coup d'état* in Canton. It had failed. The Kuomintang government had been re-established, and Chiang Kai-
shek had offered himself for punishment, only to be excused
on the grounds that he was perhaps only exerting his "great
zeal." He had, in fact, been testing his own powers. In Shanghai he showed proof that he was under no delusion about
their extent.

The massacres of Shanghai were never to be forgotten by
the Communists; and the merciless vendetta, which lasted
until 1950, had its origins during those days when, without
warning, Chiang Kai-shek attempted to put down once and
for all any opposition that might come from the revolutionary
proletariat. He excused himself by saying that information
had been received that Communists in Shanghai had been
ordered by Moscow to bury their arms, and would inevitably
endanger his rear as he pushed toward Peking; but it was
observed that he received large sums of money from foreign
and Chinese merchants to finance the northern expedition, and
it was reasonably surmised that one of the conditions attached to these grants was the extermination of Communist
influence within the party.

On the day of the Shanghai massacre, Chiang Kai-shek inaugurated a new government at Nanking. He declared
bluntly that the power had now fallen into his hands, and he
would treat with Wang Ching-wei only on his own terms.

Exactly what happened in Wuhan will probably never be
known. There seems to have been confusion, purposelessness,
sudden decisions made at night, then long periods of waiting
upon orders never made clear. Wang Ching-wei possessed a
brilliant mind, but it was hardly a clear mind; he hesitated
and delayed. In sympathy with the workmen massacred in
Shanghai, the Communists had brought about a general
strike—the first general strike in China successfully accomplished by them. At night there were Red Guards patrolling

the streets, but Borodin no longer gave orders, and Chen Tu-hsiu no longer felt any impulse to exert his authority. Three hundred thousand workers were silent, and none of them knew what to do. Meanwhile, on the highest levels, there were endless discussions, endless efforts to avoid unavoidable issues.[5]

There were reasons for the strangely hesitant atmosphere in Wuhan. The left wing of the Kuomintang was without capable leadership. Left behind during the Kuomintang advance on Shanghai, shocked by the massacres of April 12 and the bombardment of Nanking by British and American warships —with thirty-five foreign warships at anchor in the Yangtse outside Hankow—they realized that the slightest decisions would have endless, unpredictable consequences. They were not alone there. The Chinese Communist party was also in session, attended by a strange medley of Comintern advisers —Borodin, Pavel Miff, Earl Browder, Jacques Doriot, and, the most powerful of all, Manabendra Nath Roy. Most of them were incompetent, and all were useless at this turning-point in Chinese history. Chen Tu-hsiu presided over this,

---

5. The incredible confusion has been described by Tsou Lu, an associate of Hu Han-min and Sun Yat-sen: "When Wang Ching-wei sent the telegram saying he would resign, I didn't take it seriously. Suddenly I heard that Wang Ching-wei had gone to Lushan in Kiangsi, and then I heard that Chen Kung-po had gone to Kwangtung, and then I heard that a branch Political Council was established in Wuhan, and then that Wuhan opposed the Extraordinary Commission. Then I heard that Wang Ching-wei had gone to Wuhan, explaining that there was a precedent for the Extraordinary Commission, and then I heard that Wang Ching-wei proposed the opening of the Fourth Plenary Session of the Central Executive Committee to recognize the Extraordinary Commission, and then I heard that the mass meeting to support the Extraordinary Commission in Canton had been postponed, and then I heard voices in Canton proclaiming against the Extraordinary Commission, and then I heard that Wang Ching-wei had gone from Wuhan to Shanghai, and then I heard he had gone to Canton from Shanghai and proposed to convene the Fourth Plenary Session and dissolve the Extraordinary Commission, and then I heard that he had returned to Shanghai, and then I heard that Canton had been occupied by the Communists, and then I heard that Canton was recaptured. It was like a movie film." Tsou Lu, *Reminiscences*, Chungking, 1943.

the Fifth Congress of the Chinese Communist Party, but he seems to have been as baffled as the rest.

The issues were not simple. From Nanking, Chiang Kai-shek was threatening to launch a punitive expedition on Wuhan. On April 5, Chen Tu-hsiu and Wang Ching-wei issued a manifesto which exhorted the Communists to be faithful to the Sun-Joffe Agreement, and there seemed to be some hope among the left-wing Kuomintang that a common program, including wide-scale land reform could be put into operation. Moreover there were three armies, under Cheng Ch'en, Tang Sheng-shih, and Tang Yen-kai, ready to support the Wuhan government, but only on conditions presented by their commanders. These conditions included the immediate cancellation of all the plans for agrarian reform, for the army officers were themselves proprietors. Any attempt at agrarian reform would be crushed by the Army; any attempt to use the Army against Chiang Kai-shek would probably lead to defeat, for Chiang Kai-shek possessed a navy, overwhelming manpower and considerable foreign support; finally, if the three armies were not employed, they might be expected to take over Hankow and rule by military junta. All these possibilities were clearly foreseen by the government in Wuhan, and no solutions were in sight. At last, apparently through the mediation of Wang Ching-wei, Chiang Kai-shek advanced northward and abandoned his threatened attack on Wuhan. At the same time the three Wuhan armies marched against the forces of Chang Tso-lin, in the North. But the revolutionary problems remained exactly as they were before, and the most urgent of these problems concerned the peasant uprisings through Hunan and Hupeh.

THE HUNAN UPRISINGS

Early in 1927 Mao was sent to Hunan to report on the farmers' associations, traveling overland from Shanghai. He arrived in January, and spent only thirty-two days in the province, but during those few days he laid the seeds for a revolution which affected the whole development of the Kuomintang and the Chinese Communist parties. In the previous year, as secretary of the Kuomintang Peasant Committee, he had gathered considerable material concerning landowner-ship in China. The figures showed that poor peasants, num-bering perhaps 65 per cent of the population, owned only 10 to 15 per cent of the cultivable land; another 15 per cent was owned by the "middle peasantry"; the remaining 70 per cent was owned by absentee landlords, rich peasants, and money-owners. On the basis of these figures Mao concluded that the peasants were ripe for rebellion. Returning in 1927 to the counties in Hunan he knew best, he was determined to bring the rebellion about. He inspected the counties of Changsha, Lilin, Hsiang T'an, Hung Shan and Hsiang-hsiang, where he had wandered in his early youth, and secretly brought about a revolt, explaining what he was doing in a short report addressed to the Interprovincial Peasant Union.

This report should be studied at some length. Much that came later is explained by it, and the first stage of the revolu-tion as Mao saw and guided it bears a close relationship to the violent strategy evolved during the month-long walking-tour in central Hunan. In the history of revolution, this report is probably as important as the theses written by Lenin during the October revolution.

The armies of the northern expedition preached revolu-tion but hardly practiced it, with the result that the peasants came increasingly to take power in their own hands. By October 1926, the peasant associations were in control of large areas of central Hunan. They were a force to be reckoned with. Mao estimated that during the period from July to September, 1926, their total membership did not exceed 300,000 or 400,000, but after October their numbers rose sharply to 2,000,000, and half of the entire peasantry was organized under the control of the peasant associations. These were the associations which Mao himself had brought into being. He had also largely directed the propaganda cam-paign preceding the northern expedition, and his responsi-bility for the peasant uprisings was therefore twofold: he had helped to form the associations, and he had fed them with a continuous stream of propaganda from Canton. The effect was astonishing, and out of all proportion to the means employed; and the violent "revolution within a revolution," the peasants taking over power while the Kuomintang armies marched north, could only be explained by the long pent-up despair of the poor peasants in Hunan.

The flame, lit in Canton, traveled across Hunan. No land-owner's life was safe. The richer ones fled to the safety of Shanghai; those who were less rich fled to Hankow; others escaped to Changsha. Those who remained, or were caught by the peasants, were compelled to renounce their riches. Those who wore long gowns or owned more than fifty *mou* of land were fined, required to make contributions to the peasant association, and had their sedan chairs smashed before their eyes. The final affront consisted in taking their opium pipes away from them, and then the pipes were broken. With some relish, Mao noted that "the ivory beds of the daughters of the landlords were stepped upon by the dirty feet of the peasants." Revenge was in the air. Tragic excesses were sometimes committed. Landlords who had committed grievous crimes according to the peasants were killed; others were compelled to march down the streets wearing tall paper hats with their sins written on them. Mansions on large estates were burned to the ground. "There was a huge storm, and only those who bent to the storm could survive."

In his report on the revolutionary outbreak, Mao was wholly on the side of the peasants. He went to some length to defend the peasant terror. "Revolution," he wrote, "is not a dinner party, nor a literary composition, nor a painting, nor a piece of pretty embroidery; it cannot be carried out 'softly, gradually, carefully, considerately, respectfully, politely, plainly, and modestly.'" With this eightfold declaration against revolutionary gentleness—the last five terms are borrowed from the Confucian *Analects*—he launched into a studied defense of the uprisings. Even their excesses, he said, were necessary and possessed revolutionary significance. He defended the peasant leaders against the charge that they were rabble who "go about in worn-out shoes, carry broken umbrellas, wear green gowns, and gamble." No, they were reasonable men, behaving in a reasonable and revolutionary way. They fought, they organized and they performed all the complex tasks of the revolution. The report is almost a hymn to the peasantry, "who placed their muscular, sunburned hands on the heads of the gentry." The reign of the *t'u-hao,* which literally means "local ruffians" but came to mean the "local gentry," was at an end, and it was the poor peasants who were most responsible for their defeat. "To reject the poor peasants," wrote Mao, "is to reject the revolution." Sun Yat-sen had devoted forty years of his life to bringing about the revolution, which the peasants had accomplished in a few months. The real heart of the revolution was here, and— with a characteristic use of mathematical symbols—Mao came to the conclusion that if the whole revolution was repre- sented by the figure 10, then its success in the cities might be accounted as 3, and among the peasants as 7. He therefore demanded urgent action by the Wuhan government: their mistakes must be immediately corrected. Why? Because in a short time hundreds of millions of peasants would arise in China with the fury of a hurricane, and there was no power on earth able to restrain them. "All the imperialists, all the warlords, corrupt officials, and *t'u-hao* will meet their doom at the hands of the peasants. Are we to lead them or criticize them behind their backs or fight them from the enemy camp? Among these three alternatives every Chinese can choose freely."

For the first time Mao was now demanding direct action by the peasants, without the formalities of discussion with the Kuomintang, and without the agreement of the Central Committee of the Chinese Communist Party. The report was tabled before the Central Committee in Wuhan. Chen Tu- hsiu immediately ordered Mao out of Hunan and refused to allow the report to be discussed within the party. The damage, however, had been done. The peasant rising, as Mao had ex- pected, produced panic in Wuhan. And still the Wuhan gov- ernment vacillated, wondering what the consequences would be if they, who were supposed to represent the left wing of a revolutionary party, threw their military force against the peasants, who were demanding no more than Sun Yat-sen's "equalization of land."

The Communists at Wuhan were equally unsure of themselves. In one of those strange directives which Stalin occasionally issued from the Kremlin to the Far Eastern bureau of
the Comintern, then sitting at Wuhan, he had explained in
the previous year that the full-scale agrarian reforms were im-
permissible at this stage, because immediate difficulties would
arise from within the revolutionary army. Mao was presumably aware of the directive; and on his own initiative
acted entirely against it. By the time Mao left Hunan the
revolutionary flame was lit, and there was no way, except by
military invasion, to put the flames out. The Wuhan government could deliberate to its heart's content, Chiang Kai-shek
could decide to attack Wuhan, or he could march north: for
Mao none of these possibilities had any importance whatsoever, for he saw clearly, as Borodin had failed to see, that
there could be no real revolution until the absentee landlords
were dispossessed and the peasants brought into the current
of the revolutionary wave. The concessions of the Wuhan
government consisted largely in a general surrender of the
peasants to the cause of Chiang Kai-shek's betrayal. By forcing the hand of the Wuhan government, Mao hoped to
change the whole course of the revolution.

He did not succeed. He may have guessed that the peasant
rebellion would be put down with ruthless efficiency, but for
four months the peasants in the five counties resisted. In the
areas controlled by them the peasant associations possessed
the sole power, and the privileges of the landlords were taken
from them. The landlords fought back. Writing apparently
early in May, Mao said:

The Hunan peasants at the present time cannot be said to have
overthrown the landlords. We can only say that they are now rebelling against them. Those who do not know the real conditions
say that in Hunan the conditions are terrible, that too many landlords and their hirelings have been killed. But the facts are otherwise. . . . The landlords killed numbered only tens, but the
number of peasants killed by them is astounding. . . . Many
people know that the peasants are conducting a revolution in
Hunan, but few know the cunning and cruelty of the landlords. . . . It has been very common in all counties for the *min*

tuan (landlords' militia) to lynch peasants. Torture was freely
used. After being arrested, peasants would either be killed outright
or mutilated: muscles of the feet extracted, genitals cut away,
etc. . . . The *min tuan* in Tsalien burned alive in kerosene a
student who had come to the district to work in the peasant movement. . . .

After being driven from the villages by the peasants, the landlords and the dregs of the *min tuan* often sought alliances with
bandits to fight the peasant associations. Nine reports out of ten
coming from the provincial peasant association tell about the gathering of the *t'u-hao* with the bandits to drink wine and cock's blood
for the overthrow of the peasant associations, for the extermination
of the party commissioner. . . .

They also formed reactionary organizations. In Hsianghsiang
they called it the Association for the Maintenance of Town and
Village. In Henyang it was the White Party. In Lilin and Liuyang,
the San-Ai Party. In Lilin, there was also the Association for Beating Dogs, the dogs meaning the peasants. In many parts of Hunan,
there was the Party for the Preservation of Property. These organizations planned and carried out the massacres of peasants and
raids on peasant associations. Sometimes these plots were uncov-
ered by the peasants, but the organizations were never dissolved.[6]

The desire for land by the landless peasantry could not be
resisted indefinitely. In October 1926, the Kuomintang itself
had recognized that something would have to be done. Then
for the first time the peasants and workers had been given
the right to form unions. Land rents were reduced to 25
per cent of the annual income from the land. A surprisingly moderate reform program had been passed without any
serious dissensions. The peasants were allowed to form volun-
teer self-preservation corps. Now, when they applied to
Wuhan for arms with which to defend themselves, they were
turned back empty-handed, to struggle on with meat hooks,
flails, scythes, spears, and bamboos.

Only one of the members of the Comintern present,

6. Harold Isaacs, *The Tragedy of the Chinese Revolution*, London,
1938, p. 266, where the passage is quoted from the "Report of the
Delegate of the Hunan Provincial Peasant Association," *Min Kuo Jih
Pao*, Wuhan, June 12, 1927. The anonymous delegate was Mao Tse-
tung.

Sydor Stoler, a Russian, seems to have approved of Mao's action, saying that failure to help the peasants was a "fatal error." But he was fresh on the scene, and it was supposed that he understood very little about the problems of the peasantry.

The Wuhan government was in a quandary, and Wang Ching-wei carefully arranged that the Ministers of Agriculture and Labor within the Wuhan government should both be Communists. If they failed to settle the disturbance, they would be discredited.

On May 20, Tang Ping-shan, who had been a student at Peking University and possessed more experience of labor problems than of problems concerning the peasantry, was formally installed as minister of agriculture, a special position specially created for him by Wang Ching-wei. Wang Ching-Wei's duplicity—he was playing everyone against everyone else—became only too evident when, the next day, the military forces in Hunan for the first time attacked the peasants.[7]

Previously, the landlords, the gentry, and their armed defense corps had had to deal with the peasant situation alone, unaided by the three armies under the control of the Wuhan government. Now in Changsha, General Hsu Ko-chang, the garrison commander, ordered a general massacre of the revolutionary peasants and workers, throwing round the city a cordon of Yunnanese soldiers with white arm bands. These arm bands, usually provided with a single character written in red ink, were to distinguish his own men from any others who might disguise themselves in uniform. The Hunan Provincial General Labor Union, unmolested previously because of its close connections with the Wuhan government, was attacked in the early morning, and all the pickets and

7. Wang Ching-wei's responsibility for the massacres has been disputed, but the clue is to be found in a book written by his secretary. "On May 21, 1927, riots had broken out among the Wuhan forces at Changsha, the capital of Hunan, as a result of the unauthorized policy of land seizure of the Communists, working through the Provincial Kuomintang and the Provincial Government. The insurrection of military forces, *which Wang had foreseen*, had occurred." Tang Leang-li, *Inner History of the Chinese Revolution*, London, 1930, p. 273.

delegates found sleeping there were taken outside, propped against the wall, and shot. All the other organizations connected with peasants or workers were similarly raided. The west gate of Changsha, facing the river, was selected as the place where the executions would have maximum effect.

An incredible wave of terror and torture now swept over the Hunanese capital, to be remembered long afterward as one of the most terrifying of a long series of massacres. It was to avenge this particular terror that the Chinese Communists kept turning their minds to the capture of Changsha in the months that followed.

In all the five counties which Mao had visited, the garrisons received orders to strike terror among the peasants. The peasants of Liuyang fled for safety to Changsha, only to be mown down by Hsu Ko-chang's machine guns. A hundred and thirty men and women were killed outside the city gate. The peasants outnumbered the local garrison and decided upon a counterattack, taking cover in the low hills to the east of Changsha and at the same time urgently inviting the assistance of Wuhan. On May 27, the All-China Trade Union Federation and the All-China Peasant Association sent a telegram from Wuhan to the provincial unions in Hsiang T'an and Hsiang-hsiang, which read:

The Central Government has appointed a Committee of Five which left here this morning for the settlement of the Changsha incident. Please notify all peasant and labor comrades to be patient and to wait for the government officials in order to avoid further friction.[8]

These orders were not received by the two detachments from Liuyang, which marched up to the walls of Changsha, and were mown down. Tang Ping-shan headed the delegation from Wuhan, but never arrived in Changsha. Another general, Ho Chien, was sent by Chiang Kai-shek to support Hsu Ko-chang, with orders to put down the peasant uprisings mercilessly. Chiang Kai-shek was preparing his

8. Harold Isaacs, *The Tragedy of the Chinese Revolution*, London, 1938, p. 283, who gives the only complete account available in English of the Hsu Ko-chang massacre.

advance on the northern warlords, and he was determined that his rear should be protected from the uprisings of dissident peasants. The fate of the rebellion, sparked by Mao in January and February, was sealed during the last days of May.

At the beginning of June there occurred an incident which has never been fully explained. Roy, the chief delegate of the Comintern, received a telegram from Stalin addressed to Borodin and himself. According to Roy's account of what happened—an account corroborated by Wang Ching-wei's secretary—he immediately called upon Wang Ching-wei. "I thought," Roy said, "that at this juncture a final effort must be made to regain the confidence of Wang Ching-wei. I communicated to him the message from Moscow. Though not addressed to him, it was obviously meant for him, because it was a repetition of a promise made to him personally in Moscow." [9] The telegram urged that land seizures should take place, except in the areas owned by officers, and the Communist party should immediately raise an army 20,000 strong consisting only of Communists, together with battalions of armed peasants numbering 50,000. It was furthermore ordered that pressure be put on the Kuomintang to organize revolutionary courts to try anti-Communist officers. Showing Wang Ching-wei the strange telegram, Roy said: "Borodin does not like to show you this telegram, but I, on the other hand, think it is most advisable that you should know what it is about, as I am quite sure you would approve of it." [10]

The consequences of the telegram were entirely unlike those which Stalin contemplated. Wang Ching-wei immediately informed Chiang Kai-shek, whose suspicions were confirmed. Roy had acted with calm deliberation. There is no reason to believe that he did not know what he was doing. He regarded Mao as a completely unstable element, saying that he was "one of those who persistently and deliberately sabotaged all plans of revolutionary action in 1926–27." According to Roy, Mao was an opportunist who even then was planning to set up "romantic soviet republics in the

9. M. N. Roy, *My Experience in China*, Calcutta, 1945, p. 51.
10. Tang Leang-li, *op. cit.*, p. 280.

mountainous wilderness" instead of organizing proletarian
mass movements.

When Eugene Chen, the Wuhan government's foreign
minister, saw the telegram, he turned pale and said: "You
understand, this means war between the Kuomintang and
the Communist party." [11] It was a war precipitated by Mao
Tse-tung. From that moment there was never again to be any
real understanding between the Chinese Communists and
the Kuomintang. In this war, fought bitterly and without
quarter, the genuinely subversive or revolutionary forces in
China went underground, to emerge as small scattered groups
of armed peasants, destined finally to grow and to conquer the
whole of China.

In Hankow the confusion only increased during the long,
hot summer. Steam rose from the flooded yellow Yangtse, the
warships of the foreign powers still trained their guns on the
shore, and the left-wing of the Kuomintang government
fought a losing battle for power, until it submitted completely
to Chiang Kai-shek's government in Nanking. The official
power of the Chinese Communists was broken.

For a brief while Chen Tu-hsiu attempted to hold the party
together. He ordered Mao Tse-tung to report on the situation
in Szechuan, where Mao could do least harm. Instead, Mao
slipped into Hunan, only to be recalled immediately as soon
as his destination became known, with orders to remain in
Wuhan and to take no part in the organization of peasant
uprisings.

On June 30, Tang Ping-shan, who had at last been able to
make a cursory examination of the situation in Changsha,
resigned office on the grounds that he had failed to direct
the peasant movement. Two weeks later the Communist party
was officially proscribed by the Kuomintang, Chen Tu-hsiu
resigned from the chairmanship of the Central Committee,
and, on July 27, Borodin and the remaining foreign Communists prepared to leave the country which they had never
understood. Borodin was a large, quiet man, rarely given to
showing emotion, but at the railway station it was observed
that he shivered and wept unrestrainedly.

11. Tang Leang-li, *op. cit.,* p. 281.

For Mao the departure of the Comintern representatives was a blessing in disguise. Chen Tu-hsiu had stopped the Hunan uprising on the advice of Borodin, who had completely failed to understand the slogan: "The land to the tillers." Without foreign advisers the Chinese Communists were left to their own resources. There were no Borodins or Roys in attendance on the secret meeting of the Central Committee of the Chinese Communist Party which met on August 7.

The meeting was attended by Mao Tse-tung, Chang Kuo-t'ao, Li Li-san, Chou En-lai, Chiu Chiu-pei, Chang Tai-lei, Tsai Ho-sheng,[12] Peng Kung-ta, and Liu Wei-han, who was also known as Lo Man. At this meeting, Chen Tu-hsiu was drummed out of the party, although he had already resigned, and his letter explaining the defeat as due to the fact that "the revolutionary mood of the masses was not then at a high point, the Kuomintang could not be quickly overthrown, and untimely risings only weakened the power of the party" was regarded as sufficient proof of his own incapacity. A lengthy letter detailing his "errors" was sent to the remaining members of the party, and a new program, authorizing the confiscation of the property of the large landowners, but protecting the small landowners, who were merely ordered to reduce their rents, was issued by the committee, which scattered shortly afterward.

Like a moth eager for the burning, Mao immediately set out in disguise for Changsha, presumably believing that it was the last place anyone expected him to go to, and there he could hide most successfully.

The white terror of the Kuomintang was now being launched all over the Yangtse Valley, and in all the provinces of the South. The unaccountable failure of nerve in Wuhan led to the disappearance or execution of at least 10 per cent of the members of the Chinese Communist party. In Shanghai

12. Chang Tai-lei became head of the Revolutionary Committee during the Canton Commune and was killed in battle on December 12, 1927. Chiu Chiu-pei was captured and executed in Fukien during the retreat from Changchow, in 1934. Tsai Ho-sheng was executed in 1931.

alone 400 were executed, and among them were some of the highest members of the party. Others, like Chou En-lai, escaped only by ruse. Inevitably, the effect of the white terror was to harden the Communists' resolve to fight back. Only those who have known a Chinese terror know how it makes men determined upon revenge. The Communists had nothing to lose.

Proscribed, humiliated, the party dissolved by government order, their communications made increasingly difficult, the Communists had no weapons. For the most part the army remained loyal to Chiang Kai-shek. Only one section, the Twentieth Army, under Ho Lung and Yeh Ting, declared its independence at Nanchang on August 1. Nearly the whole garrison in the capital city of Kiangsi immediately drove against Swatow, hoping to establish a soviet on the coast. They were beaten back. They then turned into eastern Kwangtung, and invaded the Hailofeng area, famous because it was inhabited largely by women who remained on the Chinese mainland while their husbands went abroad to seek the family fortunes. They were a hard and handsome people, and they had already devised a kind of rule by village council which approximated to a soviet. The survivors of the battle of Swatow were welcomed, and the Communists might have thought they now possessed a base in Kwangtung from which they too might begin a new march to the North. They were mistaken. By the end of October the Hailofeng area was surrounded by Kuomintang troops, and there were only a handful of Communists left at the end of the battle. To the women who had welcomed the column under General Chu Teh, no mercy was shown. Whole villages were put to the flames, and most of the women were raped, and nearly all of them received bayonet wounds.

The failure of the Hailofeng occupation was complete. Leading a small column of three or four hundred men and women, including some railway and porcelain workers from Nanchang, Chu Teh spent the winter beating off Kuomintang attacks.

Mao's fortunes were hardly better. He is heard of for a moment in Changsha itself, a ghostly figure attempting to bring together the scattered remnants of the *Hsin Min Hsueh Hui,* only to discover that they were too frightened by the terror to go with him. He went south, to Liuyang and Lilin, his customary stamping-ground, determined once again to bring about peasant uprisings. There was every reason to believe that if he continued long enough, he would succeed in overthrowing the Kuomintang. Had not Sun Yat-sen led thirteen separate uprisings before accomplishing the revolution of 1911? Now he paid particular attention to the Henyang miners, men who seemed to belong to a race apart. Pockmarked, fearless, revolutionaries by instinct, nearly all of them deaf because underground explosions of dynamite had shattered their eardrums, they presented only one problem: it was necessary to hold them on a leash, for they thirsted for war against the Kuomintang, or against any authority whatsoever. They had been anarchists; Mao was determined to make them Communists; and he succeeded in making them the spearhead of the First Peasants' and Workers' Army.

For some time Mao had been working in the dark. Borodin's last words had been: "The revolution must now go underground." The Comintern, after a succession of hopelessly mistaken interpretations of the Chinese revolution, had come out on July 13 with a simple thesis: "The revolutionary role of the government in Hankow is finished. It is now counterrevolutionary and must be thwarted. Therefore, Communists must spread an agrarian revolution and arm the workers and peasants." How this could be done was not explained. Nor was it explained why the Comintern had ordered the workers in Shanghai to bury their weapons, thus leaving them defenseless against Chiang Kai-shek's Cantonese troops. And finally, no one had explained why the logic of revolution demanded that the Hankow revolutionaries should be put down by a counterrevolutionary force. The Comintern, previously possessed of an extraordinary influence in China, now surrendered its influence and left the Communists to their own resources; and to men of Mao's stamp it was almost unnecessary to repeat that the "Communists must spread an agrarian revolution and arm the workers and peasants."

Not all Communists, however, agreed with him. These small detachments of armed peasants, located chiefly in Pingkiang and Liuyang, with a seasoning of miners and some troops from Wuhan who had marched south after the dissolution of the Wuhan government, were derisively called "rifle brigades."

By September 12, Mao was ready. He had worked with astonishing rapidity. He planned to attack Changsha but the revolt, which came to be known as the Autumn Harvest Uprising, failed. The peasants were cut down and surrounded, and at least once he was himself captured, only to escape.

THE FORTRESS AT CHINGKANSHAN

A month later Mao was marching south at the head of three regiments. He had a thousand men and less than two hundred rifles.

Some memory of the mountain near Shao Shan, where a member of the *Ko Lao Hui* had taken refuge when Mao was a child, or one of the stories in *All Men Are Brothers,* led him to believe that the small Red army could make a fortress out of a mountain; and when he came to the Hunan-Kiangsi border, the broad pine-clad mountain called Chingkanshan suggested itself as a base of operation. It was densely wooded, with immense spurs and cliffs, and it lay close to the borders of three provinces. Attacked by an army belonging to one province, he had only to retreat over the provincial border. There were other advantages. In winter the mountain would be covered with a thick fog, and all over the mountain there were Buddhist temples which could be used as hospitals, offices, and dormitories. The monks were ordered to leave; and in the temples, the Red Army soldiers used as clothes racks the gods who were falling to pieces and who stood in rows in the dark-painted halls. A printing-press was brought from Liuyang. Within a week of establishing themselves on the mountain, the first number of the newspaper appeared, printed on the backs of Buddhist scrolls.

The interlude of Chingkanshan was heavy with future

consequences. From this moment until October 1934, the Red Army was to find itself among high mountains. Other Communist armies were being formed. Ho Lung had ridden alone to Hupeh, and there he was to found a soviet over which he ruled with uncommon gentleness and understanding of peasant problems. Hsu Hsiang-ch'ien, a former teacher, and Chang Kuo-t'ao, a former student of Peking University, were already forming soviets in northern Szechuan. But it was the army of rather less than a thousand men living in Buddhist temples above the cliffs of Chingkanshan which formed the nucleus of the main fighting strength of the Chinese Communists.

Their lives on the mountain were not without incident. Two local bandits, Wang Tso and Yuan Wen-tsai, had long ruled over the mountain with six hundred armed peasants to defend them. They threatened to attack. They had more rifles than the Communists. By diplomacy Mao succeeded in winning them over, though for about a month they kept demanding that the Red Army must be placed under their command, or be annihilated. In the end, by appointing Wang Tso a regimental commander and Yuan Wen-tsai a battalion commander, and by allowing them extraofficial powers to deal with the peasants, the six hundred bandits were incorporated into the Red Army. Mao allowed them to deal directly with the peasants only on condition that they willingly assented to undergo political training. When they agreed, their power was curbed, for they were immediately trained to obey the army commander—Mao himself.

On Chingkanshan in the winter of 1927 it was deathly cold. There was no store of food, and there were no sources of military supplies. Mao's own fortunes were at their lowest ebb, for since the Autumn Harvest Uprising had not been sanctioned by the Central Committee he could expect no help from them, and might indeed find himself summarily court-martialed by the party. Communication with the other Soviet areas was slow and independable. Mao sent his brother Tse-t'an in search of the remnants of the Hailofeng Soviet. He did not return for two months. They had no radios. They were constantly being attacked by small local forces, and they seemed to be completely isolated on the obscure mountain on the border.

Living high up on a cliff monastery, surrounded by hostile armies in command of all the roads, Mao was compelled to revise all his thinking on revolutionary tactics and strategy. Previously he had commanded small guerrilla battles where his own troops possessed swift mobility. He had suffered dreadful losses. He could no longer afford to lose soldiers. The first step was to acquire the good will of the villagers in the plains, the second was to employ them as his intelligence staff, and the third was to invite the provincial armies to attack, so that he could replenish his diminishing supply of ammunition. He said later that there was not a single machine gun among his troops at the beginning of their stay on Ching-kanshan. He ordered concealed entrenchments to be dug on the mountain, chiefly to keep the soldiers occupied, and sent couriers to link up with the other scattered Communist armies. Rice was planted in the mountains. Three crops a year could be grown there, and they hoped to hold out if necessary with their own food. Meanwhile, in the plains, Mao assembled the villagers and encouraged them to redistribute the land.

The prospect remained bleak. The winter was strangely variable, one bitterly cold day being followed by several unexpectedly warm ones. There were mutterings in the army, which was gradually increasing in numbers. A mutiny was suppressed, with terrible forcefulness. It was a time that tried men's souls. Speaking of this period, Mao said afterward that he kept remembering Wu Sung, the bandit in *All Men Are Brothers* who found himself confronted with a tiger on the Chingyang Mountains. "The tiger," he said, "would eat people whether he was provoked or not, and you had to choose between killing the tiger and being eaten by it." Wu Sung killed the tiger with his own hands.

During this time Mao introduced the first and most famous of the guerrilla slogans he invented. In the original Chinese the four lines of four syllables each are rhymed. They read:

When the enemy advances, we retreat.
When he escapes, we harass.
When he retreats, we pursue.
When he is tired, we attack.[13]

Nothing could be simpler; but these verses, which were sometimes to lose some of their effect by becoming incantations, had deep roots in ancient Chinese history. They were not original, though the new form was original, and all of them can be found in the remarkable military writings of Sun Wu, the military technician who lived at some time during the period known as the "Spring and Autumn Dynasties," between 722 and 481 B.C. Sun Wu's original statement of the last of these slogans read: "Avoid the enemy when he is vigorous, and strike at him when he is retreating wearily." Mao's merit was that he gave the ancient apothegms a modern force.

Mao's debt to Sun Wu cannot be overestimated. In his military lectures he constantly quotes him, particularly emphasizing such doctrines as: "Know yourself and know your opponents, and in a hundred battles there will be a hundred victories," or "Use the resources of the occupied country, and take your supplies from the enemy." He did not always obey Sun Wu. "If you have ten times as many troops as your opponent, surround him; if five times, attack him; if you are equal in numbers and superior in fighting power, engage him;

13. Extraordinary importance was attached to slogans by the Chinese Communists from the beginning. The original four military slogans were adapted and subtly altered to suit changing circumstances, usually after long debates. They were more than slogans in the Western sense: they enshrined principles, and sometimes they were extremely dangerous, for the words seemed to develop an existence of their own, and after the Fifth Annihilation Campaign, Mao bitterly attacked the twenty slogans employed at the time. When the Japanese introduced the scorched-earth policy under the slogan "Kill all, burn all, loot all," the Chinese Communists countered with a further development of Mao's slogan:

When he burns, we put out the fire.
When he loots, we attack.
When he pursues, we hide.
When he retreats, we return.

otherwise avoid the conflict." Here Mao violently disagreed, though he insisted that at the point of contact even guerrilla forces must outnumber the enemy. He was most completely obedient to Sun Wu in his conception of espionage. There were five kinds of spies, and all, according to the ancient military philosopher, should be used simultaneously. The first group consisted of "native spies," men who knew the terrain well; then there were "inside spies," who knew the highest secrets of the enemy; then there were "spies in reverse," who were in fact fighting for you, but were unknowingly employed by the enemy; then there "dumb spies," poor creatures who were fed with knowledge which they unconsciously gave to the enemy; finally there were "daring spies," men who went over to the enemy lines and discovered military secrets at great risk to themselves. To survive, Mao had to use all five kinds of spies.

That winter there occurred the Commune in Canton, in which Yeh Ting played a major part. For three days the Communists held the city, only to be overthrown by Kuomintang forces; and though some escaped to Hailofeng, and others survived to join forces with Mao on Chingkanshan, the destruction of Communist power in Canton was complete. The time had not come for the capture of cities, and though, as his forces increased, there were continual demands for one more attack on Changsha with Chingkanshan as a base, Mao refused to allow the Red Army to be used for a purpose which could only end in disaster.

During the whole of the year 1928 Mao remained on Chingkanshan. In May, Chu Teh arrived at the head of his ragged column. They had not met before, but they took each other's measure during a night and a day when they talked to one another without ceasing, and thereupon they decided to join forces. They provided an extraordinarily brilliant combination. Chu Teh had fought in rebellions against Yuan Shih-kai, and he had been among the first Chinese Communists in Germany. He spoke German well, and had a wider knowledge than Mao of the history of military strategy. More than Mao, he resembled a hard-bitten humorous peasant, with a broad mouth and small eyes and a habit of grin ning pleasantly at the foibles of mankind, though he could, and did, look ferocious, with the terrible ferocity of the Chinese war god, when occasion demanded. Agnes Smedley has recounted how his face turned a sickening deep green when he walked over a battlefield where his own men lay dying. Like Mao he had no instinct for adventure: he was cautious, and his boldness derived from an exemplary understanding of the enemy's powers. Yet they were antithetical. Mao remained the scholar by habit, and Chu Teh, though a scholar in his own right, desired action and thirsted for glory, though he would sometimes mock his own ambitions—as when, years later, possessing the title of commander in chief of all the Red armies, he designed for himself a purple cloak, like the one worn by the Generalissimo, and round the collar there were scatterings of frayed rabbit fur. Mao was aloof, conscious of his general superiority. Chu Teh genuinely liked men, shared their simple pleasures, joked with them incessantly, and his jokes came with the freshness of someone who understood their casual secrets. From the moment of their meeting they were almost inseparable; and together they dominated Chingkanshan, where previously Mao had dominated alone. Both had experienced the same failures, for both had attempted uprisings in southern Hunan: on his journey to Chingkanshan, Chu Teh had made one last effort to lead the peasants of Hunan against the Kuomintang. Now, having failed completely, they shared the same hopes.

In the comparative security of the mountain stronghold, they waited upon events. Their first hope was to carve out of the border villages a soviet consisting of six counties linked together. Failing this, there were possibilities of withdrawal into the uplands of Kiangsi. Most of the younger officers desired quicker profits. They would go north to Changsha or south to Canton for these were rich cities, and once established in them, the Communists could hope to provide themselves with armaments and armies. What was the use of living like bandits? Mao shook his head. He realized that the quickest advance might be the slowest. He counseled caution. They were fighting small battles all the time. They had insufficient resources for attacking the Kuomintang. Sooner or later they would have to meet the full brunt of the Kuomintang campaigns. They counted fifty-seven minor engagements, and thirteen battles during the year they spent on Chingkanshan; and though they destroyed the opposing armies, they were perfectly conscious that an almost inexhaustible manpower would enable Chiang Kai-shek to annihilate them in time.

The Sixth Congress of the Chinese Communist Party was held that summer during July and August, in a suburb of Moscow. It was attended by the leading Communists who had escaped the White Terror during the previous year, and who had been ordered by the Central Committee to take refuge in the Soviet capital. The report of its resolutions did not arrive in Chingkanshan until the late autumn. The resolutions were curiously ironical, for though Mao agreed with them in principle, it was clear that they were formed by men who had no knowledge of the situation of the Communists in China. The resolution stated:

At the present time the party must everywhere propagate among the masses the idea of soviets, the idea of the democratic dictatorship of the proletariat and peasantry, and the inevitability of the coming revolutionary mass uprising. It must emphasize in its agitation the necessity for overthrowing the ruling bloc, and the mobilization of the masses for revolutionary demonstrations. . . . It must consistently and undeviatingly follow the line of the seizure of state power, organization of soviets as organs of insurrection, expropriation of the landlords and big property owners, and the expulsion of the foreign imperialists. . . . The future growth of the revolution will place before the party as an immediate practical task the preparation for, and the carrying through of, armed insurrection as the sole path for the completion of the bourgeois democratic revolution, and to overthrow the power of the Kuomintang.

The dull, repetitive document could be read to mean anything anyone desired. It came, however, with more authority than the decisions of the Central Executive Committee, which still existed in the isolation of Shanghai; and the Central Executive Committee, disposed to believe that Changsha and Canton were the supreme objectives of the Communist campaign, had to bow before the resolutions made in Moscow. Mao and Chu Teh read the document to mean an increasing circle of village soviets and the establishment of a secure base. And when they heard in the spring of 1928 that there had been uprisings in Tungku and Hsingkuo, they began to believe that the secure base might be somewhere near these two large towns, deep in the Kiangsi hills.

Meanwhile Chingkanshan was becoming untenable. It was not only that larger and larger armies were being sent against Mao's army, but they had been unable to provide enough food for all the new volunteers who flocked to the mountain. There were now about 11,000 men, comprising Mao's original thousand, 2,000 more who had followed Chu Teh, and about 8,000 armed peasants from southern Hunan.[14] The mountain was overcrowded. Most of the military supplies they had captured were lost; they had been unable to grow much food; and they were dependent upon the peasants, who were themselves still afraid of the power of Wang Tso and Yuan Wen-tsai. The Communists were faced with a desperate situation. There were already defections to the Kuomintang. On the afternoon of January 1, 1929, Mao and Chu Teh led their small forces down the mountain, as dusk was descending, leaving Peng Teh-huei, a Kuomintang officer who had mutinied while in Ho Chien's army, in command of the mountain.

Exactly a year later the *Military Bulletin* of the Central Committee of the Chinese Communist Party published an interim account of the small column which left Chingkanshan for Kiangsi. It read very simply:

The masses completely failed to understand what the Red Army was. In many places the army was even attacked, like a bandit gang. The army had no support from the masses. There were great difficulties in finding encampments, carrying on military operations, and securing information. We marched across snow-covered and icy mountains, closely pursued by the enemy. We sometimes covered thirty miles in a single day. Our sufferings increased.

14. *Räte China—Dokumente der Chinesischen Revolution*, Moscow, 1934, p. 253.

Five Battles

The fantastically small Red Army, wandering into the hills of Kiangsi, had not the least resemblance to a real fighting-force. As they came down from Chingkanshan, they still wore their cotton uniforms, they were covered with lice, and their hair fell down to their shoulders, and many of them walked barefoot. Mao was desperately thin with the strain of commanding the mountain outpost. Less than half the soldiers on the march had rifles: it was assumed that the small column would be able to recoup its armaments from the enemy.

The mountains were deep in snow, very beautiful with their tall pines and small secluded villages among the ravines. Though the villagers supplied them, there was rarely enough food to go round, and quite often they lived on roots, and many died of exposure at night, dying silently. They were four thousand when they left the mountain, but a month later there were four or five hundred more peasant boys from the villages. They marched up mountain trails, camped on the mountaintops, and sometimes lost themselves. Of all the places they had been to in China, this was the hardest, the most legendary, and the most ripe for rebellion.

Kiangsi at this time was full of underground movements of protest against the Kuomintang. A succession of corrupt governors had left the province poverty-stricken. The landlords built large stockaded fortresses and kept their own private militia; they had power of life and death over the villagers, who were treated like serfs. Indeed, there had hardly been a time when the Kiangsi peasants were not ripe for rebellion. One of the most famous of their rebellions had been quashed at the end of the T'ang dynasty by one of the ancestors of Sun Yat-sen, who received a dukedom and a large gift of cash in reward. Here, too, among the desolate, sharp-cragged mountains, lay the heart of the Taoist religion. The Taoist temples were the richest in all China. And from one of these mountains, called the Dragon Tiger Mountain, the most famous of the Taoist popes, Chang Tao-ling, had ascended to heaven. The name of the mountain was not a misnomer: even to this day, in those hills where the bedraggled Communist armies wandered, tigers are to be found.

There were continual skirmishes, but in the first month there were no severe losses. Nananfu was occupied, and so was Namyung, but gradually it was being impressed upon them that two large towns in the heart of Kiangsi, both high up in the mountains and almost inaccessible, would provide the best base. These towns were Tungku and Hsingkuo. The last in particular was formidably defended by high mountains, for it lay in a circle of mountains whose crests were invisible in winter. All over the mountains lay the scattered Taoist temples. To get to these towns it was necessary to pass through Tapoteh. They deliberated. It was known that Tapoteh was well defended, but they needed ammunition and decided to attack, though some of them had only sticks, stones, branches and rifle stocks to fight with. It was a merciless battle, fought in late February, while the snow was still on the ground. It lasted from three o'clock in the afternoon to noon of the next day. At the end of the battle there were 2,000 dead Communists. Half the army had been wiped away.

There had been bad defeats before, but this was the worst, and the most unnecessary. "It was more like a mutual blood-letting," said Chu Teh afterward, "than a battle. It was indescribably horrible." When evening came down on the second day, Mao, who had directed the operations with Chu Teh, and who sent himself on missions to the front lines, walked over the battlefield, seeing the small clumps of dead soldiers on the icy ground, and the women coming from the villages with pots of tea and small bowls of rice for the soldiers who remained alive. There he and Chu Teh swore to avenge the defeat. By the end of February the Red Army had reached Tungku and Hsingkuo, which were to become famous bases during the "annihilation campaigns." On Chingkanshan the Red Army had flown a red banner with a five-pointed white star crossed with a black hammer and sickle. Now, as though the starkness of their purpose demanded something simpler, they flew only a red flag with a black hammer and sickle in the center.

There followed a year and a half of strange and sometimes purposeless wandering. Almost it was as though the Red Army was driven by internal forces to be perpetually on the march, in order to show itself, in order to attract an increasing number of volunteers. There were forces which held them to the remote villages of Kiangsi; other forces, following the demands of Li Li-san, proclaimed that they should launch attacks on cities. Between these two poles they oscillated.

Peng Teh-huei had been forced to leave Chingkanshan in April, four months after Mao had left the mountain. By July of the next year he thought he had strength enough—he had ten thousand men armed with bayonets, mattocks, and a few rifles—to attack Changsha, which was held by Ho Chien with 30,000 men. The city favors the defenders, but the resolution of the peasant guerrillas led to its capture. For ten days they held it, retiring only because vastly larger forces than Ho Chien's original 30,000 were being brought up against them, and because foreign warships were already bombarding the city. Thereafter, Peng Teh-huei moved south, to join forces with Chu Teh and Mao. There were long sweeping operations along the Fukien border; preparations were made for an attack on Nanchang; and once more there arose the promise of a victory at Changsha.

At Kutien, in December, Mao had warned against the Li Li-san line at a military conference. He was overruled by his field commanders, who saw no future in the aimless wandering over high mountain passes in winter: better to settle in an industrial city in the heart of China and from there spread out over the whole nation. What was the use of the small abandoned villages in Kiangsi? Would they support an army? By June 1930, preparations for the second onslaught against Changsha were made, and though the Red Army reached the walls of the city, they made no dent in the city's defenses.

Just as Changsha, to the Communists, had become the symbol of a necessary victory, and the beginning of a great campaign which would embrace the whole of China, so the same city was regarded by Chiang Kai-shek as his most important defense line; and the huge armies which wheeled into Hunan in September were designed to stamp out the small forces of the Reds forever.

They did not quite succeed. The Red Army withdrew to the pine-clad hills of Kiangsi, to face another winter; and they half guessed that at the height of the winter the Kuomintang troops would be launched against them. This was, in fact, what happened. Then, in the course of three years, while the Reds retained their bases of Tungku and Hsingkuo, five "annihilation campaigns" were thrown against them.

THE FIRST ANNIHILATION CAMPAIGN

Four of the five annihilation campaigns which occurred in Kiangsi—all of them in roughly the same region—have been commented on at length by the Chinese Communists, by the Kuomintang, and by foreigners who discussed the battles at Yenan with the Communist leaders years afterward. They were battles fought against almost overwhelming odds. The Red armies survived only by employing great mobility and ingenuity. And mostly, as the Kuomintang generals admitted later, the Red armies were successful because they knew their terrain better, because they were trained for guerrilla warfare, and because they observed all the classic tenets of guerrilla warfare without ever forgetting their main objective: loot, elbowroom, secure footholds.

The Red armies were ragged, underfed, without cannon or airplanes or any heavy equipment, without reserves, and without more than a handful of trained officers, and in all their battles they were outnumbered ten to one. Yet they nearly always succeeded in inflicting heavy defeats on the enemy, and it was by an exhaustive study of these battles that the Red armies were able to defeat the Kuomintang in 1949. From 1934 onward the study of these campaigns became obligatory in the Red Army. In the first four annihilation campaigns the Red army in Kiangsi was directed by Chu Teh and Mao. Surprisingly often, Mao's contribution to the strategical operations can be detected. Mao is the surgeon, exploring the wound, insisting above everything else on the delicate probing, the discovery of the enemy's weakened nerve, the dangerous point where weakness is balanced by strength: at this point he will order the attack. There follows a cunning interweaving among the enemy columns—as Mao describes his tactics, they have something of the inevitability of a dance —and finally there is the withdrawal to the chosen terminus, which may be within the enemy lines or deep in enemy territory or safely within the territory the Reds have circumscribed for themselves. The theory, as he relates the battles, seems to be pure Mao; the practice, the knowledge of the possible, the way in which forces can be grouped together for maximum effectiveness, seems to come from Chu Teh. Yet they learned from each other, and it is hardly possible to say where one begins and the other ends. When they came to the borders of Kiangsi and Fukien, Mao was almost entirely inexperienced in warfare. There had been the Autumn Harvest Uprising, followed by the minor guerrilla battles at Chingkanshan. None of these was of any great importance. But in Kiangsi, Mao demonstrated that he was a military genius of the first magnitude.

At the beginning there was almost nothing to show for it. there was the famous four-line slogan invented at Chingkanshan, and there was the knowledge that among the hills of southern Kiangsi the enemy might be lured beyond the reach of its supply columns—the slogan "lure enemy deep penetration" was invented by him during this time. He had not yet begun to think out all the consequences of a strategy of "luring." He was still, as he admitted later, contaminated by Li Li-san's theory of "proletarian uprisings in the large urban districts," but it was impossible to correlate this theory with the small vagrant army, consisting mostly of peasants with a sprinkling of Henyang miners, wandering in the winter hills. His mind fought for certainties, and by the use which he made later of his conceptions of the "first engagement" and the "terminus of withdrawal" it is clear that he found his certainties in these two things.

But where should the first engagement take place? Clearly, the guerrilla troops can choose their own terrain. The Red Army was concentrated along the road from Yungfeng to Hsingkuo, with its main concentrations at Kian. Should the guerrillas remain in the towns? There were heated arguments, for Li Li-san had insisted on the primary importance of the towns, but Mao and Chu Teh were already planning a withdrawal into the hills between Kian and Kwangchang; and though the debates were endless, and Mao commented ruefully that the decision to leave the towns had to be fought tooth and nail, the slogan "lure enemy deep penetration" prevailed.

By the end of December 1930, at least seven Kuomintang columns were driving down from the north under the command of Lu Ti-ping, who was governor of the province and commander in chief of the whole expedition. He had not been idle. Even during the Red occupation of Kian, he had organized what came to be known as A-B (Anti-Bolshevik) groups in the towns east of Kian, and in the Red Army itself there were these dissident elements: men who joined the army during the hurried reorganization at Kian, and who were determined to make havoc. Futien and Tungku were particularly dangerous to the Reds. But now, skirting Futien, they marched out of Kian and took Tungku in a short battle. Then they waited. The Kuomintang columns came down the Yungfeng-Kian road, and were elated to find the city aban-

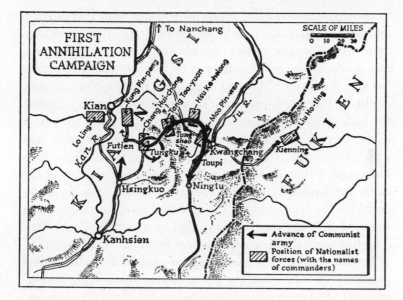

doned. Leaving Lo Ling's division to guard Kian, the rest took
to the mountains and began to pursue the Reds. It was a particularly cold winter, with mists hanging over the mountains.
Some Kuomintang columns lost their way, and there was
sporadic fighting in the hills. Reports came to the 18th
Division under Chang Hui-chang that Tungku had been
abandoned, as Kian had been abandoned before it. On December 31st, the 18th Division entered Tungku. The trap was
sprung. The Red Army made a forced march, and arrived under cover of darkness outside the walls of Tungku, capturing
the town by surprise, killing Chang Hui-chang, and making
9,000 prisoners. They also captured two radios.

Meanwhile the 50th Division under Tan Tao-yuan was
wandering among the mountains in the east, and the full
weight of the Red Army was thrown against it. The Red Army
now wore Kuomintang uniforms and carried Kuomintang
banners. Tan Tao-yuan had no radio contact with Chang
Hui-chang's division, and he was overjoyed when he saw the
18th arriving. His enjoyment was short-lived: half of his
division was virtually annihilated before he realized what was
happening.

The enemy originally possessed 100,000 troops; 16,000

were now accounted for, comprising 9,000 who had entered
Tungku, about 3,000 caught in the hills and villages, where
there were the same tactics of withdrawal and speedy return,
and 4,000 in the mass slaughter of half of Tan Tao-yuan's
forces at Tungshao. Mao had hoped that the complete division
might be destroyed, and later he complained bitterly against
the lack of concentration of the Reds at this point—it was a
lesson he took to heart. Kung Pin-pang's division pulled out
under the threat of a small independent division of Reds at
Hsingkuo, which moved up and appeared to be about to encircle the Kuomintang rear. The army under Hsu Ko-chang
and Mao Pin-wen reached Toupi, and then drove north along
the road to Yungfeng, only too glad to avoid the Red Army.
The first annihilation campaign was over.

For the first time the Kuomintang realized that the normal
processes of war were no longer applicable. The "luring"
operation had been wonderfully successful. Two divisions had
been trapped, one in a town and another in high mountains,
where its rear had been cut off. The Reds had employed a
vast knowledge of the mountain paths. The Kuomintang
troops lacked this knowledge, and they were deliberately
misled by the hostile villagers; also, many of the village
people slipped out of their villages and took to the hills,
sniping at them, or leading them to small concentrations of
Red troops, who mowed them down from their higher positions. The Kuomintang troops had no training in mountain
warfare, did not know the strength of the Reds, or realize
the desperate poverty of the villagers and all its consequences,
and they did not co-operate with one another, each divisional
commander hoping to avoid the responsibility of a direct
engagement with the Reds. The most prominent commander,
Chang Hui-chang, had been killed at the very beginning of
the battle, and he had made the basic error of leading his
troops too close to the main concentration area of the Red
Army; the forces of Tan Tao-yuan and Chang Hui-chang were
outnumbered. Finally, three divisions at Kian, Futien, and
Kienning, made no effort to support the 18th Division, probably because they had no idea what had happened to it. The
Kuomintang generals had hoped to annihilate the Red Army

between the Kan and Ju rivers, but they were themselves annihilated. There were skirmishes until the end of February, and at least one major engagement was fought near Ningtu, the original "terminus of withdrawal" selected by the Reds. There, once again, Mao complained of the Communists' occasional inability to concentrate all their forces at the psychological moment on the enemy: too many were allowed to retreat. But the lessons had been learned, and with the destruction of the 18th Division they discovered their own power for the first time. Also, they now possessed the two captured radios, which were to be of inestimable use to them in the kind of guerrilla warfare they practiced. "In this battle," said Mao, "we faced the enemy with poise and ease."

THE SECOND ANNIHILATION CAMPAIGN

One of the major advantages possessed by the Red Army was the completeness of its intelligence. The positions of the enemy were known, if only because the Kuomintang forces allowed their positions to be published in newspapers; the positions of the Red Army, hiding among the hills, were nearly always unknown. There were also disadvantages. The Red resources were limited. They had lost about 7,000 men in the first campaign, and they had made up their forces to the original 30,000, but they knew that Chiang Kai-shek was preparing to launch an even greater expedition than before. Lo Ling's division was retained to guard Kian, but from the north, east, and west seven columns were advancing on Ningtu. In the first campaign Mao fought his first battle against the strongest opposing force; in the second, he deliberately hurled himself at the weakest, avoiding the Nineteenth Route Army under Tsai Ting-kai, who was regarded as the best of the opposing generals. In the following year Tsai Ting-kai was to achieve lasting fame for his valiant resistance to the Japanese attacks in Shanghai, and for some time to come he was to remain a thorn in the flesh to the Communists.

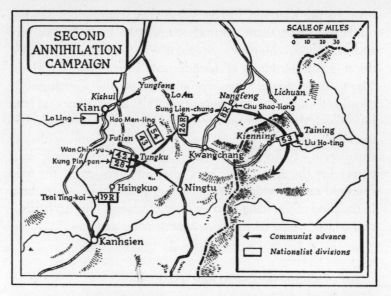

8th Route—Chu Shao-liang   42nd Division—Wang Chin-yu
19th Route—Tsai Ting-kai   43rd Division—Kuo Hua-tsung
26th Route—Sung Lien-chung   54th Division—Hao Meng-ling
28th Division—Kung Pin-pan   53rd Division—Liu Ho-ting

Now that they possessed radios, diversionary movements of guerrillas—even on a large scale—became easier, and Red forces were scattered behind the enemy lines. The main forces, however, were to travel 250 miles in fourteen days, fighting four battles and capturing more than 20,000 rifles. Nanfeng was taken, and then abandoned, and exactly as Mao had calculated they were to find a "terminus of withdrawal" inside the Fukien border, south of Kienning.

Mao's notes on the battles, compiled with the help of Chu Teh, give an impression of illusory ease to the whole campaign. It is almost a dance, or a game of skittles. In fact, far greater risks were taken by the Reds in this campaign than before. Absolute superiority in manpower did not exist. There were none of the advantages which come with winter mists—the attack began in late spring—and the country was less mountainous. The enemy was learning his lesson. Ho Ying-ching, in command of the expedition, urged the commanders to move more slowly and cautiously, consolidating the territory recovered before advancing further; and already there was emerging in embryo the idea of an enclosing ring of blockhouses. Mao's deliberately dry account of the campaign is here quoted in full:

The situation was:

1. The advancing enemy forces numbered 200,000 with Ho Ying-ching as the commander in chief with headquarters at Nanchang.
2. As in the First Campaign all the troops did not belong to Chiang Kai-shek's own faction. The strongest units were the 19th Route Army (in the southwest) and the armies under Sung Lien-chung and Chu Shao-liang (in the east, inside the border of Kiangsi province). The rest were weaker.
3. The A-B group was purged, and the Red Army enjoyed the support of the people of the Soviet Area.
4. Wang Chin-yu's division (in the Futien area northeast of the 19th Route Army position) had just arrived from North China, and was frightened. A similar situation obtained with the two columns of Wang's left wing, the divisions of Hao Meng-ling and Kuo Hua-tsung.
5. If we were to attack Futien first and then sweep to the east, we could extend the territory of the Soviets in the vicinity of Chien-ning, Lichuan, and Taining on the Fukien-Kiangsi border and amass provisions for smashing the coming encirclement campaign. If we strike in the western direction, then we would come up against the Kan River, leaving no space for expansion after the conclusion of the campaign. If (after the western operations) we turn back to the east again, our army would be fatigued and our time lost.
6. Though the strength of our troops was slightly reduced to 30,000 odd, our men had had four months for rehabilitation and training.

Basing ourselves on these considerations, we decided to engage the forces of Wang Chin-yu and those of Kung Ping-fan (on Wang's western flank), totaling eleven regiments, for the initial battle, and after defeating them, we would beat the troops of Sung Lien-chung, Chu Shao-liang and Liu Ho-ting (in the Tienning and Taining area in Fukien). For fifteen days in succession, from May 16 to May 30 1931, our troops covered a distance of 700 *li*, fought five battles, and captured more than 20,000 rifles. The encirclement was broken dramatically and punctually.

Our battle with Wang Chin-yu took place between the positions of Tsai Ting-kai's (19th Route Army) and Kuo Hua-tsung's division some ten *li* away from Kuo and forty *li* from Tsai. We were derided for forcing ourselves into a tight position, but we succeeded in getting in. This was mainly due to the condition of the Soviet area, plus the disunity among the enemy's units. After the defeat of Kuo's division, Hao's division fled to Yungfeng during the same night and was saved from disaster.

This is not, of course, an attempt to tell the whole story. Mao contents himself with offering the *logical* plan of a guerrilla campaign, a plan which revolves around the utmost daring and the reversal of generally accepted rules of warfare. Deliberately, the Red Army set itself the task of entering a fortified area, smashing a comparatively weak army, though strong armies were on both its flanks, and then slicing through the three remaining armies in the northeast, taking each by surprise. Elsewhere, Mao has remarked that the battles were not completely satisfactory, and dangerous risks were taken; but when he speaks of these risks, he does not mention the first onslaught against Wang Chin-yu, but the fact that the Red Army, after the capture of Nanfeng, was compelled to divide its resources, and he regards it almost as an act of weakness that they did not possess absolute superiority at Kienning. 10,000 Red Army troops were employed against the 7,000 of the 53rd Division. The superiority was not great enough. "Even in guerrilla war, there is complete assurance of victory only when a vastly superior force strikes at any given point: in this way a very small army, by concentrations, can *eat away* at a vastly superior enemy."

Mao's campaigns suggest a brilliant daring, but their success came from caution, from a very careful evaluation of the enemy's strength, and from the patient study of "the first engagement" and "the terminus of withdrawal." Mao places an almost mystical trust in these concepts. During the second campaign, the Red Army, after a night march, actually occupied Tungku, and then, just as silently, evaporated. For twenty-five days they led a secret existence in the town, waiting for Wang Chin-yu to advance from his strong position at Futien. "During the interval of waiting we were closely quar-

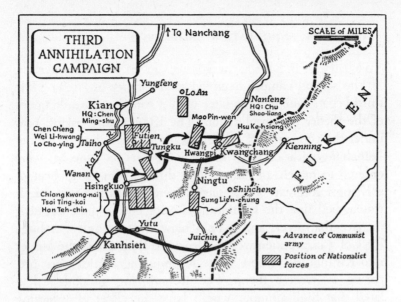

tered by the enemy," Mao relates in his book *Strategic Problems of the Revolutionary Wars.* "Despite the danger that information about our presence might leak out, we rejected all impatient suggestions for a quick attack. At last our desire was realized."

The success of the second campaign was evidently even greater than the Communists had hoped. Near Tungku the Kuomintang Fifth Army was cut to pieces, and the equipment of two divisions captured: more equipment was captured in the three remaining battles, and once again their losses were made up by the prisoners. It looked as though the same tactics—a quick break-through at the weakest point followed by a quick succession of battles while they were still flushed with their first victory, and then withdrawal into the mountains—would be continually successful. But the third campaign was to last longer and was to be fought harder than any of the others. By the middle of June the second campaign was over. On July 2, Chiang Kai-shek launched the Third Annihilation Campaign, which was to last for three long months. This time there were variations of the theme of guerrilla warfare, and this time the Reds escaped encirclement largely by luck.

THE THIRD ANNIHILATION CAMPAIGN

The second campaign ended on February 29, 1931. The third began four months later with a complete abandonment of the theory of consolidation. The Kuomintang troops, now under the command of Chiang Kai-shek, who had arrived at Nanchang with a staff of German advisers on June 22, were ordered to march 25 miles a day through the torrid heat of a Kiangsi summer. Their tactics were carefully prepared. It was agreed that the Communists were now a more pressing menace than ever, and a final blow was necessary: a huge force of 300,000 men were to drive the Reds across the border into Kwangtung, where other Kuomintang armies were preparing to receive them. The Kuomintang generals calculated that high summer would have the effect of wearying the Reds, whose extraordinary mobility would perhaps be reduced; and this time the Kuomintang armies were heavily equipped, with about 200 cannon and a hundred airplanes, and they were under some of the best commanders the Reds had ever fought against.

The map on page 121 shows a series of battles fought toward the end of the campaign. At the beginning the area between Tungku and Kwangchang was in the hands of the Reds, who were compelled to retreat within the borders of Fukien. Tungku, because it had harbored the Red forces, was treated like Lidice: it was burned to the ground and all its inhabitants massacred. In the first stages of the campaign the Reds lost heavily; airplanes were able to bomb their concentrations in the forests and make careful reconnaissances. But after August 1 the tide began to ebb. Heavy rains set in, and the lines of communications of the Kuomintang armies were already too long and unwieldy. Having occupied the triangle Kian-Kwangchang-Yutu, they concentrated their forces on the right bank of the Kan River, though four divisions were left in the mountains. In an effort to cut the rear of these "lost divisions," the Reds deliberately courted danger by taking the least likely path to the north. Intending to make a wide encircling movement, they found themselves detected near Futien, two divisions rushed down to intercept them, and they were then compelled to return to a small village west of Hsingkuo. They were exhausted and bedraggled. They knew they had only a single day in which to reform their ranks, and they had been fighting continuously for over a month. Then, by one of those chances which came to them with surprising frequency, their patrols discovered a fifteen-mile gap between a single division in the north and a huge army numbering some 100,000 men in the south. Through this, at night, they fled, only to encounter two divisions driving south under the famous commander Shankuan Yun-hsiang. They destroyed these divisions in a battle lasting forty-eight hours, marched for three days in the direction of Hwangpi, and there destroyed still another division, under Mao Pin-wen. A few days later they destroyed the army of Hsu Ko-chang, an act of destruction which gave them exceptional pleasure, for it was this general who had been responsible for the massacres in Changsha in May 1927.

Heartened by these victories, the Reds drove west to Tungku after occupying Kwangchang, deliberately inviting a close encirclement, while spreading a net of partisan forces in the hills. Here they were almost trapped. As the ring closed tighter, they attacked the Nineteenth Route Army, the one army which they respected most. Finally, after heavy losses, they were forced to disengage. Once more they found a providential gap between the opposing armies, and after climbing some high mountain paths they emerged again at Hsingkuo, where they were able to rest. The enemy did not find them: it was too busy operating against groups of guerrillas who kept descending from the mountains and sometimes gave the impression of being a whole army. When the Red Army was at last detected at Hsingkuo, the rains had set in with a vengeance and Ho Ying-ching was already counseling retreat. As he retreated toward Kian, he fought continual rear-guard actions. An entire Kuomintang division commanded by Han Teh-chin was destroyed, and a brigade commanded by Chiang Ting-wen was also lost.

Mao could now observe with satisfaction that the strange

serpentine movement of the Red Army completely confused
the enemy. About 35,000 deserters from Kuomintang ranks
joined him with their rifles and machine guns intact, and the
entire territory taken by the Kuomintang troops in July was
retaken by the Communists by the end of September.

On September 18 occurred the Mukden Incident, which
became the signal of the Japanese occupation of Manchuria.
Shortly afterward the Kuomintang divisions withdrew from
southern Kiangsi, leaving only some supporting troops at
Kian. The Kuomintang contended that their morale had
been affected by the Mukden Incident and that this was the
sole cause of their withdrawal. It seems unlikely. The destruction of Tungku resulted in a widespread increase of
peasant partisans. As so often before, a huge, unwieldy army
had disintegrated because every divisional commander had
been anxious that every other divisional commander should
bear the brunt of the fighting. The Kuomintang troops were
underfed because the Reds had carefully hidden all food supplies in the villages; their officers were corrupt; and both the
troops and the officers terrorized the local populations. Toward the end of the battle one of the Kuomintang brigadiers
was heard to say sadly: "The fat has worn thin, and the thin
has been worn dead."

Of all the engagements which occurred during the third
campaign, Mao was proudest of the first, the short, sharp
battle near Lientang which was fought by a weary army after
marching three or four hundred miles continually in the hills,
after a single day's rest, and after a dangerous march between
the enemy armies. It was a battle fought with the energy of
despair, with tremendous speed and fury, and it could not be
otherwise, for they were encircled and hopelessly outnumbered. Tactically, the decision to fight this battle went against
all Mao's military beliefs except one: the belief that the first
engagement determined all the rest. He was least proud of
the dogged battles fought against the Nineteenth Route Army,
which wasted the efforts of both armies, and ended in stalemate.

The third campaign was decisive. They had defeated, or
broken, seventeen out of the enemy's thirty-three divisions,

and increased their own strength. They had set up soviets throughout the south, and there were even soviets behind the enemy lines. They had made some military mistakes—Mao came to the conclusion that it was probably a mistake to have made the long march through Juichin to Hsingkuo, when it should have been possible to lure the enemy into the hills of western Fukien, for the idea of "lure enemy deep penetration" had not been utilized during this campaign; but he was dubious whether the victory would have been so complete. He noted with pleasure the remark of a Kuomintang general: "Wherever we go we are in darkness; wherever the Reds go, they are in brightness." It was a shadow game, played by one invisible enemy against another only too visible—a game played with exquisite cunning and furious violence. At its best, it was played by gradually circling around the enemy, threatening him, feeding him with suspense, and finally accomplishing his demise with a blow falling from an entirely unsuspected quarter, so that he was almost unconscious that the blow had fallen at all. Not only was Mao good at the game, but in a sense he had invented it, and no one else knew the rules.

These rules were re-examined after the conclusion of the third campaign. A completely new set of operational principles was formulated. There were developments in tactics and strategy, and the rudimentary character of the earlier principles was abandoned, though their essentials remained. In particular, Mao found no quarrel with the sixteen-word slogan he had made up at Chingkanshan. They were simple words, but they contained the answers to all the problems of encirclement. They rang like a bell, and Mao said that if you wanted to put the matter in more pompous military terms they provided "the basic directives for a countercampaign against encirclement, and the phases of both the strategic defensive and the strategic offensive, as well as those of strategic withdrawal and the strategic counteroffensive in a defensive operation." They are long words, in Chinese as in English, and Mao preferred his simple doggerel. "In a sense," he wrote, "all that came afterwards was but an elaboration of those sixteen words."

THE FIRST ALL-CHINA CONGRESS OF SOVIETS

For a few months the Red Army rested on its laurels. Preparations were made for holding the First All-China Congress of Soviets. The Kuomintang had reached a crisis in its activities: it had failed to prevent the Japanese occupation of Manchuria, just as it had failed to prevent the growth of the Red Army. In December 1931, at the end of one of China's most fatal years, which had seen floods in the Yangtse valley and the failure of crops over large areas, and the first onslaught of the Japanese as well as the third annihilation campaign, the congress was convened.

This congress is important, for here the Communists drew up their blueprints for the "democratic dictatorship of workers and peasants," and this blueprint was to remain relatively unchanged throughout the course of Communist expansion. When Mao came to power, exactly the same phrases, the same laws, and the same interpretations were used. Most of the declarations of the congress bear Mao's characteristic imprint. Nearly all of them are signed by him as president of the provisional government, though the names of the two vice-presidents, Han Ying and Chang Kuo-t'ao, are included.

In the constitution, the aims of the "democratic dictatorship" are defined. These aims include "the destruction of all feudal remnants and the destruction of the power of the warlords; the unification of China; the systematic delimitation of capitalist expansion; the development of the organization and class-consciousness of the proletariat; and the rallying of the broad masses of the village poor to our banners in order to effect the transition to the dictatorship of the proletariat." Not all of the constitution is so dry or so formidable. A special article is reserved for education—"all the peasants and toiling masses are guaranteed the right to education." Another article gives minority races equal rights and privileges. The electors are given the right to recall their deputies. Nationalization is to be on the broadest scale. The concessions are to be unconditionally returned to China. Outright confiscation of custom-houses, railways, mines, and factories in foreign ownership is demanded. Asylum is offered to foreign revolutionaries. Compulsory military service occupies a special place in the constitution. Finally, "the Soviet Government in China proclaims the Soviet Union, the land of proletarian dictatorship, to be its loyal ally."

The constitution outlined a rigid program, and though it spoke of rights, it spoke more often of harsh duties and final judgments. The labor code, on the other hand, though some of its articles were clearly impracticable, did show a desire to improve labor standards in a way which had never been seen in China before. It called for a universal eight-hour day, a six-hour day for youths between sixteen and eighteen, a four-hour day for younger workers, and special privileges for women. No work would be allowed on New Year's Day, the anniversary of Lenin's death, the anniversary of the Paris Commune, the anniversary of the inauguration of the Soviet Union, May Day, and the anniversaries of the Canton Uprising and the Shanghai Massacre. Only six hours of work was permitted on days before holidays. Wages were to be arranged by collective agreement. A list of places where women and children were not allowed to work was provided, including "forest work in places too high or too low." Women were to receive the same wage rates as men. Special machinery to prevent the exploitation of apprentices was put into force, and labor inspectors were given complete powers over the establishment of all new businesses. Unions were granted the right to strike, and two per cent of all wages were to go to union funds, and another one per cent to cultural undertakings. Social insurance, with benefits of free medical attention, unemployment relief, disablement and old age pensions, and special relief to cover funerals, childbirth, and payments to the survivors after the death of the wage-earner, were also introduced. The whole labor code was to go into effect on January 1, 1932.

Admirable in many of its provisions, impracticable in others, the new labor code was never completely put to the test. But it did show the direction in which the new soviet state was progressing. Curiously enough, it had more to say about the conditions of the workers than of the peasants, as though preparation was already made for the moment when the proletariat would take over power according to the Marxist theory. Yet the proletariat was noticeable by its absence.

At this conference, too, Chang Kuo-t'ao prevailed upon the Communists to accept a new interpretation of strategy. The old and well-tried principles of guerrilla warfare and the breakthrough during encirclement were to be abandoned, or at least partially abandoned, in favor of the wresting from the enemy of whole provinces. He argued that it was wrong to lure the enemy into deep penetration, because so much Communist territory was necessarily abandoned: it would be better to defeat the enemy without abandoning any territory. Were they not two states confronting one another? The Soviets possessed huge settled areas, with regular armies, and for such armies guerrilla warfare must be accounted an anachronism. In this war of theory against practice, no final decisions were made, though the ghost of Li Li-san's ideas, which tormented them in 1927, now confronted them again at the moment of their triumph. It was a ghost which was not entirely to be laid for many years.

On this subject Mao had brooded at length with a kind of derisive horror against all those who objected to his simple and constantly repeated maxims of guerrilla war. He mocked at the strange new concepts: "absolute centralized command," "lose not an inch of land," "the division of the army into six advancing columns," "a war of blockhouses against blockhouses," and the strangest of all, which can be translated as "big-rearism." "All these theories," he wrote, "are undoubtedly erroneous. They are mechanical expressions of revolutionary hysteria and impatience. This is the theory and practice of reckless and naïve elements who, when circumstances become difficult, move from sheer desperation to conservatism, and from conservatism to escapism."

In 1932 no annihilation campaigns were fought. In February the Nineteenth Route Army under Tsai Ting-kai found itself battling the Japanese at Chapei, without help from Chiang Kai-shek. They were forced to withdraw to Fukien, where they set up an independent state. China was beginning to crack along the seams. The provinces of Manchuria were under Japanese control, the Japanese having employed the same tactics as the Communists: night marches, sudden surprise attacks, the wearing of enemy uniforms. Against the constant use of surprise, Chiang Kai-shek, with a faulty system of intelligence, had no weapons. Through most of the year the Red Army continued its sporadic attacks against the Kuomintang armies. On April 20, the Red Army attacked Changchow in Fukien, and held it for six weeks. There were short guerrilla attacks in the areas between the Kan and Ju rivers. Lo An, Kienning, and Lichuan were stormed, and more deserters from the Kuomintang ranks came to join the Red Army. Even airplanes were captured, only to be burned, because at this stage there were no pilots available. Gradually the Red Army had come to possess about 80,000 front-line troops, and perhaps 50,000 partisan units. Yet it seemed to be losing its original vitality. Observers noted a curious sense of apathy, arising perhaps from the failure of the revolutionaries to solve the economic problems of the border regions.

In April the Communists prepared a solemn declaration, urging the Kuomintang troops to destroy the Kuomintang before launching an attack against the Japanese. Exactly the same kind of demand had been made by the Kuomintang, who urged that the Communist armies should be destroyed before the Kuomintang armies were thrown against the Japanese. When winter came, and the mists closed in on Kiangsi, Mao decided that the time had come for a complete revaluation of policies, he abandoned his role as military commander and set about creating a new survey of conditions in the Soviet areas under his control. One thing was evident: the soviets in China, spread out in pockets over Hunan, Hupeh, Szechuan, Honan, Anhwei, Fukien, and Kwangtung had completely failed to form a large central soviet. Different policies ruled in the different Soviet areas. Worse still, as Chu Teh admitted to the American writer Nym Wales: "the economic situation was not good, because we had already expropriated all the landlords and had no further sources of revenue."[1]

Meanwhile, the fighting went on. A fourth annihilation campaign was launched, and then a fifth. The fourth lasted from April to October, 1933, and was fought out in the area between Lo An and Nanfeng, ground which the Reds knew intimately. The Kuomintang armies made the mistake of driving south in three columns. Two columns were cut to pieces, and the third was turned back. Mao described the battle briefly, and without much interest. The opening battle near Nanfeng had been a failure, and though the encirclement was broken and a battle at Hwangpi led to the capture of 13,000 men, the tactical employment of the Red Army no longer showed its former brilliance.

The fifth campaign followed immediately on the fourth. Chiang Kai-shek had concluded a truce with the Japanese and thought his rear safeguarded. He destroyed part of the Honan-Hupeh-Anhwei Red Army, which could no longer provide diversionary assistance, prevailed upon foreign bankers for loans, and promised that within three months he would completely annihilate the Red armies. He very nearly succeeded. The first battle was inconclusive. Mao complained bitterly against the commanders who allowed the retreat. From that moment the Red armies lost their advantage.

THE SECOND CONGRESS

On January 22, 1934, while the Fifth Annihilation Campaign was in full swing, Mao called the Second National Soviet Congress, at Juichin, and there, before about 800 delegates, he made a speech outlining the successes of the Chinese soviets. It was a curiously perturbing speech. He made great claims, and admitted mistakes. He claimed, for example, that the Chinese soviets now controlled so vast a population that numerically they were second only to the

1. Nym Wales, *Inside Red China,* New York, 1939, p. 256.

Soviet Union. He admitted that there were economic difficulties, and the system of land tenure had not yet been completely worked out. He spoke with pride of the victories of
the Red Army, and anyone reading the speech today could
derive the impression that the position of the Soviet armies
could not be bettered and that all five annihilation campaigns
had proved unsuccessful. In fact, the military position was
alarming. The Red Army was being bled white. Only a few
days before the speech was delivered, the Kuomintang had
sent a naval landing party to Fuchow, captured it from Tsai
Ting-kai, and put an end to the independent Fukien government. Thus they established a Kuomintang base southeast of
the Communist forces.

With the help of his military adviser, General von
Falkenhausen, Chiang Kai-shek now introduced a maneuver
known as the "fiery wall." Small, heavily fortified posts were
carried forward into Communist positions, and all the land
traveled by these posts, and all the land between them, was
put to the flame. It was the scorched-earth policy. But worse
than the scorched-earth policy was the growing hysteria of
the peasants, who turned to the Communists in alarm, but
could no longer be relied upon to fight. Hysteria led to
panic, and for the first time there appeared a strange process
of dissolution. It was as though, under the weight of fear, the
whole Communist system was about to crack wide open. New
sects appeared. Quarrels, which at other times would have
been settled amicably, now acquired increasing acerbity.
There had been, as Agnes Smedley noted, a Red Terror, but
the White Terror which followed was incalculably more terrifying, for the Kuomintang soldiers no longer trusted the
peasants, and because they could not trust them, over a million
peasants of Kiangsi were starved to death or killed as the
"fiery wall" drew closer to the Communist concentrations.
Years later, Mao blamed his German adviser, Li Teh, for
strategical errors at this time. The Communists should, he
said, have linked up with the independent Fukien government under Tsai Ting-kai, and later they should have thrown
all their available forces in the direction of Shanghai.

At the conference Mao spoke at moments as though they

were faced with no pressing dangers. With memories of four successful campaigns, he conjured up a picture of vast accretions of Communist power. He stated unequivocally the party's reliance on the peasantry, and at the same time he announced that "the war is becoming more acute with every day that passes, and the time must come when the two contending parties must fight a decisive battle." "The whole world," he said in the same speech, "is passing through a transitional phase leading to a new development of war and revolution." But he did not define the new development, and indeed he did not know which direction the revolution would take. Not for a moment did he suggest that ten months later the Chinese Communists would have to break through the encirclement of Juichin and begin their long wandering march through nine provinces of China.

Yet there were occasional hints of shadows, disturbing repetitions, strange emphases. He was perfectly conscious that the revolution would assume more and more violent proportions, and with the Fifth Annihilation Campaign a critical stage had been reached, so critical indeed that he urged the formation of an army a million strong and demanded the immediate strengthening of the Central Revolutionary Military Committee.

However, there were good prospects in store. "The enemy has far more difficulties than we have," he said, "since his soldiers are continually wavering, the broad masses of the peasants hate them, the militarists themselves are disintegrating, there are continuous clashes and conflicts between the Kuomintang supporters, and they are facing economic and financial bankruptcy."

Mao's speech at the Second National Soviet Congress was the most important of the statements he had made since the famous report on the conditions of the Hunan peasantry in 1927. It is not, however, easy reading. It seems to have been composed hurriedly, and under considerable strain. Three times, in slightly different terms, as if he felt it necessary to remind his listeners repeatedly of the basic problems involved, he defines the task of the revolution:

The fundamental task of the Soviets is revolutionary war and to mobilize all mass strength to fight this war. Around the fundamental task are gathered many urgent tasks. We have to practice a broad democracy; we must suppress with absolute determination the counterrevolution within our territory; we must promote the class struggle of the workers and the agrarian revolution of the peasants; we must promote the militancy of the masses of workers and peasants under the principle that the workers shall lead the alliance of workers and peasants; we must administer correct financial and economic policies in order to guarantee the material needs of the revolutionary war; and we must wage the cultural revolution in order to arm the leaders of the masses of workers and peasants. All these are directed toward a single goal: to overthrow the imperialist rule of the Kuomintang through revolutionary war, to consolidate and develop the democratic dictatorship of the workers and peasants, and so progress toward the stage of proletarian dictatorship.

Here were the seeds of the "new democracy" he advanced six years later, and it is significant that the "new democracy" appears under the guise of a "democratic dictatorship of workers and peasants."

Though reliance on Marxist theory gives a curious air of unreality to his discussion of the stages through which the Chinese revolution must pass, the speech only rarely refers to theory. The practical benefits of Communist rule, as distinguished from "the desperate stratagems of our enemies," are related at length. In the soviets, women share equality with men; corporal punishment is abolished; real wages are raised; the period of apprenticeship has been shortened; marriages may be arranged by simple registration; private investments are permitted, for "the soviets shall not monopolize all the productive enterprises but concentrate on those beneficial to the state." Usury is prohibited. The eight-hour day is enforced. School children may spend only a small part of their day working in the fields: the rest of the time must be spent in playing and reading in school. Private merchants are to be encouraged to break the enemy blockade, and taxes are no longer to be paid when goods travel from village to village.

Mao notes sadly that the blockade has effected two of the things he has always held most precious—paper and tobacco. He reveals that during the land inspection conducted in the summer of 1933, "in the central Soviet district 6,988 landlord families and 6,638 rich peasant families owning a huge excess of land were discovered and their land siezed and money taken from them to the total of $606,916."

He shows the men and women of the soviets at work on the farms, with their slogan: "Liquidate all fallow land." He admits that the Soviets have not progressed as far as they should have done. New tactics are necessary. "A struggle," he says, "must be waged against bureaucracy and the habit of dictation among Soviet functionaries: persuasion must replace dictation in everything that concerns the masses." It is a theme he was to repeat many times later, but the very repetition of the theme suggests that bureaucracy was inefficient, and often culpable. In fact, though very remarkable changes had taken place under the Kiangsi Soviet, and the best of them followed the principles of the Taiping rebels, the Soviet had not yet proved itself. Sometimes the government was ignorant. An eight-hour day must be meaningless to farmers during the spring sowing. It was absurd to take children off the land when all the traditions of Kiangsi made it inevitable that children should work as soon as they could walk. As the Kuomintang armies, numbering half a million, drew nearer, the apathy of the peasants increased, and Po Ku, one of the wisest of Communist commissars, could say with some truth that "there is only the peasant: if he should lose faith with us, it is all over." It was Po Ku also who spoke openly about the "Lo Min line," saying that Lo Min, a Fukien party leader, was perfectly right to make complaints. What Lo Min had said was: "Even if our best leaders were to come, or to bring Stalin himself, or even resurrect Lenin from the tomb, and were to speak all together to the masses for three days and three nights, I do not think it would help change the mood of the people."

In spite of the defeat which came shortly afterward, Mao's speech contained too many truths to be neglected. In Nanking it was read as the testament of an expiring leader-

ship, and Chiang Kai-shek thought hopefully of clearing all
the Reds out of Kiangsi by June. "The long drawn-out campaign is now coming to an end," he said, "and only three
counties, out of more than a thousand, remain infested by the
Communists. These are isolated by a ring of troops and will
be cleared up soon."

This opinion was not shared by Dmitri Manuilsky, who
claimed in Moscow that the Chinese Communists were on
the eve of important successes and had already emerged as the
second great Communist power, "in control of territories
larger than France or Germany or any other imperialist
country outside the United States." He praised their offen-
sives against "English tanks and armored cars, French artillery and American airplanes," and he prophesied an immediate and final defeat of the Kuomintang armies. Both Nanking
and Moscow were wrong. The war dragged on through the
summer and autumn and by the beginning of July, Chiang
Kai-shek was regrouping his forces for the long promised
thrust at the heart of the Soviets. The end did not come until
October.

Mao's speech had defended the Communist case as well as
it could be defended. Most of the time he was speaking
about reconstruction, about the need for consumers' co-
operatives, about the ways in which the peasants could be
freed from bond slavery, about increases in real wages, facili-
ties for education, and the improvement of land tenure. For
the peasants in that hard-bitten province these were matters
of huge importance. Though the "fiery walls" of General
von Falkenhausen burned the countryside, and whole villages
and towns were depopulated, the need for a social program
comparable to the one he had outlined had never been greater.
The Red Army might be defeated; the message of the Communists to the Chinese peasants, in the absence of any comparable message from the Kuomintang, would remain.

DEFEAT

The end came with surprising suddenness. Early in the campaign there had been a furious victory at Hsingkuo, a model village where "experimental sovietism" had been tried out successfully. In this battle a corps of women soldiers, fighting with spears and sabers, had distinguished itself and a whole enemy division had been defeated. But thereafter the tide turned. Repeated attacks against enemy strong points failed. The Red armies were reduced, in Mao's words, to "moving backward and forward as we sought battle between the enemy's main forces and his chain of blockhouses, so that for long periods we sank into a kind of passivity, retaining no initiative at all." The strategical directives were given by the German Communist Li Teh. They were almost fatal. The ring grew tighter. The Communist leaders seemed to be hypnotized by the huge forces arraigned against them. The cardinal mistake was the division of their forces into six columns, for it was thought hopeless to engage the enemy at any one place on the circumference: the Kuomintang was advancing from every direction. The old axiom was: "Lure the enemy into the depths of our territory, then attack with all our force at the enemy's weakest place." Unaccountably, the axiom was now reversed. There were no assigned points of withdrawal. The Communists might have broken through with their captured tanks, but they had no gasoline; and though they now had three airplanes on active commission, their pilots were inexperienced. At the beginning of the campaign the Red Army possessed 180,000 men under arms; by August 1934 there were less than 100,000. The young Hunanese Hsiao K'eh broke through the ring with a column of about 10,000 men in August. There was still sporadic fighting, with the Communist forces withdrawing as well as they could toward Yutu on the Fukien border. From there, on the night of October 14, receiving news of Hsiao K'eh's successful escape and some not too accurate information about a weak point in the enemy lines, some 90,000 of them, soon to be increased by another eight or nine thousand gathered from the neighborhood, set out on the Long March.

For years afterward the experience of the fifth annihilation campaign remained a nightmare to the Red military command. For the first time they had seen how a modern army, under capable direction, equipped with mechanized units, could force its way into guerrilla strongholds. When he came to write *Strategic Problems,* Mao admitted quite frankly that appalling errors had been made. "The main error," he wrote, "is that we did not plan organically: we had not thought out the campaign. Elated by the victory at Hsingkuo, we regarded it as a triumph, but in effect it was a defeat, for it led us to unwise decisions. The enemy's supreme command was far-sighted in its strategy: we only thought of what was under our nose. There are three essentials: an assurance of victory, an understanding of the campaign as a whole, a knowledge of the next strategic move." More bluntly, he wrote: "We panicked, and we fought stupidly."

The Long March

The story of the Long March already belongs to Chinese legend. The extraordinary adventure—a march of 6,000 miles, continued against all odds and with an enemy hot on their heels—had the effect of placing the Chinese Communists on the path of the Japanese invasion. It gave authority to their rule; it provided a hard training-ground for the future Red Army; and it settled once and for all Mao's dominance within the party, for the march was led by him and by Chu Teh, who regarded Mao as the guiding genius and for the most part bowed to Mao's decisions.

No complete and readable account of the Long March has yet been prepared. The Chinese Communists have published in two large volumes, printed in Yenan, a statistical survey of the battles they fought, the ammunition and prisoners captured, and the military strategies evolved. It includes maps and documents, most of them piously collected by Chu Teh, and the whole is printed on fraying brown paper in almost illegible type. By far the best readable account is that made by Edgar Snow in *Red Star over China*, though this was written before the march was completed—more straggling columns reached northern Shensi after Edgar Snow had left. Edgar Snow wrote the stories of the survivors before their memories had dimmed. Arriving in Yenan ten years later, I was struck by the gradual decay of memory. They still told stories of the legendary Long March willingly enough; they remembered their long night marches, how hungry they were, and how close to extinction; they remembered sickness and despair; but often the details escaped them. The same incident, told by different people, became different incidents. The crossing of the Tatu River, told by three separate people, seemed to be three separate crossings, at different times and at different places, yet all three survivors had been within a few hundred yards of each other. The stories of the battles were even more difficult to piece together. "There were so very many battles," General Peng Teh-huei told me. "Now, when I look back, it seems to be one enormous battle going on forever." Once, drawing the plan of a break through in an encirclement campaign in Kweichow, he paused suddenly— he had made a mistake: the battle he had intended to describe occurred in Szechuan several hundred miles away. So it was with all the commanders: they remembered small details and forgot the decisive events, and most of all they remembered the marshes and the snows, the strange landscape on the edge of Tibet where Lin Piao nearly perished and Mao was sick and only Chu Teh, gifted with amazing physical energy, seemed to be wholly and completely in command of himself.

For Mao the responsibility of the journey weighed heavily. He was the president of a provisional government on the march. During the last stages of the "annihilation campaigns" he deferred to the experience of the German Communist, Li Teh, but from the beginning he felt that positional warfare was wrong. He still believed that small compact groups of guerrillas could do as much harm as a division armed with automatic rifles.

At Kwangchang, on the Fukien-Kiangsi border, there had been the last shattering defeat, a defeat so terrible that when he came to describe the concluding stages of the Fifth Campaign in *Strategic Problems,* he completely omitted any reference to this battle in which 4,000 were killed and 20,000 wounded, as though too painful to contemplate. Suddenly, there came the order, signed by Mao and Chu Teh, to abandon Juichin. Documents were destroyed. The machinery in the arsenal was taken to pieces and buried in the forests. Everything that could conceivably aid the Kuomintang was destroyed, and everything that could aid the Red Army on its march was placed on the backs of pack animals. Every man was ordered to take a rifle and fifteen *chin* of food. Two diversionary columns were set out: one under Fang Chih-min, with orders to establish itself in Yuying in the northeast of the province, and the other under Han Ying, with orders to hold out in the south along the mountains on the borders of Fukien, Kiangsi, and Chekiang. The first perished, and the second led an exhausting existence through years of guerrilla warfare in the south, the remnants of this army only reappearing in Shensi in 1938. Orders were given for all forces to concentrate at Yutu. There were skirmishes during the comparatively short journey from Juichin to Yutu, but the Red armies were helped by the rain and the moonless nights.

Now, with their armies exhausted and the villagers no longer daring to help them for fear of immediate reprisals from the Kuomintang armies in the neighborhood, Chu Teh and Mao could reflect that they were once more in the same situation in which they had been on Chingkanshan. Without cannon, sometimes armed only with sabers, often barefoot, the soldiers marched to the point of concentration with little hope of any immediate respite, followed by a small army of sick and wounded men from the hospitals, for it was generally agreed that the sick and wounded would be treated unmercifully by the Kuomintang in their triumph. Those who survived the first month speak of the agony of wandering in the dark, in the rain, but it is possible that if there had not been this continuous rain which concealed their movements, the Kuomintang would have completely destroyed them.

Where were they going? No one knew. Years later, when Mao was asked what direction they had intended to take, he answered: "If you mean, did we have any exact plans, the answer is that we had none. We intended to break out of the encirclement and join up with the other soviets. Beyond that, there was only a very deliberate desire to put ourselves in a position where we could fight the Japanese." He had no idea, nor had anyone else, that they would find themselves close to the frontiers of Tibet within five months.

Hsiao K'eh had broken through, and they intended to follow him, and if possible consolidate all the separate soviets, none of them approaching the original Kiangsi soviet in size, for it was evident that these small soviets could no longer exist alone. The main objective was the largest of these soviets, in Szechuan, where Hsu Hsiang-ch'ien was in command of the Fourth Front Red Army consisting of around 100,000 trained soldiers. As Mao realized later, this was still another fantastic error: to march so deliberately toward the largest remaining soviet camp was to invite the Kuomintang to straddle their path.

Other errors were committed. In their anxiety to retain as much as possible of their spoils, great quantities of food, ammunition, bank-notes and even silver bullion, were being transported on pack animals, and this delayed their advance. It was a characteristic mistake: from the beginning, Mao had attached a great deal of importance to the spoils of war. Worse still, two columns followed the identical road taken by Hsiao K'eh without suspecting that the Kuomintang might have deliberately allowed Hsiao K'eh's escape in the hope of trapping larger columns; and the early days of the march, as they fought their way through the rings of blockhouses, were the most desperate and the ones in which they suffered their greatest losses. In the first three weeks twenty-five thousand men perished in the skirmishes around the blockhouses.

There was to be little rest for the men on the Long March as they skirted Hunan and Szechuan. Driving into Kweichow they met relentless opposition from the combined armies of the local warlord and from those sent down the Yangtse to Chungking by Chiang Kai-shek. Immense efforts were made to impede their progress. From Chungking, armies drove across the Szechuan border into Kweichow: an attempt was made to surround the Red forces with another ring of iron. The phrase "a ring of iron" recurs frequently in Chiang Kai-

THE LONG MARCH

← approximate route of the Red Army

shek's manifestoes of that time. Hill forts were rapidly built, crossings were guarded, bombing planes were sent out. But the Communists were invisible from the air, because a low-lying cloud hovers over Kweichow for five months of the year, and the hill forts could be taken by assault.

A classic encounter occurred on the Wu River, where the Communists found themselves surrounded. They had already crossed the river, but the enemy lay on both banks, waiting to spring the trap. The Communists had a firm belief in the power of one man to win a battle. They sent a single soldier over at night after they had silenced the enemy guns with mortars. The solitary swimmer managed to capture one of the boats hidden against the shore, and this single boat was afterward sent backward and forward across the river crammed with Red soldiers until a beachhead was established. Later all the boats were captured. The Kuomintang forces, who had not expected the Communists to turn back and attack the shore they had just left, were routed by a surprise maneuver— one which looked ludicrously simple when Peng Teh-huei drew a map of the small campaign for me in the dusty loess soil outside his cave. It was by such ruses that they won their battles; and more and more they were forced to regard themselves as guerrilla forces, dedicated to ruses, to the endless game of cunning and surprise.

The successes in Kweichow were paid for at enormous cost. They were fifteen weeks in the province, with minor engagements taking place every day. The heavy cloud which hides Kweichow, as it hides Szechuan, in autumn and winter did not always succeed in keeping the bombers away. Occasionally, low-flying bombers did come down through the clouds and seek out the Red Army. Their casualties from air raids were slight, but Mao's wife, Ho Tzu-ch'un, who was heavy with child, was seriously wounded during one of these bombings. Her wounds were almost fatal. Eighteen or twenty pieces of shrapnel entered her body. She was still suffering from the wounds long after the Chinese Communists settled in northern Shensi. Mao had married her after the execution of his first wife by Ho Chien in 1928. She was a Kiangsi girl, seventeen years younger than Mao, and she appears to have spent some time at the Normal College in Changsha, where Mao had studied. She bore him five children in seven years. Three of them were abandoned to the peasants they met on the Long March. In later years, when an effort was made to trace the children, they had completely disappeared. Mao was intensely moved by Ho Tzu-ch'un's fortitude during the march, and said afterward that the women showed far greater courage than the men. Only thirty women survived the march, though hundreds had set out from Juichin.

A MEETING AT TSUNYI

The bloodletting in Kweichow could not continue if the Red Army was to survive. After a short, bitter engagement at Tsunyi, on the road between Kweiyang, the capital of Kweichow, and Kunming, a meeting of the political bureau of the party was held in the captured yamen of the provincial governor, Wang Chia-lieh, on January 4, 1935. It was necessary that a new program should be elaborated. They had already lost a third of their army, and there were moments when, in spite of victories, their march across China was coming to resemble a rout.

As Mao saw it, they were still dominated by the philosophy of Li Li-san, who had been deposed by Pavel Miff from the Central Executive in January, 1931, though his uncanny influence could still be felt. Mao had a close acquaintance with Li Li-san. He had known him cursorily when they were youths together in Changsha, and he had come to know him intimately within the Chinese Communist secretariat.

Unlike Mao, whose romanticism was tempered by an astonishing regard for facts, Li Li-san was almost the pure romantic revolutionary. In March 1930 he had declared: "Prepare for the establishment of revolutionary power. When the revolutionary high wave arrives, 90,000,000 can be organized in three days." In June 1930, he declared: "The aim of local uprisings is the capture of local cities. The perspective in view is convergence upon the central cities, so bringing about a victorious insurrection through the whole country." This declaration had even been adopted by the Political Bureau of the Chinese Communist Party. It was as though Li Li-san suffered from an almost neurotic obsession with revolution in cities, an obsession which sprang perhaps from the fact that his major achievements had all taken place in cities. He had been a successful labor agitator, and had organized the anti-foreign campaign which broke out in Shanghai following the May Thirtieth Incident in 1925.

Against the desire to attack cities, Mao now raised his

voice. "There is no way to accomplish this," he pointed out, "with the resources we command. The desire to fight positional wars and to capture cities springs from the same adventurism. Our duty is to fight a protracted war, avoiding the enemy if possible, never engaging him unless it can be made certain in advance that the engagement is to our advantage." He attacked the policy which Li Li-san had encouraged with extraordinary invective. Li Li-san had desired to transform Communist-dominated trade unions into action committees. What was this but "the game of insurrection"? And surely the Long March, as it was being fought, savored of adventurism? He attacked all the principles by which Li Teh, the German military adviser, had fought, and proposed that thenceforward the column should be directed by Chu Teh and himself. He went over all the experiences of the annihilation campaigns in detail—it was through Li-Li-sanism that the first campaign had failed in its main objective, and the fifth campaign had failed as the result of the same kind of adventurism. "Adventurism," he wrote later in *Strategic Problems*, "continued to arouse opposition against luring the enemy into deep penetration, but it ended in conservatism." The proper direction, he reminded, was an advance in the direction of the Tibetan tribesmen and the Mohammedans "until we hit a stone wall." He outlined the conditions of the advance. They were extremely simple. Once again the Communists must become "an army on the border," and the border this time was the border, not of provinces, but of China itself.

The argument was accepted, but the fighting went on. Chiang Kai-shek was determined to prevent the Red Army from escaping to Tibet, or to the borders of the Soviet Union. From Kunming, he himself directed operations, just as previously he had directed operations from Kweiyang. Mao determinedly opposed the idea of attacking the large cities, but he could not prevent the Red Army from flaunting its powers by skirting both these places. The Red Army, passing through Kweichow and Yunnan, took a good view of the two provincial capitals from the neighboring hills.

In Yunnan the Yangtse River is known as the Gold Sand

River. It was necessary for the Red Army to cross the river to reach the uplands near Tibet. The Kuomintang removed all the ferry-boats to the northern shore. The Communists made a forced march in three columns across the plain until they reached the river, while a fourth column was sent moving backward and forward between Kunming and the river to distract the enemy. The first column covered 45 miles in a single day. They found a boat tethered on the south side of the river, and some of the men boarded it, disguised as civilians. The enemy was in no hurry. At the river crossing at Chouping, the Reds discovered a tax officer, explained that they were Kuomintang troops in disguise and wanted the boats sent over to the south bank, together with fuel and food. This daring group of soldiers found themselves invited to dinner with the local landlords; all the time, unknown to the landlords, Red Army troops were being ferried over to the north bank. The Red Army soldiers camped that night on the banks of the river, attended by the landlords, who solicitously provided for their comfort and offered them a feast. The next day at daybreak they climbed a mountain and were on their way toward Tibet when the landlords, who had begun to suspect these sunburned, hardened men, sent the *min tuan*, or local garrison troops, after them. These fired a few ineffectual shots, but they came nowhere near the Red Army forces, which had spent the night ferrying themselves over the river.

The pattern of their passage through Chouping was to be repeated. Ruse and cunning, exactly the same kind of ruse and cunning that was displayed by the heroes of *All Men Are Brothers* now became the pattern of the Communist advance. Positional wars were to be avoided; food, if possible, was to be supplied by bowing landlords who complimented them on their achievements against the Reds!

Ten miles from Chouping lay Tungchow, guarded by two battalions of Kuomintang troops. They, too, were unaware of the Red advance. They were sleeping with their weapons scattered all round them when they were discovered. Their arms were captured, including some good machine guns. It was the Communists' easiest victory, and here they waited while their remaining troops, numbering now nearly 60,000, caught up with them. They had lost 30,000 men on their march from Juichin, but most of the losses were replaced by new recruits. They had held innumerable mass meetings, and on the march they practiced the same form of communism they had practiced in Kiangsi. The landlords were expropriated, the title deeds were destroyed, and the land was given to the villagers, together with arms with which to defend themselves. Here, too, for the first time they came in contact with the tribespeople, the Lolos and the Miaos, who lived among the mountains of Kweichow and Yunnan, in a primitive communism of their own. Some of these tribespeople they took with them; others were encouraged to fight against the Kuomintang—though they needed little enough encouragement.

In Yunnan, north of the Gold Sand River, the Red Army was generally a few days ahead of the most redoubtable of all the generals sent against them, Hsueh Yueh, the future victor at Changsha. Once a column of Szechuanese soldiers discovered their hiding-place and attacked, but their morale failed at the moment of counter-attack. The Chinese Communists afterward remembered with pleasure how the whole column suddenly began screaming to be allowed to surrender. Here, for the first time since they crossed Kweichow, they allowed themselves to rest, and there were to be no more forced marches with the enemy hot on their heels—one forced march had lasted two days and one night. Their enemies now were mountains, precipices, flooded rivers, marches, and bitter snows.

APPROACHING TIBET

The Red Army was approaching Tibetan territory. In this rugged landscape there were few trees, little vegetation, almost no houses, though here and there they came upon an immense gray, flat-roofed, fortresslike palace surrounded by stockades. Their food was running out, and now more than ever they depended upon their Lolo guides, who led them along the mountain trails to the defiles of the Tatu River.

It was May, and the river was in spate. They came to the small town of Anshunch'ang, which overhangs the river.

Oddly enough, none of them knew until they came here that in this region a vast Taiping army had been crushed to extinction. The advance posts, sent to meet the villagers, had learned to their horror that Prince Shih Ta-k'ai had waited for two days on the banks of the river to celebrate the birth of his child, and as a result of the delay had met defeat in the wilds above Mienninghsien, trapped in the gorges.

There was nothing to be done except to hurry, before the Kuomintang forces were able to encircle them. They found three boats and sent 500 men over the river; then two of the boats sank, and it was decided not to send any more. At a conference at Anshunch'ang, Mao and Chu Teh worked out a plan of campaign. The men already on the other side of the river were ordered to continue the march to Lutingch'iao, and at the same time the major part of the Red Army would follow the trail along the gorges. It was hoped that those already on the other side would be able to reduce the regiment holding the bridge at Lutingch'iao before the main forces came up.

They had not reckoned, however, with the treacherous nature of the gorges. Astonishing luck had followed them. At Anshunch'ang they had captured the regimental commander at the bridgehead; he happened to be visiting his father-in-law. The maps, codes, and deployment orders of the Kuomintang forces in the neighborhood were captured with him. But though the maps were useful, and the codes might conceivably become useful later, and the deployment orders might be regarded as reasonably accurate, the main enemy remained: and the enemy was the rugged nature of the country through which they would have to pass. The trails along the cliffs were rarely more than five feet wide. A reckless company of Kuomintang troops concealed along the cliffs could have held them up indefinitely. The bridge at Lutingch'iao might already be destroyed. To surprise the enemy, they made forced night marches. There was no moon. They were compelled to light flares, and the news of their advance became known. Meanwhile, the men who had reached the north bank of the river were unaccountably delayed; the pathways scratched on the rock were often dangerous, so that tired men occasionally fell down the cliffs and disappeared in the river; and many of the pack animals had to be left in Anshunch'ang.

The sixty miles that separated Anshunch'ang from Lutingch'iao were more nightmarish than anything they had experienced during the Long March. For years afterward men talked of the cold nights, the darkness, the threat of the black river below, as they wound among these gorges where sometimes the cliffs were less than twenty feet apart.

But at Lutingch'iao, which means the "Town of the Iron Bridge," their luck held. Here in 1701 an iron bridge had been built under the orders of the Emperor Kang Hsi. Nine immense cables, each over 300 feet long, made of charcoal-smelted iron, were secured to the cliffs. On these, loose planks were laid; the guardrails consisted of thin iron chains. The bridge swayed and creaked in the wind coming down the gorges, and since the wind came every afternoon, this was always the most dangerous time to cross over. When the Red Army arrived on the small cliff edge with its cluttered hamlet, they found that the Kuomintang regiment on the south bank had already heard of their progress, and most of the planks had been removed. This was the only bridge lying on the frontier of Sikang and Szechuan. If they failed to capture the bridge, their only course would be to retire along the road they came by.

Once again a council of war was held. An attempt to cross the river by rafts and pontoons failed. At any moment they expected the Kuomintang to blow up the bridge, for nothing would have been simpler: a single stick of dynamite tossed at its moorings would have destroyed it. The bridge was three hundred feet above the level of the river; they heard the river booming below. All the fighting at the bridge occurred to the sound of the deafening roar of the river. They called for volunteers who would cross the bridge, making their way hand over hand, their only weapons hand grenades and pistols, for a rifle would have been useless. And the bellying of the iron chains as they hung over the middle of the river partly concealed the hundred volunteers who inched their way across, to the splatter of machine guns.

To divert attention from these volunteers, machine gun fire was directed on the Kuomintang entrenchments from farthur up the river. The small force which had already crossed over was nowhere in sight. One by one the soldiers making their way across the bridge fell down into the ravine, either because they were struck by machine-gun fire or because they were swept off by the wind. Nothing could be done for them.

In the end a solitary soldier climbed up on the planks on the farther side—the planks were already being drenched in kerosene, and the flames were rising—and by a lucky throw of a hand grenade put an end to the resistance at the bridgehead, though there was further resistance from the entrenchments behind. The passage of the one soldier had an electric effect. Fifteen or sixteen soldiers reached the burning planks. Almost at the same moment the advance guards of the 500 who had taken ship across the river at Anshunch'ang came into sight, and shortly after their appearance the Kuomintang forces retired. A hundred Szechuanese soldiers surrendered and offered to join the Red Army. The planks, stored in the retrenchments, were put back on the bridge, and toward evening the whole of the Red Army had crossed the river. It was May 30, 1935.

The brilliant and carefully thought-out maneuver cost less than fifty lives, and of those only twelve perished by falling into the river. To make up for this loss, fifty soldiers were admitted into the Red Army ranks from among the villagers. "We were always at our best," said Mao later, "when we were faced with impossible odds. We knew that there was every reason to believe that we would fail: that was why we did not fail. Besides, the enemy thought we were trapped." He had watched the whole scene from the cliffs, with the Lolo chieftains at his side. Once they were over the bridge, there were no more decisions to be made: they would follow the mountain trails until they came out into the low-lying forests of western Szechuan. The maps, however, were sketchy, and none of them knew the dangers ahead.

They climbed the Ma An-shan Pass, ten thousand feet high and five thousand feet higher than Lutingch'iao. Here there were red rhododendrons and small waterfalls and charcoal-burners' huts; and beyond Ma An-shan lay the terrible white mountain known as the Great Snow Mountain.

During the crossing of the Great Snow Mountain, Mao was sick and suffered from fever; during part of the journey he had to be carried. The hardships were beginning to tell. It was absolutely necessary that the mountain should be crossed in a single morning, for by some freak of the weather tremendous winds occurred in the afternoons and at the same time the air pressure dropped alarmingly. But even during the mornings there was so little air that people could hardly breathe on these high mountain paths. Mao endured the journey better than Lin Piao, who suffered from a weak heart and was compelled to rest half-way up the mountain—a dangerous and wildly exciting three hours during which he suffered the full violence of a storm. At least half of the pack animals perished on the heights, and some of those who remained on the mountain at night were killed by whirling hailstones, an inch round and as hard as rock.

On some Chinese maps the height of the Great Snow Mountain is given as 16,300 feet. Mao himself is inclined to believe, perhaps on insufficient evidence, that it is considerably higher. The prodigious height of these mountains—the Great Snow Mountain was the highest, but there were more to follow—was something he had never faced before. The mountains in Kiangsi, for example, are hardly more than hills, ranging up to 2,000 feet. The prolonged marching through the snow mountains seriously weakened his army, and when at last his troops reached northwestern Szechuan, meeting the Fourth Front Red Army under Hsu Hsiang-ch'ien and Chang Kuo-t'ao at Ta-wei, they were prepared to enjoy a long rest. They were in a comparatively safe area at last. They were also well protected by their numbers, for Hsu Hsiang-ch'ien's army numbered about 40,000 men and there were about 40,000 survivors of the long ordeal over the mountains; moreover, the Communist troops from Szechuan were well armed.

The column under Mao rested for nearly a month. At the

beginning of August, Mao decided that the time had come for the continuation of the march. News had come of the establishment of soviets in northern Shensi, and he was eager to establish a base there before the coming of winter. He had hoped to arrive in Shensi by the end of September, but he had not reckoned with the dangers ahead.

There were many dangers. The Kuomintang troops were driving down on the Communist armies. It was high summer, with the rivers in flood. There was disagreement between Mao, the chairman of the Kiangsi Soviets, and Chang Kuo-t'ao, chairman of the Honan-Hupeh-Anhwei Soviets, which had achieved bases over large areas of northern Szechuan. The western route—the only one open to them—was un-mapped, and ruled over by tribesmen far more suspicious than the Lolos of Yunnan. With Lin Piao, who was already being regarded as a strategist of a high order, and Peng Teh-huei, who now ranked immediately after Chu Teh, Mao set out with about 30,000 men in the direction of the Grasslands, his numbers reduced as the result of severe, sporadic fighting in Szechuan.

THE GRASSLANDS

The Great Snow Mountain, with its deceptively smooth slope, had been their introduction to their running battle with nature. There was more to come. In the Grasslands there was nothing but plain and swamp, the earth soft under-foot, few trees, the grass a foot high. By ill luck, August was a month of perpetual rain or fog. There was a thick haze over most of the swamp, and the mosquitoes were the size of horse-leeches. Nothing they had gone through up to this moment was quite as bad as the Grasslands. There were no houses or villages where they could pass the night. The tribespeople picked them off from well-concealed hiding-places. They lost their few remaining pack animals, many of them drowning in the swamp. A small column would be seen walking across a sea of thick, damp, foggy grasses, and then the whole column would disappear. Occasionally they came upon ancient forests, where there were layers of dead leaves beneath the trees. Here they could rest, search for mushrooms, and even light fires. But these were the lucky ones who were able to skirt the Grasslands. For the most part they struggled through the grass along trails which they had either to discover for themselves or which were pointed out to them by captured tribespeople. Sometimes these tribespeople led them straight into ambush, but more often they were won over by the diplomatic skill of Ho Lung and Mao.

Meanwhile, the columns were near starvation. Occasionally they had to fight for food, and sometimes it would happen that a whole column would find itself engaged in a military operation where the total spoils consisted of a single sheep hidden among the reeds and grasses, defended by the Mantzus with poisoned arrows. The tribespeople hid their cattle well. Often the guerrillas were reduced to eating the roots of grasses and turnips, or chewing on hides.

People who went through the Long March still remember the Grasslands with horror—the long plains of black and yellow grass, the rain, the poisonous mud which made their legs swell with red blisters, the way the marshes would suddenly give place to slow-moving nearly stagnant rivers, the mudholes, the ambuscades. At night it was deathly cold. They made shelters of clumps of grasses knotted together, but the cold penetrated. Worst of all, they had lost most of their medical supplies, and those who were ill were simply left behind—impossible to carry them on litters in a place where everyone was fighting for survival. The only treatment for infected sores was boiling water. Columns became lost or detached from one another. To collect the columns together, Chu Teh found it necessary to go three times across the Grasslands, spending an entire month walking among treacherous pathways, for the radios were out of order. When Mao was asked what he remembered most of the Grasslands, he said: "Just this: that Chu Teh crossed it three times, and I found the greatest difficulty in crossing it once."

During this stage Mao took little part in the military decisions. For the first time he was coming to grips with foreign relations. He met the tribespeople and attempted, not too successfully, to barter with them. Unfortunately, the Red Army had almost nothing to offer them in exchange for their cattle and wheat except rifles and these might be used against them. He found interpreters and did everything he could to bring them over to the Reds, but they were sullen against the invaders. He feared the tribespeople, and half envied them. Quite naturally, without any preparation, as though by instinct, the Mantzus waged war against the Red columns in continual skirmishes which showed a surprising knowledge of the technique of guerrilla warfare. He confessed that he learned much from them, and he was especially impressed with their art of concealment.

The strain of the Long March was beginning to tell. Mao was very lean, with dark hollows under his eyes, and often ill. His stomach suffered most. He missed his cigarettes, and most of all he missed the red Hunan peppers. He wore a faded blue uniform, carried no weapons, and there were usually books in his pocket—a copy of the monkey tale, *Journey to the West,* and the old dog-eared copy of *All Men Are Brothers.* The book *Journey to the West* described a pilgrimage by a learned monkey through China, Tibet, and India; and what was surprising was the accuracy of the author of a medieval fairytale when it came to describing the borderlands of China and Tibet. Meanwhile he wrote poems. One of the longer poems was called "Grass." It appears in the collection of poems called *Wind Sand Poems,* which Mao collected together in Yenan, though nothing about the poem except the title is known.

The Long March was at last coming to an end, though a year was to elapse before the columns under Chu Teh and Hsu Hsiang-ch'ien, which had been left behind, were to arrive in northern Shensi. They had still to face short, sharp engagements with the Mohammedans who straddled their path in Kansu, but they were approaching territory where the Kuomintang forces were too far from their bases to offer effective opposition. Moreover, northern Shensi was part of the area which the "Christian General" Feng Yu-hsiang owned as a kind of private reserve, and he was not unsympathetic to many of the Communist demands. He was not a Communist; he had executed Communists in the past. But he possessed a considerable knowledge of the peasantry, and he believed in the urgent necessity of agrarian reforms.

The columns under Mao had succeeded in forcing a passage through China. He had employed the characteristic "wide curve" he used in the three annihilation campaigns. Success had been achieved at a frightful cost. A hundred thousand set out from Kiangsi. Fewer than 20,000 remained, and many of these were recruits who joined the Red Army on the march. Many of the leaders were killed; those who survived bore traces of their sufferings for years afterward. In spite of the huge losses, Mao believed firmly that the expedition had proved the superiority of guerrilla tactics: the Red Army had shown the utmost strategical mobility. Above all, a legend had been created. Mao was perfectly conscious of the power of legends. In later years, when he came to examine the causes of the Long March, he came to the bitter conclusion that it was all entirely unnecessary. The Fifth Annihilation Campaign was itself ill-directed, and the Communists in Kiangsi should not have panicked so easily. There were at least two untried maneuvers which would have enabled them to escape the Kuomintang net and establish themselves in the region of Shanghai. He refused to regret the journey, just as he refused to regret his own inability to force the issue. "A revolution," he wrote, "does not march in a straight line. It wanders where it can, retreats before superior forces, advances wherever it has room to advance, and is possessed of enormous patience." When the Red Army reached Shensi, the surviving guerrillas could tell themselves that a revolutionary patience had won for them all their battles.

Mao tends to be unrevealing about his personal life, and he generally dislikes to discuss himself, but on the subject of the Long March he has often talked at length. It was the time, he says, when he came to maturity. There were terrible battles, but he felt perpetually exhilarated. He had not thought he would survive, but at the same time he was perfectly aware, in an almost mystical way, that the Communists would develop bases in North China and demonstrate the authenticity of their experiment in battles against the Japanese. He says—there is no particular reason to disbelieve him—that he never faltered in this simple faith, and though he was conscious that the Kuomintang armies, which would also meet the Japanese, were being weakened by their wars against the Communists, he could see no other way out. The armies tested one another before being tested by the Japanese.

Mao was also a little bewildered by his continuing good luck. He was never wounded. His health stood comparatively well the enormous strains of the journey, a fact which he attributed to his long walks in his youth. He observed, with a kind of ironic detachment, that it was possible to live on nothing except a furious hope. He took a deep interest in herbal medicine and began to propound theories which have something in common with psychosomatic medicine. He was delighted with the strange flora he came upon—the trees, the herbs, the grasses, the different uses to which they could be put. He prized his knowledge of new tobaccos. Most of all, he was astonished by the virgin quality of these unexplored lands on the frontiers of Tibet. He saw colors he had never seen before, mountains so preposterously grand that they resembled the feverish dreams of some Chinese painter, tribespeople of whose existence he had been completely ignorant. Above all, having passed through so many provinces, he had come to know China.

In October 1935 Mao's column reached Pao An, and a year later most of the columns which had taken part in the Long March, and many others from various Red areas came to join him. The march, with all its failings and miseries and splendors, had been successful. The time had come to put the new knowledge into practice. "It was not a miracle," Mao remarked later. "It was a logical plan, logically and correctly pursued, and in this it differed from much of our fighting during the annihilation campaigns." But it is permissible to believe that the Long March was a miracle of human endurance.

The Years in the Desert

"The years disappear like the jade birds who fly into the yellow hills," said the Chinese poet; and the small group of Communists living in northern Shensi might have disappeared among their loess hills if external events had not brought them once again into prominence. Gradually they built up their armies and joined forces with the small scattered Communist armies all over North China. They introduced village government and dispossessed the more exacting landlords; they coined money and set up small arsenals. But they were weakened by the Long March, and might have been erased altogether from the map of China if Chiang Kai-shek had foreseen the danger and swept the peasants with a program of social reform. Less than twenty thousand had arrived at this small outpost in the North. To anyone except a Communist it would have been inconceivable that an obscure walled village would soon rival Nanking as the center of imperial power. Yet it was so. From the mud huts and small caves of Pao An there came a continuous stream of commands, pronunciamentoes and manifestoes destined to change the

Chinese scene. Sooner than anyone could have foreseen, Pao An became a legend.

From the beginning Mao gave all the appearance of negligently doing nothing. He seemed, like the old Chinese sages, to be waiting on events. He spent the nights working; most of the day he slept. He lived in a cave. He smoked incessantly —homemade cigarettes or a yellow pipe with stringy, yellow, home-grown tobacco—and he read omnivorously. There were almost no government buildings or ministries: the affairs of state were conducted from the small caves, among the walnuts and the date palms. Chiang Kai-shek might have been excused when he said: "Now that they are sedentary, it will be easier to destroy them." Even some of the Communists took alarm. For the first time they were living beyond the reach of the Kuomintang, and safety seemed dangerous to men who had lived in danger nearly all their lives.

In the years that followed, Mao was to grow bored with Shensi. The high loess hills cut off the light of the sun: there was always the sensation of living at the bottom of a yellow valley. The land was poor, the nearby cities were under Kuomintang control, and in relation to the rest of China it was as though they were living in a remote village of Arkansas, their only means of communication with the outside world being a pedal-operated radio transmitter. Yet it was oddly satisfying. Mao's health had not been broken during the Long March, but he was slow to recover from some of its effects. He needed a rest to think out the next moves in the incalculable game of chess. Besides, legend demanded that the sage should be silent and unmoving, then power would come to him of its own accord. Confucius said in the *Analects*: "To govern by means of virtue may be compared to the North Star which remains steadfast and unmoving: all the stars are turned respectfully toward it." Simply by existing quietly in northern Shensi, he was acquiring power.

There were vast advantages in this extraordinary position, and not the least of them was that every move made by the Generalissimo only increased Mao's power. He had by now acquired a double eminence: he had shown at Tsunyi that his knowledge of tactics was superb, and throughout the Long

March he had acted as political leader of the main column, and his policies had completely succeeded. Others coveted his eminence. Chang Kuo-t'ao, in particular, seems to have fought against him with some bitterness. He had been vice-chairman of the Kiangsi Soviets, and later chairman of the Honan-Hupeh-Anhwei Soviets, and regarded himself as at least the equal of Mao. During the summer of 1935 there were stormy discussions between Mao and Chang Kuo-t'ao concerning the bases of Chinese Communist operations. Chang Kuo-t'ao would have preferred to remain in Szechuan, where his personal power was established, and he offered to integrate the Kiangsi columns into his own army. Mao violently disagreed, pointing out that the Communist armies were still weak and unproved—their battles against the Kuomintang had never been decisive, and it was absolutely necessary for the Communists to prove themselves by their actions. Soviets in northern Szechuan were inherently unstable. Tragic excesses had been committed by Chang Kuo-t'ao's army, and the peasants had been alienated. With some reluctance, faced with the determined opposition of Chu Teh and Peng Teh-huei, Chang Kuo-t'ao signed an agreement to follow Mao's army to the northwestern areas of Kansu and Shensi.

When they met a year later at Pao An, Chang Kuo-t'ao assumed an attitude of intolerant opposition to the Communists who were already there. He accused them of adventurism, a charge which was greeted with distaste, for it was precisely Chang Kuo-t'ao's adventurism which Mao was fighting against. It was necessary, however, that he should be treated with respect, and toward the end of 1936 he was sent in command of the Fourth Front Army to Kansu, to establish bases among the Mohammedans. Once again, as in Szechuan, tragic excesses were committed, and in a sudden rebellion in February 1937, the Fourth Front Red Army was attacked by Mohammedan tribesmen. Thereafter Chang Kuo-t'ao was in disgrace, and in 1938 he fled from the Soviet areas to Hankow, announcing that "no compromise is possible between the Kuomintang and Communist parties. An entirely new party must be formed." The Communists accused him of working for the Kuomintang secret police.

The defection of Chang Kuo-t'ao was not the first. Chen Tu-hsiu, who had led the new youth of China, had been drummed out of the party in 1927, to be arrested in 1932 by the Kuomintang government and sentenced to thirteen years imprisonment—in the eyes of the Kuomintang a comparatively light sentence, since without Chen Tu-hsui there might not have been a Communist party in China. He was released in the autumn of 1937 as the result of popular clamor for the release of all those who had fought against the Japanese, either as intellectuals or as soldiers. He died in Chungking in 1942. Mao's third adversary, Li Li-san, disappeared to the Soviet Union, returning to Manchuria at the end of the war as General Lin Piao's political adviser, and vice-chairman of the All-China Federation of Labor.

But on the whole defections were rare. The Chinese Communists were coming into their maturity. They had experienced many of the possible forms which communism could undergo in a country like China, and the experience of the Long March had taught them to have faith in the simplest and most easily manageable forms. More and more Mao came to personify the peasant virtues of primitive communism. He believed that in some remote era of China's past there had been a kind of primitive communism; he also believed that feudalism came about as the result of invasions of barbarian tribes. The Japanese were the modern equivalent of the ancient barbarians, and he waited patiently for the moment when they would attack, convinced that the choice of northern Shensi as a base was justified by the menace of Japan. Not far away lay the Great Wall, and beyond that lay the Ordos Desert, where, if necessary, they could go on still another Long March, secure from any pursuers.

Meanwhile he devoted himself to a study of the peasantry, and for some time he immersed himself in the study of a strange language called Latinxua. Mass education had become, he believed, the key to the revolution. What could not be done with an educated peasantry? Latinxua, which consisted of romanized Chinese, and resembled the romanized languages introduced by the French into Indo-China and by the Russians into Siberia, might provide a key, for it involved the learning of only twenty-six letters, while the most elementary knowledge of Chinese was impossible without the learning of at least a thousand characters. Newspapers were printed in Latinxua; they were also printed in a Chinese which deliberately used only the simplest words. He compared their successes. Somewhere, there may be still in existence letters written by Mao in that strange hybrid Latinxua, which he at one time embraced with the fervor of a new apostle. It was ugly and ungraceful: the horrible combinations of consonants offended the eyes, and though Latinxua was never entirely abandoned—there are still newspapers printed in it—it gradually lost importance.

Meanwhile, the guerrilla armies which remained in Central China were gradually growing more powerful, and Mao began to believe that if the Japanese did attack there would be two large centers of Communist resistance against them. There was still sporadic fighting against the Kuomintang. Telegrams were exchanged between Nanking and Pao An. By one of those arrangements which seemed strange to foreigners but had become accepted policy in Chinese civil wars, a telegraph office under Kuomintang jurisdiction was opened near Pao An, just as later a telegraph office was opened at Yenan. Increasingly, Mao assumed control of the organization of the peasantry, leaving the military decisions to Chu Teh. He traveled through the border regions, addressing the peasants. "We must hasten," he said. "Only with an awakened peasantry can we fight the Japanese."

INCIDENT AT SIAN

By November 1936, Mao's suspicions that the Japanese were ready to launch their attack on China were being confirmed. Since the summer of 1935 he believed that the attack would come, probably from the north, through Mongolia, and it would be launched first through Communist territory. The Anti-Comintern Pact had been signed, suggesting that the Fascist powers were drawing more closely together.

In Mongolia itself strange events were taking place. On November 17, the Generalissimo flew to Taiyuan and interviewed Prince Ah, the vice-chairman of the Suiyuan-Mongolian Autonomy Council. It looked as though the Generalissimo were preparing to arrange that the forces in this half-Mongol province, where the lamas still ruled and bannermen still possessed power, would be thrown against the Reds.

Mao was not particularly disturbed by this development. He was more disturbed by the discovery that the Japanese were arming irregulars in Manchukuo and sending them across the border in disguise. There was a short, fierce battle at Pailing-miao, in northern Suiyuan, and afterward, in an abandoned lama temple, documentary evidence was found proving Japanese complicity. There were rumors that the Kwangtung army in Manchukuo was preparing to come over the border.

The atmosphere was ominous. Mao had expected war, but not in winter. Worse still, there came reports that the Generalissimo was preparing a last effort to sweep the Communist Army from the face of the earth. He had sent Hu Tsung-nan's First Army against the Reds. It was severely defeated on November 21, with the capture of large supplies of ammunition. Stung by this defeat, was the Generalissimo about to make the long-promised "final and eternal liquidation"?

It seemed so. Calling upon his troops to prepare for a short but determined war against "the enemies in our midst," the Generalissimo flew to Sian, arriving there on December 7. He immediately set about preparing plans for a massive attack on the Communist strongholds. He wrote in his diary that "the bandit-suppression campaign has reached the stage when it will require only the last five minutes to achieve final success." The general order for mobilization against the Communists was to be issued on December 12. On December 11, the Young Marshal, Chang Hsueh-liang, in command of the Tungpei forces, struck and ordered the arrest of the Generalissimo, his staff, and all the government officials, gendarmes, and special-service men loyal to him. If there had been no general order for mobilization, the Generalissimo might have been allowed to go free and nothing more would have been heard of what came to be known as the Sian Incident.

What had happened was very simple. Chang Hsueh-liang was not prepared to attack the Communists. He had said as much in an interview with an American correspondent, Nym Wales, in October. His soldiers were largely Manchurians, who were anxious to return home after driving the Japanese out of Manchuria. They had no particular quarrel with the Communists, who were now established in Yenan. It was four days later before the Young Marshal sent an airplane to Yenan, with the request that Yenan send three responsible officials to take part in the trial of the Generalissimo.

The trial never took place. Chou En-lai, Yeh Chien-ying, and Po Ku flew to Sian. An immediate meeting of the Executive Committee of the Communist Party was summoned in Yenan on December 15. Mao was chairman. He reviewed briefly all the information which had come by radio, and though the Moscow radio was to claim that all kinds of strange forces were at work, he guessed from the beginning that only Chang Hsueh-liang was responsible for the arrest, and from that moment he gave it as his opinion that "it was pure mischief, and Chang Hsueh-liang himself should be arrested."

No final decisions were made at the Yenan meeting, except one—that the Generalissimo's life and dignity should be spared, for otherwise a Japanese attack could be expected at any moment, or worse still—Ho Ying-ching would assume command of the Army, and make a treacherous agreement with the enemy. The memory of the Ho-Umetzu agreement, by which Ho Ying-ching had agreed to a Chinese surrender along the Great Wall at the time of the Fifth Annihilation Campaign was still fresh in their minds.

Chou En-lai had three secret conferences with the Generalissimo, who deliberately treated the Communist general with the utmost disrespect. All these conferences, and many others, were referred back to Yenan. The Young Marshal had compiled eight demands to be made of the Generalissimo, who refused them all. For the Communists only one of these eight demands was important: the immediate cessation of the civil war. When this was agreed to, they urged that the Generalissimo be freed.

"Mao saw it all very simply and directly," Yang Shan-k'un,

the young Szechuanese chief of staff, told me later in Yenan.
"He stripped the problem to its essentials, when we were all
confused. The Young Marshal wanted the Generalissimo put
on trial—a people's trial and a people's verdict, and this was the
last thing Mao wanted. He wanted, and kept repeating that
he wanted, the Generalissimo in command of all the Chinese
forces. It was the only way he could see in which the Chinese
would be able to oppose the Japanese successfully. He still
thinks it was the only way. When all the reports were received
from the delegates, he sent a strongly worded telegram saying
that if necessary the Communists in Sian—many had been
released from prison—should stage a coup, free the Generalissimo, and take him back secretly to Nanking. The Young
Marshal wanted the Generalissimo sent to Yenan because he
was afraid of the responsibility he had assumed. Mao absolutely refused. Under no condition did he want the Generalissimo in his own power, for the Japanese would have immediately suspected some kind of alliance between us and
used this as an excuse for launching an attack, and Ho Ying-
ching would have seized the opportunity of taking over power
in Nanking. As soon as we knew that the Generalissimo
loyally wanted to unite the Chinese against the Japanese, the
die was cast. Even before that, we wanted him to return un-
harmed. At the final meeting of the Central Executive Committee there was only one dissenting vote: it came from Chang
Kuo-t'ao, who later went over to the Kuomintang!"

In conversation with Yang Shan-k'un there emerged a more
complex interpretation of the event. At the back of Mao's
decisions there was always the fear of Ho Ying-ching's
treachery, but there were also other fears. In his annihilation
campaigns Chiang Kai-shek had shown the greatest insensi-
tivity to the losses of his armies. An immense army would be
thrown against the enemy, and annihilated; immediately afterward, another immense army would be thrown into combat.
He regarded China as an inexhaustible reservoir of men, and
it occurred to Mao that the Generalissimo was quite capable of
trying to solve his problems by setting the Tungpei and Hsipei
armies against the Communists, and these would annihilate
one another. "Mao believed that the real reason for the

Generalissimo's visit to Sian was precisely what he said it was: he would order the Tungpei and Hsipei armies to launch a campaign against the Reds with the certain knowledge that we would destroy the Young Marshal's forces. After all, we had just defeated Hu Tsung-nan's army. And after we had destroyed the Young Marshal's army, the Generalissimo reasoned, we would be too weak to attack him for a little while. If this was the plan, and we had very good evidence of it, it was remarkably shortsighted. If we had been destroyed, the Japanese would have taken the opportunity to sweep through Shensi and Shansi."

By the end of 1936, the Generalissimo now safely in Nanking, Mao could reflect that the year had passed with an increase of power to the Communists. In the spring the Red Armies had invaded Shansi, the "model" province of Marshal Yen Hsi-shan, returning with considerable supplies of captured equipment, and adding 10,000 highly trained troops from among the prisoners. The Generalissimo's threatened annihilation campaign had petered out, and the danger of civil war while the Japanese were preparing to launch an offensive against China no longer threatened.

There were other advantages. He had maintained his hold in Shensi for more than a year, and his armies, which numbered less than 20,000 survivors in October 1935, numbered considerably more than 100,000 by December 1936. Moreover, he was no longer under the orders of the Comintern,[1] and he could use his own knowledge of the situation to determine what he came increasingly to call the "correct strategy." Directly or indirectly he now controlled vast areas of China. There was not only the border region in northern Shensi; there were other Red partisan areas in southern Shensi, another on the Fukien-Kiangsi border, another on the Shensi-Szechuan border, and still another on the Hunan-Hupeh-Kiangsi border. There were yet others in Anhwei and

1. In a speech delivered on the disbandment of the Communist International in May 1943, Mao said: "Since its Seventh Congress in 1935, the Chinese Communists have received no assistance or advice from the Comintern." The Chinese Communists were first placed under the orders of the Comintern in 1923.

northeastern Kiangsi. All of these comprised redoubtable fighting forces, though the Kuomintang continued to consider them as bandits. There were evidently some bandits among them—it has been calculated that there are 20,000,000 bandits in China, people who live in the hills and prey on the villages. Various estimates of the forces under Chinese Communist control were published, but they differed widely, and it is doubtful whether in 1936 they controlled more than a few million inhabitants. They were a force in being: they were not yet a force which had grown powerful enough to challenge the hegemony of the Kuomintang.

In December 1936 the Soviet government moved from Pao An to Yenan. There were considerable advantages in the change. Yenan had long been a prefectural capital, and one of the most important cities on the road from Sian to the Great Wall. Here, in 200 B.C. the Huns under Mao Tun had made a prodigious attack on the heart of the Chinese Empire, retiring after capturing an immense quantity of spoils. The poet Tu Fu is supposed to have wandered here during his travels, for one of the city's suburbs bears his name. More important, historically: the capture of Yenan by Li Tzu-ching had led to the downfall of the last purely Chinese dynasty, for the Mings perished when Wu San-kuei invited the Manchus into the empire against Li Tzu-ching. Yenan had seen the beginning of the downfall of a great Chinese dynasty. Mao, who was passionately interested in history, began to believe that it might see the beginnings of a new kind of Chinese dynasty altogether. The choice of Yenan, not far from the burial place of the Yellow Emperor, was perfectly deliberate, and was based largely on its historical associations. There is one other reason for the choice which may have unconsciously influenced Mao. In *All Men Are Brothers* the city where much of the action takes place is also called Yenan, though it is another town altogether—in Shantung.

AGREEMENT WITH THE KUOMINTANG

In the spring of 1937 Mao was largely concerned with the increasing menace of Japan and with efforts toward closer military liaison with the Kuomintang against the Japanese. On March 14, 1936, he had already declared his intentions. "It goes without saying," he wrote, "that we shall never allow Chiang Kai-shek to lay a finger on the Red Army. If his army will only cease hostilities against us, then we shall extend to him the hand of friendship again on the field of battle against The Japanese." He had repeated the offer in August 1936, with a plea for a united front against the common enemy, but it was only after the Sian Incident that he was assured of an end to the protracted civil war. At some time in the spring of 1937, and under conditions of some secrecy, a closer liaison was established, with Chou En-lai as the official Communist representative in Nanking. At this time four promises were made to the Kuomintang. They were:

1 The Communists propose to abandon the agrarian revolution they have practiced in the past.
2 They promise not to overthrow the Kuomintang by force.
3 They promise to reorganize the Soviet government in the border region as a democratic, local government.
4 They agree to reorganize the Red Army as a national revolutionary army.[2]

2. Gunther Stein, *The Challenge of Red China*, New York, 1945, p. 114. These four promises were recited by Mao to Gunther Stein. The official *China Handbook 1937-1945*, New York, 1947, p. 67, gives the Kuomintang version of the agreement:
1 The Chinese Communist Party shall struggle for the realization of the Three Principles of the People.
2 They will abandon the policy of overthrowing the Kuomintang regime, give up the Communist movement, and discard the policy of confiscating land by force.
3 They will dissolve the present Soviet organization, and by carrying into practice the principles of democracy, they will help to bring about the political unity of the whole nation.
4 They will disband the Red Army.

The consequences of the new agreement were far-reaching. They prepared the way for a decisive change in Communist-Kuomintang relations. The first promise was perhaps the easiest to accomplish. Experience in Yenan and Pao An had proved that a moderate socialist party, retaining many of the landowners in possession, was a perfectly "correct" policy in wartime; and Mao's own views of the rich farmers had changed remarkably since the time of the Kiangsi Soviets. The second promise implied a reciprocal agreement on the part of the Kuomintang not to attempt to destroy the Chinese Communists. The third was carried out with a great display of elections and balloting. The fourth led to the formation of the Eighth Route Army later, while already, on August 10, 1936, Mao had announced that "the Workers' and Peasants' Government" had been renamed "the Peoples' Government," and "the Workers' and Peasants' Army" had been renamed "the Peoples' Red Army." The changes in the names were significant of the changing atmosphere of the times. It was proposed that the "four promises" should officially be made public on July 15, 1937. Suddenly, early on the morning of July 7, there was an unprovoked attack on the Marco Polo Bridge. The disastrous Sino-Japanese War had begun in earnest. It was not until September 22, ten weeks after the beginning of the war, that the Chinese Communists published their version of the agreement with the Kuomintang. In it they expressed willingness to fight for the realization of the Three Principles of the People and pledged themselves to renounce the policies of insurrection, and land-confiscation. They did not pledge themselves to abandon their army.

The war, long foreseen by Chiang Kai-shek and by Mao, came unexpectedly. It was thought that the Japanese might invade China in August or September. It is possible that even the Japanese were unaware of the implications of the incident at the Marco Polo Bridge. The Communist forces were mobilized, and with Chou En-lai directing their mobilization from

---

It is clear that the official version of the "four promises" published by the Kuomintang is weighted against the Chinese Communists and includes matter which the Chinese Communists were incapable of accepting.

Nanking, there seemed to be every possibility of a close liaison between the two armies. The Red Army became officially the Eighth Route Army—the *Pa lu chün;* and out of the scattered guerrilla forces in Central China the New Fourth Army was brought into existence. In Hopeh, Peng Teh-huei met his old adversary, Wei Li-huang, and for a brief space their armies were joined.

By 1939 it was clear that the Japanese could advance little farther, and that Chiang Kai-shek, with his policy of vacillation, was incapable of making up his mind on the proper method of attack. He distrusted the guerrillas. He had no desire to fight positional wars. Behind the Ichang gorges, in the mountainous and thickly wooded areas of Szechuan, he felt secure; and this fatal sense of security prevented him from organizing his large armies on any firm basis. Factions broke out within the Kuomintang. It was the period when Chen Li-fu began to exert a strange domination over the Kuomintang. The landowners of Szechuan threatened trouble. When winter came at the end of 1939, Chiang Kai-shek was organizing security under the heavy protecting clouds that covered Szechuan.

THE FOURTH ARMY INCIDENT

Security, as so often in China, involved a balance of forces. There existed, even during the period of the Sino-Japanese War, semi-private armies, only theoretically under the control of the Kuomintang. In Yunnan, General Lung Yun ("Cloud Dragon") behaved like an independant satrap. The Kwangsi generals retained their armies near their capital in Kweilin. Most of these generals were fighting for position and power, and their loyalty depended upon the armaments and money they received from the central treasury.

Chiang Kai-shek, confused by conflicting loyalties and obsessed by an ancient hatred for the Chinese Communists, determined that at least one of the conflicting factors in the struggle for power should be eliminated. In December 1940

he ordered that the New Fourth Army should cross the Yangtse. The order was carried out. By early January, most of the
army, except for some headquarters and combat troops, had
crossed over. Passing through a long mountainous defile on
their way to the river, these were suddenly attacked by some
80,000 troops operating under the orders of General Ku
Chu-tung, commander of the Third War Zone, and General
Shankuan Yun-hsiang. Both of these generals had fought in
the annihilation campaigns in Kiangsi on the side of the
Kuomintang. It is possible, but only just possible, that they
acted in defiance of the orders of the Generalissimo. For eight
days there was a massacre. The headquarters staff and some
5,000 combat troops were cut down. Han Ying, once vice-
chairman of the Kiangsi Soviets, was killed. General Yeh
Ting was captured. Fewer than 2,000 escaped.

It was a sign of the times. From this moment onward there
was distrust and suspicion on both sides. The Communists
observed that the attack was entirely treacherous and against
all the accepted canons of war. General Yeh Ting had sent a
message to the Kuomintang commander, reminding him that
they had both been cadets at the Whampoa Academy together: then why the attack? Invited to visit the Kuomintang
headquarters under a safe conduct, he was immediately put
in irons. For the next five years messages were to be exchanged
constantly between the Kuomintang and the Communists,
but no one could ever tell whether these messages meant
anything at all.

Five Books

During the course of the anti-Japanese war, Mao's authority in the Communist areas remained unchanged: he was the theoretician of the Communist revolt. His speeches and reports were usually recognized as final. There were party discussions; there were elections; there were continual conferences at Yenan; but the main brunt of working out essential strategies had been left, as though by common accord, to him. He invented slogans, and he was constantly called upon for advice.

In 1940, northern Shensi suffered from a drought, and he began a campaign for self-sufficiency in food. Soldiers, sent out to till the land, complained of difficulties. He wrote back: "Remember you work for the people. Enlist their enthusiasm. Learn from their experience, and develop mutual benefit." The last phrase was purely Confucian. The slogan, "Move your own hands," and the later one, "Move your bottoms over"—referring to intellectuals who sat away from the peasants—were, however, his own. For long periods during the war he was concerned with discovering the theoretical solutions, while Chu Teh and Peng Teh-huei were left in complete charge of the Army.

During this period he wrote a number of short books. They were written with grace and learning and a hard-bitten power. In the early guerrilla campaigns he seemed to order his columns as though he was ordering a dance. His arguments in the books have something of the same effect. He often writes in apothegms. He frequently quotes the classics, and sometimes when he ridicules them, he gives the impression of a man who protests too much.

These books are major sources for an understanding of the Chinese Communist revolution. Logical, complex, deliberately designed for the widest possible audience, they occasionally show signs of being written with some difficulty, against the grain, each word chipped off the chest-bone. These signs of strain arise, perhaps, from the fact that he uses Chinese proverbs, classical allusions, and quotations from Marxist literature; and the algebraic Marxist symbols mingle uneasily with the grace of Confucius and the rough common sense of the peasants. There are elements in his style which derive from Confucius and Han Yu and from the great Chinese novels, but he has also been influenced by the spare ironical prose of the story-writer Lu Hsun. Mao has been a journalist: sometimes he writes as a journalist. He is a poet: sometimes he writes prose as only poets write it. He is a politician: he is not always free from demagoguery. He is a general: he will sometimes write as though each word is being sharpened for battle. He reads voluminously—he said once that he counted a day wasted if he had not fought a battle or read sixty pages —and sometimes he gives the impression of desiring to throw pell-mell into his own prose everything he has ever read.

His five major works are all short and could be bound together to make a single 300-page book, though another 300 pages of notes would probably be necessary if they appeared in an English edition. Though most of his works have been translated in full, they are surprisingly little known. It is doubtful whether they have been read by the foreign secretaries most concerned. They are important books, because they reveal his mind and the temper of the Chinese revolution he led; and it would be a pity if their continued neglect led us to underestimate the quality of his thought. The five major books are, *On a Prolonged War; The New Democracy; The Strategic Problems of China's Revolutionary Wars; The Chinese Revolution and the Communist Party of China;* and *Coalition Government.* In the pages that follow his main conclusions are outlined and many of the more illuminating passages quoted.

"ON A PROLONGED WAR"

Like most of Mao's published work, the book was originally a series of lectures. They were delivered before the Yenan Association for the Study of the Anti-Japanese War, between May 26 and June 3, 1938. They were later published in *Chieh-fang (Liberation),* in July, where they occupy only 39 pages.

On a Prolonged War was an attempt to grapple with the problem of the war, and to discover its main outlines: how it should be fought, how long it would last, the circumstances of final victory. Methodically, Mao examined the stages the war would pass through.

The first stage was described as Japan's geographical advance and China's defensive retreat. The enemy would occupy all the large cities and lines of communication east of a front which links Canton, Hankow, and Lanchow. To bite off so large a portion of China would involve, of course, inevitable strains on Japan's economy, but at the cost of 50 divisions, amounting to a million and a half men, an expenditure of ten billion yen and after a campaign lasting 18 to 24 months, Mao believed, the Japanese would succeed in their purpose.

In fact, the Japanese campaign did come to a standstill within eighteen months, did cost ten billion yen, and did involve an army numbering more than a million. The Japanese did not, however, succeed in all their objectives: they occupied only two-thirds of the area they had intended to occupy.

The second stage of the war would be one of stalemate and watchful sparring, of indecisive conflicts and a kind of shadow play, prolonged in time but short in maneuver—the graceless heaving of two giants who, though wrestling furiously, give the impression of simply standing against each other. During this time the Chinese might be expected to summon up their forces and mobilize on all levels, while the Japanese would weaken; and as the international situation grew more favorable to the Chinese, the Japanese rear would be placed increasingly in jeopardy. Upheavals in the homeland, the determined opposition of guerrillas operating behind the Japanese lines, short, sharp attacks at critical points along the front would force the Japanese to retire, or else they would be driven to wild excesses. Whatever happened, if China could endure a prolonged war, and if she was sufficiently mobilized, the destruction of the Japanese Army became certain. "China will beat the nose and pull the tail," forcing the Japanese to fight in two directions, on two fronts.

The third stage would be that of the counteroffensive and the final Japanese collapse as a result of defeat in China, economic exhaustion, revolution, and internal pressures—a collapse which might appear quite suddenly and unexpectedly. In this final stage, mobile war would give way to positional war, and guerrilla warfare would lose its importance.

The thesis is simple, but it is most revealing. Mao contended rightly that war must be considered in terms of its inevitable stages. There are progressions and retrogressions; the ultimate solutions are discovered when nothing is apparently happening at all, during those periods of stalemate, wavering, and defection. The simplest, or two-stage kind of war occurred in 1904. There a Japanese offensive was followed by a Russian retreat. The war in China was clearly comparable with the Napoleonic invasion of Russia. There was Napoleon's offensive, a short period of stalemate, and a Russian counteroffensive. In China the period of stalemate would, for various reasons, become almost unbearably long, but its very length must be regarded as part of the price of victory.

Again and again, using the three simple stages the war must take, Mao analysed the situation, now in terms of military straegy, now in terms of tactics, now in terms of resources. He worked out the relative importance of mobile, positional, and guerrilla warfare during the three stages. "In the first period," he wrote, "mobile warfare will be primary, but afterward positional warfare will assume the primacy. Guerrilla warfare will tend to become far less important that before, though both of the other tactics will be assisted by it." In the second stage, "China will advance increasingly in bureaucratic and military power, and there will be a general mobilization of people and their culture. Guerrilla warfare will expand. In the economic field, there will be a process of expansion in small industries and considerable agricultural expansion. There will be an increase in international aid. There will be great changes."

The casual analysis of the stages assumes something of the form of prophecy. It is as though Mao was saying: "Tomorrow will be fine, the day afterward windy." Even the phrase, "There will be great changes," seems to go back to the Confucian *Book of Changes,* which is concerned with just such political prophecies. Actually, Mao was outlining a rigid scheme which would embrace all the conceivable possibilities of the war according to very simple laws. He is not primarily concerned with guerrilla warfare, as so many have thought. He regards it as auxiliary to the war of movement. Mobile war is the aim, but guerrilla warfare is a fundamental device to be employed relentlessly on every occasion where it can be justified. There are even moments when he seems appalled by the temptations of guerrilla war. "Guerrilla war," he wrote, "is fundamental to us, but there must be no slackening of mobile war." And again: "In the area as a whole a mobile war is primary, guerrilla war secondary; in the area considered as small parts, guerrilla war is primary, mobile war secondary." It is a typically Chinese statement, but the force of it can be realized only when we consider how vast were the temptations to fight a ceaseless guerrilla war against the Japanese.

As early as the summer of 1938 Mao examined the Japanese mistakes. He assumed that they would continue to make the same mistakes throughout the whole invasion. He found five major mistakes: (1) They mobilized too slowly because they underestimated Chinese resistance. (2) They failed to concentrate their main strength on one objective, but dissipated their forces. (3) Except in relatively small areas, they were incapable of co-ordinating their forces. (4) They failed to follow up. (5) They failed to take prisoners, in contra-distinction to the Chinese Communists, who attempted, not always very successfully, to capture rather than kill the Japanese. A captured Japanese could be used against the enemy.

He was equally critical of the mistakes of the Chinese. They, too, failed to mobilize sufficiently. He said: "We are weak because there was no general mobilization of the political consciousness of the people before the war." The Chinese were, in fact, too passive, but "passivity is fatal to us; our task is to make the enemy passive." Against passivity, he inveighed passionately. Only a deep, serious political consciousness had power to change the situation for the Chinese. "The nation's internal political progress is inseparable from a determined waging of the war. The greater our political progress, the greater our ability for determined resistance; the greater our determined resistance, the greater our ability to progress politically." Here he was saying exactly the same thing three times, but each time with a different inflection and a different accent. Passivity was one kind of weakness; there remained others. There was the inevitable weakness of the Chinese compelled to wage war against a highly industrialized enemy. Under some conditions, China could not possibly win. One of these conditions was the absence of outside aid, and he particularly mentioned Great Britain, France, and America as possible allies. He wrote:

Since our own strength of itself will still remain insufficient, we shall have to depend upon aid from abroad and on internal changes in the enemy's country. If not, we cannot be victorious. It is for this reason that we stress the importance of Chinese propaganda abroad and our work in foreign relations.

He was writing with the long view. In 1938 there was comparatively little belief that foreign aid would be forthcoming. The powers seemed to be disposed to welcome Japan as the arbiter of China. Yet he was completely convinced that after a long war China would emerge victorious. "Those who believe we can win a speedy victory are as incorrect as those who say we cannot win."

Not all the book is written with this professorial air. There are moments when a hard passion breaks through, when the horror of the invasion is allowed to penetrate the bleak schematization of a threefold war. Referring to a prince of the Spring and Autumn Period, and equating his hatred of the four feudal virtues with his hatred of Japan, he wrote:

We are not Sung Jang-kung. We do not want the stupid pig-like *jen, i, tao,* and *te.* We want to take the enemy's eyes and ears and seal them as completely as possible. We want to make them blind and deaf; we want to take out the hearts of their officers; we want to throw them into utter confusion, driving them mad.

A great deal of matter that appeared in *On a Prolonged War* appeared in Mao's report to the Sixth Plenum of the Chinese Communist Party delivered on October 12, 1938. The report bore the title *The New Stage,* and though it dealt with an infinity of other problems, it was mainly concerned with the fact that the anti-Japanese war had already reached the stage of stalemate. The time had come, according to Mao, for the complete mobilization of China's resources. He quoted widely from the previous book, and *The New Stage* is admittedly indebted to *On a Prolonged War.* This long speech, written very carefully, with a multitude of subheadings and paragraph titles, is less convincing than it might have been. It is a deliberate propaganda speech, without grace, and almost excessively repetitious, and it is surprisingly full of blandishments to the Kuomintang. Mao quoted with approval Chiang Kai-shek's message to the people: "The center of gravity of China's ultimate victory does not lie in Nanking or any other large city. It lies in the stout hearts of the people all over the country." He payed tribute to the Kuomintang, calling it "the party of the brilliant revolution," and he set forth a program for the numerical strength of each: The Kuomintang should have a membership of 5,000,000, while the Communist party should reasonably limit itself to a membership of 1,000,000. Following the party line, he demanded that the united front should be continued. "There are no real differences beween us, for we too desire that the Three Principles of the People should be put into operation." As though answering the perpetual question raised within the ranks of the Kuomintang concerning the theory of the class struggle, he said in a revealing paragraph: "We do not deny the existence of the class struggle, but the struggle itself can be adjusted for the sake of our national unity against the enemy. There can be formulated a proper policy of the relations between the classes which will be acceptable to all classes." It is doubtful whether he believed a new orientation could come about during the stress of war, but the hope remained. The class struggle, as he said again and again in his articles and books written in wartime, is the first casualty of the war.

The New Stage is most revealing when it continues the arguments of On a Prolonged War. For the first time there appears the casual statement, later to assume tremendous implications: "The villages and the countryside will defeat the cities and the towns." Here, too, Mao brought his mind to bear on the larger perspectives of a peasant revolt. There were only a few conditions which could bring about a large-scale peasant revolt. "It would be impossible, for example, to imagine a peasant revolt in modern England, France, the United States, Germany, Italy, or Japan being maintained for any length of time; nor is a peasant revolt possible in a small semicolony. It is only because China is a vast semicolony, with untapped resources of its own, that the peasant revolt can be brought about." He was talking of the peasant revolt against the Japanese invaders, but there is more than a hint of a perpetual revolt—the revolt that continues until in the end the Kuomintang surrenders its power.

Mao's concern through much of his life has been to discover the relationship between Chinese and Western civilization, and in The New Stage he stated his final opinion categorically:

The idea of "unconditional westernization" is a wrong one. China has suffered greatly by blindly absorbing foreign materials. Chinese Communists should never break this rule, even in the application of Marxism. We must unify appropriately the general truth of Marxism and the concrete practice of the Chinese revolution, i.e., we must adopt the national form before we can find Marxism useful, and we should never subjectively or mechanically apply it.

Dry, precise, logical, rarely very penetrating, *The New Stage* is a rough sketch for the far more powerful *The New Democracy,* written a year later.

THE NEW DEMOCRACY

With *The New Democracy* which Mao published on January 19, 1940, the stage was set for a possible compromise with the Kuomintang. It was written hurriedly, and first delivered as a speech lasting eight hours. It has a number of minor inaccuracies, and like *The New Stage* is almost excessively repetitious; but it represented a hardheaded and practical program of reform and a new approach to the problem which had obsessed the Chinese Communists from the beginning: under what conditions would Communism develop in China? The situation had changed since the Kiangsi Soviets. The Communists were no longer a small harassed force fleeing from the Kuomintang. Steadily, with extraordinary patience, they were gathering together a vast army in the North and they were perfectly aware of their power. What was necessary was to develop a program which would not exasperate liberal sentiment within the Kuomintang. But at the same time the Communists had no intention of retreating from their advanced positions. To solve the problem, Mao invented an entirely new political category, "the new democracy," which differed from all other democracies, not by its newness, but by the fact that it represented the discovery that there might reasonably be an interim stage between feudal China and a purely socialist China. "The first stage," he wrote, "is new democracy, the second is socialism. But the duration of the first stage will be rather long. It certainly cannot be completed in a morning and an evening, for we are not visionaries: we cannot divorce ourselves from the reality of the situation."

Mao never made clear the exact length or the exact kind of development he proposed for "the new democracy." It manifestly represented a period of political experiment, and Mao

probably derived his new insistence on "gradualism" from
the British Fabians. The theory on which the Chinese Communists reposed was no longer the expropriation of the landlords, the Commune, the sudden flash of a proclaimed dictatorship. He was feeling his way cautiously. The Nazi-Soviet Pact
had occurred just before the book was written. The Kuomintang was sending out feelers toward the Communists, and
there existed passages in Sun Yat-sen's *Three Principles
of the People* which were evidently acceptable to the Communists. If a compromise could be effected, it could be arranged on the basis of a gradual transfer of power.

Once again, Mao reposed his faith entirely on the peasantry.
"The war of resistance," he wrote, "is really a peasants' war.
Everything we use in resistance, everything we live on is
really given to us by the peasants." Elsewhere, he amended the
statement to include the workers, the intelligentsia, and the
petty bourgeoisie. As for the class of people he described as the
"national bourgeoisie," the upper middle-class supporters of
Chiang Kai-shek's regime, he was prepared to accept that
they possessed a revolutionary quality but held that they were
also innately treacherous. "They are revolutionaries, but they
are also prepared to compromise," he wrote. "They have a
dual nature and belong to both camps at the same time." In
this, at least, there was a remarkably accurate diagnosis of a
whole class, which supported Chiang Kai-shek but drove him
almost insane because he knew its support might be withdrawn at any moment.

Basically, *The New Democracy* remains a Marxist-Leninist textbook written to support the thesis of revolution by
gradualness. Mao inveighs against those who desire the socialist dictatorship immediately. Such miracles, he says, are
eminently desirable, but they are clearly unobtainable:

If we say that of the two revolutionary stages, the first is the pre-
requisite for the second, and that the two must be consecutive
without allowing any stage of bourgeois dictatorship to intervene,
then this is correct. But if we say that the democratic revolution
does not have its own definite task or its own definite time, but can
tackle other tasks, such as those of socialism, which in fact can
only be brought about at another time, and if we heap all these

tasks together with the democratic tasks and attempt to carry them out simultaneously—that is "trying to do everything at once". Such an attempt would be clearly utopian, and will be rejected by all true revolutionaries.

Though the statement could hardly be more repetitious and shows clearly that it is a part of a speech, yet it conveys exactly what Mao intended to convey. The time for socialism was not yet. There were possibilities of canalizing Communist doctrine with the doctrine of Sun Yat-sen. There were tasks which could be called "democratic," and these had to be confronted before the tasks which could be called "socialistic." Eventually, when the Communists had taken power, "new democracy" came to mean something which could hardly be distinguished from "socialism"; but neither Mao nor Chiang Kai-shek could have forseen the swift defeat of the Kuomintang in 1949.

The New Democracy leaves many questions unanswered. It could hardly do otherwise, for the political configuration of China was still fluid. Except in one particular, *The New Democracy* avoided dogma, but that one particular was fraught with alarming consequences. Having traced the changes in the character of the revolution from the May Fourth Movement, he insisted that the revolutionary front could only be understood as part of the world proletarian socialist revolution:

With all the imperialist countries as her enemies, China cannot obtain independence without the aid of the one socialist country and the international proletariat. The world now lives in an era of revolution and war, a new era, where capitalism is definitely dying and socialism is beginning to flourish. In the international environment of the middle of the twentieth century, there are only two ways open to all decent people in the colonies and semicolonies. They must either go over to the side of the imperialist front and take part in the world counterrevolution, or come to the side of the anti-imperialist front and take part in the world revolution. They must choose between these two. There is no other way.

The implications of his later journey to Moscow were thus stated quite clearly in a pamphlet issued ten years previously. Here for the first time Mao introduced a completely dogmatic theme. The world was divided into black and white. There were no half-lights. Only the Soviet Union, which had given almost no assistance to the Chinese Communists and had indeed interfered gratuitously with their development, was to be relied upon. That other democratic and near-socialist states would emerge among those whom Mao professed to call imperialist did not occur to him; that even America with its TVA and New Deal was gradually progressing toward a welfare state apparently had no meaning for him. For once he was content to rely on dogma, on the inevitability of an exclusive alliance between China and the Soviet Union. "The whole world now looks upon communism as its savior," he wrote, "and so does China." He had listened to the radio and studied the textbooks. He did not know that over large sections of the world there was bitter disappointment over the course the Russian revolution had taken, and for once he found himself talking of matters of which he had no direct knowledge.

Except for the reference to the Soviet Union and the almost casual manner in which he dismissed all other alliances, *The New Democracy* did prepare an intelligible blueprint for the future. He insisted upon a poised, scientific attitude and deliberately set himself against arrogant theorizing. He summed up most of his past revolutionary experience when he wrote:

A scientific attitude should be one that seeks the truth in concrete facts, and problems can never be solved with the arrogant attitude of considering oneself always right or of acting with self-assumed authority. The catastrophe facing our nation is so grave that only a scientific attitude and a spirit of responsibility can lead us along the road of liberation. There is only one truth. This truth is determined, not by subjective boasting, but by objective practice. Only the revolutionary practice of millions of people can be taken as the gauge for measuring truth.

Here, as elsewhere, he is dogged by ambiguities, for there is arrogance in his statement that "there is only one truth," and he is not altogether free of "subjective boasting." But on the whole the book is unusually humble, and it lacks altogether the wildly unrealistic approach of the Generalissimo's *China's Destiny*. The similarities between the doctrine announced in *The New Democracy* and Sun Yat-sen's *Three Principles of the People* are amazing. Mao accepts all of Sun Yat-sen's theses, with four qualifications. First, he insists on the eight-hour day. Secondly, he refuses to accept Sun Yat-sen's philosophy of history. Thirdly, he sees no hope that the revolution can be established "in a single throw." Finally, he says that there will be a difference in the thoroughness of the execution of the revolutionary policies: the Communists have the habit of thoroughness. With this oblique reference to future wars and past campaigns, he dismisses the *Three Principles of the People* only to include them within the orbit of his own *New Democracy*.

Whatever its defects, *The New Democracy* was appropriate to its times, and Mao's brief analysis of the forces at work commanded the respect of Chinese students, especially those who found *China's Destiny* indigestible. He claimed with some truth that the bourgeoisie unites with the workers and the peasants to oppose the external enemy, only to combine with the external enemy when the workers and peasants appear as an emerging force. Something like this happened in France, when it became clear that Weygand preferred German military occupation to a revolution of the workers and peasants. In China, there was always the danger that Chiang Kai-shek would make peace with the Japanese in order to crush the Communists. Unfortunately, as so often in Communist literature, the simple theory assumes the character of an axiom, and the fact that it is no more than a theory is conveniently forgotten; for the truth is that people are so complex that they can never be divided into these simple categories, and those who subscribe to these theories are culpable before history.

In one of the more engaging passages of *The New Democracy*, Mao appealed for an ever increasing absorption of the culture of foreign nations. China, he said, must never remain static. It must learn from all nations, from all cultural movements. In a curiously involved passage, he suggested that learning introduced from abroad must be regarded as food, "which is first chewed, and then introduced into the stomach and intestines for digestion, where saliva, pepsin, and other secretions of the organs separate it into essence and residue, and so the essence becomes our nourishment and the residue is passed out of the body altogether." Just as Marx, in the *Communist Manifesto,* praised the bourgeoisie for its great triumphs, so Mao praised the feudal empires of China "which created such brilliant cultures in ancient times." He went out of his way to praise the great writer Lu Hsun as "the bravest, firmest, truest, most correct, and most zealous of our national heroes," forgetting that there were others who deserved the honor more. But his greatest praise is reserved for the peasants "who are our all."

"THE CHINESE REVOLUTION AND THE COMMUNIST PARTY OF CHINA"

Written shortly after *The New Democracy*—the actual writing of it took place in November 1939—the three lectures which comprised *The Chinese Revolution and the Communist Party of China* attempted to provide a theoretical basis for the "new democratic revolution." *The New Democracy* deals with practical affairs. *The Chinese Revolution* is almost wholly devoted to theory of a kind which is peculiarly Chinese, for it is based on premises which have little enough to do with historical fact, and a great deal with the ethos of the Chinese nation. It is a strangely unequal work. A list of uprisings and an examination of class categories will be followed by a burst of passionate poetic prose. There are constant hints of the ancestral greatness of the Chinese and the coming proletarian empire, and there is a complete absence of the blandishments to the Kuomintang which characterize *The New Stage.* In its own way the work is comparable to some of the works of Lenin during the early stages of the Russian revolution, and it possesses an authority which places it among the most important documents Mao has published. The Chinese Communists themselves recognize its authority; they place it highest among his works. Yet it is a work which is fundamentally visionary—a sociologist trained in Western sociology could hardly be expected to recognize the peculiar resonance it possesses for the Chinese. It is important, also, to remember that it was written when the coastal cities were occupied by the Japanese and the wartime capital had been moved to Chungking.

The work begins with a vision of the ancient, classless China which existed before the feudal empire was established:

China has gone through thousands of years of primitive communist society, equal and classless. Afterward, there was a collapse of this primitive, classless society, and the era of class distinctions began. First there was a society based on serfdom, and from this arose feudalism. The process has lasted five thousand years.

No evidence is brought forward to prove the existence of an ancient communistic society three thousand years B.C., nor is there any reason why he should bring forward such evidence. It is a statement which belongs to Chinese beliefs, to the legends which became crystallized in Chu Yuan's story of the Peach Blossom Fountain, with the vision of a white- or yellow-haired people who live in a state of pure anarchism, every man ruling himself within the village community. The omission of supporting evidence for the existence of such a classless society is less important than the omission of reasons for its collapse. He adduces none, and we are left to wonder how it is that feudalism develops. Why did these peasants assent to become serfs? Did the collapse occur as a result of inherent weaknesses within the archaic society? What impulses brought about the victory of feudalism? It is easier, and more necessary to his present purpose, to discuss the characteristics of feudalism, and so he continues with a brief examination of these characteristics. Curiously enough, he omits here any reference to the possibility that feudalism arose as the result of the invasions of barbarian tribes. It arose, in Mao's view, simply and solely to perfect the machinery of exploitation. "Let us examine," he says, "the economy of feudalism. It was clearly a self-sufficient economy with the peasants producing their own food and making most of the articles they used with their own hands. But while the Emperor, the nobles, and the landlords owned most of the land, the peasants owned little or none. They used their own tools to plough the land, and to their overlords they were compelled to present forty, fifty, sixty, or even seventy per cent of the crop. And not only did the Emperor, the nobles, and the landlords live upon the exploited peasants, but the government monopolized by the landowning class compelled the peasants to support a vast bureaucracy, an army which suppressed the peasants, making them pay tribute and taxes and conscripting their labor." It is a familiar picture, and if it is perhaps excessively simple, the general outlines are probably correct. At this point, following the classic argument of Sun Yat-sen, Mao explains how the feudal society broke down under the impact of the West:

But we must recognize that China is no longer a feudal society. Since the Opium War of 1840, Chinese society has gradually become semicolonial and semifeudal, and since Mukden it has become (as the result of Japanese occupation) colonial, semicolonial, and semifeudal. The invasion of foreign capital broke up the economy of Chinese society by destroying the self-sufficient natural economy of town and rural handicrafts, substituting a commodity economy. The destruction of the previous economy created markets for capitalistic commodities, while the widespread bankruptcy of the peasants and handicraftsmen enabled the capitalists to exploit cheap labor.

What is to be done? Clearly, he says, the battle is engaged for the subjection of foreign capital to Chinese needs, the capitalists must no longer possess the authority they possessed in the past, and the aims of the Chinese revolution must be reconsidered in the light of the most urgent demands. But it is not essentially against capitalism that Chinese communism must wage war: there are more important enemies. The argument of *The New Democracy* is repeated with some significant changes, and remembering the recent defection of Wang Ching-wei to the Japanese, he enlarges upon the roles of the various classes in a long paragraph which successfully summarizes his position. It is written in the dry, algebraic formu-

las of Communist theory, but it is so important that it should
be quoted in full:

Since our present Chinese society is still colonial, semicolonial, and
semifeudal, the chief enemies of the Chinese revolution are still
the imperialists and the semifeudal forces. Since the task of the
Chinese revolution is to carry out national and democratic revolutions to overthrow these two enemies, and since the forces which
will overthrow them are sometimes still joined by the national
bourgeoisie and by part of the upper bourgeoisie, even though the
upper bourgeoisie has betrayed the revolution and joined the
enemy, yet the dagger of the revolution should not be directed
against capitalism and the private property of the capitalists, but
against imperialist and feudal monopolies. Therefore the nature
of the Chinese revolution at its present stage is not that of proletarian socialism, but of bourgeois democracy. But the present
Chinese bourgeois revolution is not the old and ordinary kind of
bourgeois revolution, for this kind of revolution is already out of
date. No, on the contrary, it is a new and special kind of bourgeois
democratic revolution. This kind of revolution is developing in
China, and in all the other colonial and semicolonial countries, and
we call this kind of revolution the New Democratic Revolution.
This new kind of New Democratic Revolution is a part of the
world proletariat socialist revolution, which resolutely fights against
imperialism, i.e. international capitalism. Politically, it is formed
by several revolutionary classes which unite together to form a
revolutionary democratic dictatorship over the imperialists, traitors,
and reactionaries, and to oppose the transformation of Chinese
society into a society of bourgeois dictatorship. Economically, it
strives to nationalize all large capital interests, and all the large
enterprises of the imperialists, traitors, and reactionaries, to divide
up the large estates and to distribute them among the peasantry, at
the same time helping middle and small private industries, while
making no attempt to abolish the economy of rich farmers. Con-
sequently, while this new kind of democratic revolution clears the
way for capitalism, yet in another sense it is also creating a precedent for socialism.

The argument, which has the appearance of being am-
bivalent, stressing the necessity of capitalism at the same time
that it stresses the necessity of a socialist dictatorship, is not
new: it is one which Mao had acknowledged almost from the

time when the Communist government was established in Yenan. It differs completely from the classic Stalinist argument, and there is no sign of the acceptance of capitalism in the speeches he made when he was chairman of the Kiangsi Soviets. He says further: "It may be expected that a form of capitalism will survive as an inevitable result of the New Democratic Revolution in an economically backward country like China."

But the force of *The Chinese Revolution and the Communist Party of China* lies less in its theoretical aspects than in its affirmation of revolutionary values. The Chinese revolution is set against the long history of China. He shows a fierce pride in Chinese inventive genius, recalling that papermaking was invented 1700 years ago, while printing from wooden blocks was invented 1200 years ago. He ranges across the centuries for examples of Chinese peasant revolts and introduces long lists of the more successful revolts which accomplished the overthrow of dynasties. The real meat of the work, however, occurs in three long paragraphs buried in the middle, where in a kind of poetic prose, each paragraph beginning with an affirmation of danger, and ending with an affirmation of the "correct" policy to be pursued, he announces the revolution. It is in such passages, which marry revolutionary logic with poetry, that he most clearly reveals himself, and they should be studied carefully by those who attempt to come to grips with the man. He begins casually enough with a statement that the main enemies are the imperialist powers (meaning Japan), the semifeudal forces (meaning the bureaucrats and the landlords on the side of the Kuomintang), and the upper bourgeoisie who have betrayed the people by collaborating with the imperialists (meaning Wang Ching-wei and the class he represents). Then he continues:

Faced with such enemies, the prolonged and bloody state of the Chinese revolution becomes inevitable. Because our enemies are so powerful, our revolutionary forces can only be strengthened and accumulated over a long period of time, so that it may become an invincible force in achieving ultimate victory over our enemies. And while these enemies ferociously suppress the Chinese revolution, our revolutionary force must be persistent and strong in guarding its own camp and defeating the enemy. It is incorrect to imagine that our revolutionary strength will quickly become overwhelming or that the Chinese revolution will succeed easily.

Faced with such enemies, it is clear that the method to be adopted and the predominant pattern of the Chinese revolution cannot be peaceful. Success can be achieved only through armed struggle. Our enemies do not allow the Chinese people to carry out peaceful activities or to possess any political freedom. Stalin has rightly said: "The special feature of the Chinese revolution is the revolt of the armed masses against the armed reactionaries." It is incorrect to ignore the principles of armed struggle, revolutionary wars, guerrilla warfare, and political work in the army.

Faced with such enemies, questions arise concerning the special revolutionary bases. The great imperialist powers, and their reactionary allied armies in China have always indefinitely occupied the important Chinese cities. If the revolutionary force refuses to compromise with foreign imperialism and its servile underlings, but contrarily, struggles to the very end, and if the revolutionary force is to accumulate and nurture its own strength and avoid fighting decisive battles with powerful enemies when its own strength is not yet ascertained, then it must turn the backward remote areas into progressive, strong bases, making them great military, political, economic, and cultural revolutionary strongholds. Then, from these strongholds, the revolutionary force can start to drive out those malicious enemies who are based upon the large cities and who encroach upon the villages. Also, from these strongholds, the revolutionary force may, through prolonged struggle, gradually achieve total success. Under such conditions, and because of the unbalanced nature of Chinese economic development (the rural economy is not entirely dependent upon the urban economy), and because of the vastness of China's territory (there are immense spaces for the revolutionary forces to fall back on), and because of the disunity and conflict existing within the anti-revolutionary camp, and because the main force of the Chinese revolution, which is the Chinese peasantry, is under the leadership of the Communist party: so there arises the great possibility that the Chinese revolution will succeed first and foremost in the countryside. Thus the revolution is driven to its conclusion within a totally unbalanced atmosphere, which increases our difficulties and causes the prolongation of the revolution. Thus, too, we are enabled to understand why it is that these prolonged revolutionary struggles, starting out from such special strongholds, are composed chiefly of peasant guerrilla wars under the leadership of the Communist party. It is incorrect to ignore the principle of making and establishing revolutionary bases in the countryside, and it is equally incorrect to ignore the need for strenuous work among the peasants, and the need for guerrilla wars.

What he is doing in such passages is to ascribe logic to a state of affairs which had come about as a result of the failure of the Kiangsi Soviets. He passionately defends the existence of the border government, and he has no illusions about the struggle with the right wing of the Kuomintang, whatever he may say at other times, for the trap is sprung in the opening words of the extraordinary panegyric of revolution: "Faced with such enemies, the prolonged and bloody state of the Chinese revolution becomes inevitable."

THE STRATEGIC PROBLEMS OF CHINA'S REVOLUTIONARY WARS

In February 1941, almost immediately after the New Fourth Army Incident, *Strategic Problems* was published in Yenan in a small volume of fifty pages printed on thick brown paper. In many ways it was the most revealing of the five books which he published in the space of three years. Intended as the first volume of a general survey of guerrilla war, Mao's book is concerned to discover the fundamentals of guerrilla warfare, and how a small force can destroy a greater. "There are," he explains, "no mysteries whatsoever in the strategy of defeating superior forces. This is how it is done. In this way, and only in this way, can our armed revolutionary forces succeed in destroying an enemy twenty times our number."

There was nothing secret in *Strategic Problems*. Copies of it were received in Kuomintang headquarters in Chungking, and presumably, for the book was issued as a textbook for the Red Army, copies fell into the hands of the Japanese. What was ominous both for the Kuomintang and for the

Japanese was that Mao considered that the Red Army had reached a position where it no longer needed to conceal its methods. He explains almost casually all the tricks of the guerrilla trade, admits his mistakes, describes with his own maps the various phases of the five annihilation campaigns waged against the Red Army on the borders of Kiangsi and Fukien, enlarges on "centripetal withdrawal" and "defensive retreats," and explains the conditions under which small armies can break through an encirclement. The writing is unusually close-knit, and large parts of it appear to have been written as early as 1936. Often, the book is more significant for its omissions than for what it includes. He shows no knowledge of having read deeply in military books by European writers. For the most part his sources are Sun Wu, the ancient military commentator who appears to have lived about 400 B.C., *The Spring and Autumn Annals,* which may have been compiled by Confucius and which certainly relate to battles of the sixth century B.C. and the novel *All Men Are Brothers*. Also, it is clear that he had made a special study of the military campaigns of the Han Dynasty. He praises the Russians for avoiding a positional war with Napoleon in 1812 at Moscow, and he twice praises the French for their strategic withdrawal on August 21, 1914. For the rest, there is a careful discussion of all the innumerable forms of guerrilla campaigns. Combat disposition, command, camouflage, concentration, deployment, night fighting, antiaircraft defense, ambush, feints, and the various types of encounters and operations are all passed under review. He explains that the whole purpose of guerrilla war is the capture of spoils. Guerrillas are not interested in a war of attrition; they are interested in mobility, the quick thrust, disguise, the physical annihilation of enemy troops. The temptation to engage in a war of attrition must be avoided at all costs. "While such a game of 'matching pearls' is nothing between two dragon gods of the seas," he writes, remembering a fairytale written by Prince Huai Nan-tzu, "it is ridiculous for a beggar to match pearls with a dragon god." In *Strategic Problems* the ancient past continually obtrudes, and he discusses at length a battle between the states of Lu and Ch'i which occurred in 684 B.C. It is one of the merits of the book, and one of the peculiar distinctions of Mao, that the discussion of this ancient battle becomes entirely relevant to the war against the Kuomintang or the Japanese.

There are moments during his recital of military problems when Mao seems to delight in the inevitable contradictions of guerrilla warfare. "Our strategy is one against ten, while our tactic is ten against one—such contradictions provide the laws by which we overcome the enemy." Or again: "A revolution or a revolutionary war is on the offensive, yet it has its defensive and retreat. To defend in order to attack, to retreat in order to advance, to take a flanking position in order to take a frontal position, and to follow a corkscrew path in order to go directly to the objective—these are inevitable phenomena in the development of all events, and why should we suppose that military events are otherwise?" He can also be brutally humorous, as when he writes: "A communist war which lasts ten years may be surprising to other countries, but for us this is only the preface. The introduction and the preliminary remarks have been written, but there remain many delightful paragraphs for the future." The concluding remarks show a characteristic effrontery:

Now that we have reached a stable period, and can now make our own ammunition and our own guns, we are in danger of depending on our own resources. Such an attitude is unwise. We should not depend upon our own war industry, but on that of the imperialists and our enemy at home. We have a claim on the output of the arsenals of London and Hanyang, to be delivered by the enemy's transport corps. This is not a joke, but the truth. *Where the Red Army was able to provide a limited quantity of good ammunition, producing it in its own arsenals, it scored the least victories.*[1]

But though a constant, unrelenting effrontery was demanded of the Red commanders, and he insists that guerrilla war is fought for the sake of spoils—the American government might have sent less ammunition to Chiang Kai-shek if it had known

1. He is referring to the situation during the Fifth Annihilation Campaign when the Reds possessed a large arsenal at Juichin.

how ardently the Communists in Yenan were waiting for the moment when they could capture them and turn them against their enemy—the study of strategic problems is not always pitched to this high, romantic key. Guerrilla warfare introduced peculiarly difficult tactical problems. The Red armies were forever faced with encirclement. Even when the Kuomintang armies were not immediately encircling them, they were still conscious of being distantly encircled by the huge weight of Kuomintang power. Mao never underestimated their power, nor their capacity to recover from the blows inflicted upon them. In all his accounts of his battles he shows little respect for Chiang Kai-shek, but he not infrequently shows respect for some of the Kuomintang commanders. "There were a few men among them," he said, "who knew our minds, and how we were fighting. If there had been more, we would not have won so often or so easily."

One day, at the guerrilla base in Chingkanshan, some peasants had asked the question: "How long can the red flag wave?" He answered: "As long as there is space to move in." In *Strategic Problems* he turns the statement into poetry: "No one need worry about whether there is enough room to move around in. In our country, 'when night falls in the west, the day breaks in the east; when light recedes from the south, the north is bright.'" Other things beside time and space conspired to help the Communists. The land is incredibly mountainous, with the result that most of the modern implements of war are hopelessly ineffective. In mountain defiles it is difficult to make use of cannon, and still more difficult to use tanks; and though airplanes took a heavy toll in the fourth and fifth campaigns, it was only because they were unexpected and because the Red armies allowed themselves to be caught in the open. Afterward, they developed a simple method of "scattering," and airplanes rarely troubled them, even during the Long March. A hundred other things came to their defense. The very nature of Chinese civilization, its furious contrasts, the divisions between the people, between the provinces, between the warlords, all these supplied the inevitable basis for revolution. Mao was, of course, perfectly conscious of these contrasts, and he ranges through them at some length when he comes to discuss the characteristics of the revolutionary war. It was a consideration of these contrasts which led him, after the Sixth Congress of the Chinese Communist Party, in 1928, to decide that the conquest of China was possible once the Red Army possessed a convenient base of operations. He wrote:

If we analyze the question, we see that throughout China there exists an uneven political and economic development, and this is indicated by the coexistence of a frail capitalist economy and a predominant semifeudal economy; a few seemingly modern industrial and commercial cities and boundless expanses of rural districts in medieval stagnation; of several million industrial workers and hundreds of millions of peasants living under a decaying regime; of great warlords administering the Central Government, and lesser warlords administering the provinces; of a regular army and a variegated collection of local armies; of great steamship lines, motor roads, and railways, together with field trails and wheelbarrow paths such that even a pedestrian has difficulty walking on them.

For hundreds of generations the Chinese had celebrated the "golden mean," but he could see no evidence of it anywhere; and the absence of a tolerable median civilization made revolutionary warfare only the more possible.

"COALITION GOVERNMENT"

For some years Mao had been watching the growing dogmatism within the party. Dogmatic himself, he recognized the danger signs. He had fought against dogma at the Tsunyi conference, and even before. Now, as the war came to an end, he was conscious that the time had come to restate the case for the Communists in the light of all the experience the party had undergone. On April 24, 1945, he called the Seventh Congress of the Chinese Communist Party into existence at Yenan, and on that spring day, while Chu Teh presented a report on the battles in the liberated area, Mao proclaimed that the Chinese Communists had fought the Kuomintang too long. It was time for a marriage.

He began by announcing that a compromise was entirely possible; that the Kuomintang and the Communists could exist together; that a single government composed of members of both parties might work reasonably well. The statement seems to have been made with intense conviction. The Japanese were reeling under American attacks, the war against Germany was over, and the time had come to formulate a convincing blueprint for the future. He distrusted the Kuomintang, and was prepared to fight it if necessary. At the same time he was prepared to envisage a period of relative calm, and even of co-operation between the two parties; and it is probable that at this time he underestimated the corruption which already existed within the Kuomintang ranks.

Coalition Government is the most carefully constructed of all Mao's published political writings. It breathes a kind of confidence which is not always present in his works. He called for reforms within the Kuomintang, but he also called for reforms within the Communist party; and he insisted on a "bedrock," absolute reliance on the demands of the people. Again and again he says: "The people must rule. There is no rule without the people. We must find what the people want, and then satisfy them." The implications are clear. The Kuomintang has not interested itself in the demands of the peasants, and just as long as it refuses to interest itself in those demands it will fail. He wrote:

Our starting-point is to serve the Chinese people earnestly and wholeheartedly, and never to be severed from the people; to set out always from the point of view of serving the people's interests, not serving the interests of a small group or oneself; to give equal responsibility to the people and the guiding organization. Experience during the last twenty years has taught us that all tasks, policies, and methods that were correct corresponded to the demands of the people at that definite time and place, and all that were incorrect were separate from the people's will.

The principle of reliance upon the popular will was one which was rarely, if ever, followed by the Kuomintang, which operated as though the people were simply counters to be moved at will. The war had made the Kuomintang more authoritative than ever, demanding from the people sacrifices so great that they were already in a state of passive non-co-operation over large areas of Nationalist China. In return for their sacrifices they were offered nothing but the continuing corruption of the high officials. It was as simple as that, and among these simplicities Mao knew himself at home. The Kuomintang government no longer led. The Communists had not yet begun to lead. The leadership must come, if it was to come at all, from "the broad masses of the people." To prove that popular will may sometimes be in advance of the government, Mao wrote:

Our comrades must not think that what is unintelligible to us is also unintelligible to the masses. Very often the masses stride ahead of us and want urgently to advance forward, while our comrades do not act as leaders of the broad masses, but on the contrary reflect the opinion of some backward interests. Every comrade should be made to comprehend that the highest criterion of all our statements and activities is whether they correspond to the highest interests of the broadest masses, and whether they are supported by the broadest masses. Every comrade should be taught to comprehend that as long as we rely on the people, firmly believing in the infinite creative power of the people, then we may be able to overcome all difficulties, no matter how serious they are, and no enemy will be able to overwhelm us, but will be overwhelmed by us.

This was not essentially the policy pursued in the early days of the Communist revolution in China. It was a policy hammered out of the war against the Japanese, out of the extraordinary conditions in North China, and out of a clear understanding of the error committed by the Kuomintang, an error that was finally to destroy them.

Though, technically, *Coalition Government* constitutes an appeal for a government of the Communists and the Kuomintang, it is also an attempt to analyze the basis of any government in terms of the popular will: the absolute primacy of the popular will is accepted. But here a doubt arises. There is never any attempt to analyze the nature of the popular will. What does it consist of? On what forces does it rely? How does it express itself? To some extent, of course, it expresses itself in the ballot box. It also expresses itself in the deliberations of the village councils, in the opinions seeping up through the ranks of the army, in the resolutions of county governments, in the overt signs of change which appear in the political atmosphere of our time. "The main task of the leader," Mao wrote elsewhere, "is to keep his ears to the ground." It was in this way that he understood "the popular will," but there was always the danger that "the popular will" might be another name for the incantatory editorials of the *Liberation Daily*. It was a danger he faced, though he did not always face it squarely, and it is significant that he demanded "equal responsibility for the people and the guiding organization," in the same breath in which he demanded the primacy of "the popular will."

The appeal for a coalition government had already appeared in *New Democracy*. In the new book the argument was reinforced and given weight by the successes of the Communist armies in North China. Here, too, Mao defined more clearly than elsewhere his attitude to investment capital. He insisted that capital was not in itself an issue: there were some forms of capital that were perfectly acceptable, for the need had never been greater. "To develop industry," he wrote, "enormous capital is required. Where will it come from? It can come from only two sources: the capital accumulated by the Chinese people themselves and from foreign loans, and we shall welcome all foreign investments as long as they obey the laws of China and are advantageous to our economy." This was not a sop to the capitalists, but a statement of simple truth. Wrecked by war, China could hardly expect to survive without enormous capital investment from abroad. But he refused, with considerable bitterness, to accept a state of affairs by which China would become a semicolony at the mercy of foreign capital:

Some people refuse to understand why the Chinese Communists do not fear capitalism, but on the contrary develop it as much as possible. Our answer is simple: we have to replace foreign imperialist and native feudalist oppression with capitalist develop-

ment because this is the inevitable course of our economy, and because the capitalist class is benefited as well as the proletariat.
What is superfluous today is foreign imperialism and native feudalism, not native capitalism. On the contrary, our capitalism is
indeed too little.

There was nothing original in this complaint: it had been
made repeatedly by Sun Yat-sen. What was new, and strange,
and encouraging was that Mao seemed to have worked out an
answer to the pressing question: how shall we have peace?
Capital would provisionally remain; the Kuomintang capitalists would have some of their powers clipped away; but the
need for capital was so great that he seemed prepared to accept an interval of "new democracy by means of a coalition
government," where power centered in an elective assembly
and the Communists would be represented for the first time
in the legal government. There is no reason to believe that
Coalition Government is a dishonest document. For ten
years the Communists had been gathering power to themselves by default of their enemies, the Japanese and the Kuomintang. The time had come for a careful evaluation of policies. Eventually, the Communists believed, they would take
over power peacefully, either by sapping at the foundations
of Kuomintang rule or by proving that their own policies
answered more closely the needs of the people. Though civil
war was conceivable, the Communists hoped to avoid it, and
Coalition Government suggested a possible alternative to
war.

With the publication of *Coalition Government,* the die
was cast. Mao made it perfectly clear that the Communists
were no longer to be treated as bandits. They would fight
back against any further annihilation campaigns. The alternatives were: coalition or war; and though the first was prefera-
ble, there was no reason to believe that their armies would
be unable to fight. The Communists were not prepared to
accept isolation, and they refused to be swallowed up within
the Kuomintang. The Kuomintang was therefore placed in a
dilemma: it must either accept coalition, or be faced with a
war even more heart-rending than the campaigns fought in
the early thirties. Unfortunately for the Kuomintang the

Communists had assured themselves of victory if war broke out by possessing a social program superior to their enemies', and nothing in all Chiang Kai-shek's writings speaks with so much assurance as Mao, when he said:

People must understand that no matter how tortuous the path may be, the independence and liberation of the Chinese people will be realized, and the time for it is already at hand. The great aspirations of countless martyrs during the last hundred years must be fulfilled *by our generation.* Whoever desires to prevent these aspirations from being translated into fact, that man will fail.

The Storm Breaks

With the end of the war against Japan, the Chinese Communists were solidly entrenched behind Japanese lines. Unknown to the foreign press, they had fought a series of hard campaigns. They had taken part, with Lin Piao as commander, in the first engagement of consequence between the Chinese and the Japanese at Pinghsinkuan. They had destroyed railroads and coal mines under Japanese occupation, and combined with General Wei Li-huang, who fought against them in the annihilation campaigns, in the battle of Chekuo. In 1940 there occurred the "Hundred Regiment Campaign," which came to an end, after four months of bitter fighting, in December. Almost immediately afterward occurred the New Fourth Army Incident, and the Chinese Communists were compelled to secure their flank against the Kuomintang. They continued, however, to fight the Japanese, and an endless war, taking place in hundreds of separate areas, a war fought in tunnels underground and in forests and in the outskirts of cities and in the plains, drained the Japanese of their strength, so that the Tokyo radio clamored for some way of preventing the continual bloodletting. Openly, the Tokyo radio proclaimed that the main enemy to China was the Chinese Red Army. It was hardly an exaggeration, for the Kuomintang had lost its offensive. By early 1945 the Kuomintang government no longer possessed the power or the authority for a counterattack, and less than a hundred miles of railway remained in its hands.

While the Kuomintang waited for the war to end, the Chinese Communists were busy extending the areas under their rule and removing them from the rule of the Japanese. Their guerrilla wars went on. To the Americans who flew to Yenan and established the Yenan Observation Group, they provided admirable intelligence. Radios were sent to them. Special apparatus was flown in. It was observed that the Red Army was a fighting force, trained to guerrilla warfare on a scale unsuspected before. It was also observed that Mao and Chu Teh possessed an authority over their troops denied to Chiang Kai-shek.

As the war came to a close, Mao and Chu Teh were openly preparing to exert the authority of the Yenan government to the uttermost. Mao had no knowledge of Russian intentions: the occupation of Manchuria was clearly decided upon at the last moment. He thought the war in the Pacific would end with an American thrust against Japan and the southeast coast of China. He had considerable admiration for the Americans who visited Yenan, and showed it in countless ways to the military officers who came to stay at Whittlesey Hall on the south bank of the Yen River. At the same time he was perfectly aware that the Kuomintang-Communist negotiations, which continued throughout the war, had ended in complete failure. What was to be done?

In an address, "Our Task in 1945," delivered before the People's Congress of the Shen-Kan-Ning Border Region, on December 15, 1944, Mao outlined the main strategy. The Americans had reached Leyte and might at any moment land on the Chinese coast. The Japanese had just driven a continental line through China which joined Tokyo to Singapore. The war was still in a state of stalemate. He still hoped for an all-out offensive by the Chinese armies, but it was clear that no political basis for such an offensive existed until a coalition government had taken power, or until the people, like the French *maquis,* rose in a *levée en masse.*

The specific problems facing the Chinese Communists, said Mao, were fifteen in number. The first was the expansion of the liberated areas by continued calculated attacks on weak enemy-held garrisons. The second involved attacks on their battle fronts. The third involved the training of the self-defense corps and the people's militia, and in discussing the training of the self-defense corps he returned, as he was to do again, to the necessity of expanding the liberated areas:

Except in some areas, where it is impossible to expand further, we must try our best to expand. Among the ninety million liberated people every man and woman citizen, except the old, young, and sick, must be organized into self-defense corps, while never giving up their production at home; and they must do this to defend their homes and villages, and to help the army . . . Of our ninety million people, at least five per cent, that is four and a half million, should join the people's militia. This means that the present people's militia must be doubled.

It was still, of course, guerrilla war. Mao pointedly remarked that the chief weapon of the people's militia must remain the land mine, which was often no more than a stone hollowed out to contain gunpowder. The fourth objective—the most ominous for the Kuomintang and for the Japanese—was the training of a regular army on modern principles, which presumably meant an army trained to fight positional wars. The fifth objective was economic: the new areas must be supported by the old. The sixth involved the Red Army itself: he demanded the utmost solidarity between the officers and the soldiers. He admitted that there were still "militaristic" habits among the officers, who sometimes neglected the soldiers when they were ill, deprived them of their food, and punished them arbitrarily, insulting and shooting deserters. "All these," Mao commented, "are utterly bad habits, and must be rooted out relentlessly." He ordered every unit to launch a "support-officer-love-soldier" movement, based upon adequate political training. The soldiers must keep the trust of their commanders, and the defects and mistakes of both should be publicly explained and swiftly corrected.

So far Mao had dealt largely with the state of the Communist military forces in relation to the enemy. Many of the remaining proposals were devoted to internal politics. The seventh concerned a "support-government-love-people" movement. The eighth demanded that all those who held posts under the government should work for a coalition government. The ninth asked for a careful examination of the problems of rent reduction—rent *must* be reduced in the newly liberated areas, for it was only by reducing rent that the peasants in the new areas would be made to rally round the Yenan government.

The tenth proposal concerned production and mutual aid groups. "The people must have sufficient food and clothing to acquire a surplus. Our slogan should be 'three years' cultivation, one year's surplus,' for within a few years we must strive to be completely, or at least nearly, self-sufficient. To this end, division of profits to private persons according to the quality of their work can and should be put into practice."

The eleventh proposal concerned intellectual and cultural work among the peasants. Culture he defined as art, newspapers, schools, and public health. A vast effort must be made to raise the standard of education. "Tyrants," he said, "feed on the ignorance of the people, but we rely on the intelligence of the people." The sly challenge to Chiang Kai-shek was followed by another, for he carefully pointed out in the twelfth proposal the necessity of the widest possible expression of popular elections.

The fourteenth proposal involved the education of cadres, or government personnel. He did not have a very high opinion of them and thought their inefficiency due to lack of education. He continued the charge in the fourteenth proposal, which attacked the dogmatism and pride of these same officials. "There are cadres which hate to hear criticism, delight only in praise, and never receive suggestions from the people, because the people are afraid to offer them, and are afraid of being humiliated or retaliated against." He proposed to wage

a pitiless war against these cadres and he ordered that no one
should be punished for speaking out:

Anyone, as long as he is not an enemy and does not attack with
malicious intent, should be allowed to speak, and it does not matter
if he is wrong. It is the duty of the leaders of all ranks to listen to
others. The following principles should be observed: First, say
what is on your mind and without reservation. Secondly, the
speaker is not to be blamed, while the listener should take notice.
If the principle that the speaker is not to be blamed—this is a real
and not fictitious principle—is lacking, then the full effect of the
principle cannot be obtained.

The fifteenth and last proposal introduced once again the
necessity of a coalition government. "We must think of all
the ways and means which will help to promote the establishment of such a government. One way is to continue negotiations with the Kuomintang; another way is to urge the entire
population to demand a coalition; and there may be other
ways." On this note the speech to the Border government
comes to an end.

The speech has been quoted from at length because it
conveys the thoughts going through Mao's mind toward the
end of the war. The civil war was still far away. The Japanese
war could be expected to last at least another year. The Chinese Communists were still concerned with an immense
number of small-scale operations. Shortly afterward, on
April 24, 1945, during the Seventh Congress of the Chinese
Communist Party, held at Yenan, Mao made his report "On
Coalition Government," and here he was elected chairman
of the Central Committee. It was an odd title, for he had
been in fact if not in name chairman ever since the Tsunyi
conference, and even in Kiangsi he had been addressed by
this title.

When the Japanese government accepted terms of unconditional surrender five days after the dropping of the first
atomic bomb, the position of the Chinese Communists suddenly changed. The dynamics of their expansion demanded a
race to the coast between the Communists and the Kuomintang. Chu Teh, as commander in chief of the Red Army,

issued an order to the guerrilla forces besieging Japanese-occupied cities to advance and accept the enemy's surrender, an order immediately countermanded by Chiang Kai-shek. By August 15, Chu Teh and Mao were urging that the United States cease lend-lease aid to the Kuomintang, who might use the guns, airplanes, and ammunition shipped into China against the Communists. It was a reasonable request; it was not followed; and the guns, airplanes, and ammunition eventually fell into the hands of the Chinese Communists.

By the end of August the danger of civil war was imminent. Chiang Kai-shek may have hoped that he could launch an immediate "annihilation campaign" with American military support, but there was popular clamor for a meeting between the two adversaries in a final effort to solve outstanding problems. The initiative had passed into the hands of Chiang Kai-shek. He dispatched a telegram to Mao, humbly requesting a meeting in Chungking. Mao answered: "My humble self is most willing to come to Chungking to discuss peace and national reconstruction with you." The letter was signed: "Your younger brother." For the first time in eighteen years the two adversaries met face to face.

It was an unhappy meeting. It was the first time Mao had flown in an airplane. The Americans had guaranteed his safety, but he could not avoid wondering at the prospects ahead: he distrusted Chiang Kai-shek too firmly to believe in the proffered good intentions. They drank toasts, commended each other in public. There were long conferences and strange, tortured interviews between them. Both were ill at ease. Chiang was politely cold, Mao warmly ironical. But gradually a basis of agreement was discovered. There would be a termination of "the period of tutelage," all political parties would receive equal rights, a People's Consultative Council would be assembled, and there would be popular suffrage. The agreement, which Chou En-lai and Wang Jo-fei signed on behalf of the Communists, was completed on October 10, and on the next day Mao flew back to Yenan. He was not convinced of the Generalissimo's good intentions. He still hoped for peace, but he saw little signs of it. No final decisions had been made about the status of the Eighth Route

Army or the New Fourth Army, and the question of the
Chinese Communist authority to accept the Japanese surrenders was still unsolved. Bitterness against Chiang Kai-shek
had increased. "He treated me like a peasant," Mao said afterward. The wound had not healed; it had only opened wider.

At this point American intervention in Chinese problems
became a factor of considerable importance. General Hurley,
working sometimes heroically and sometimes with an incredible lack of knowledge of the Chinese mind, attempted
to grapple with the problem. He had visited Yenan. For a
brief while he had been accepted by the Chinese Communists as an earnest mediator, in spite of his strange habit of
breaking out with Indian war cries at inopportune moments.
But when United States forces landed at Tientsin in September and established themselves in Chinwangtao and Peking
on the pretext that they had come to guard the railways, it
became clear that the American government was firmly resolved to protect the Kuomintang against the Communists.
"On the one hand," exclaimed Chou En-lai, "we see American ammunition fired at Communist troops, while on the
other hand the Americans are trying to bring about peace."
The tragic ambivalence, which is visible in so much of American foreign policy, was now at work. In despair of understanding the forces unleashed by the dubious peace, General
Hurley resigned.

With the increase of American intervention, the forces
making for civil war also increased. On November 15, the
United States government declared its intention to continue
lend-lease aid to the Kuomintang government amounting to
$777,638,292 up to June 30, 1947. A few days previously
Chu Teh had protested to General Wedemeyer, who commanded the United States forces in China, against continued
American intervention in Chinese affairs. The reply was un-
favorable to the Communists. The Communists believed that
the crisis had come, and in December the evacuation of Yenan
began. Kalgan, which had been captured in August, became
the industrial capital of the Communist empire; and though
Mao and Chu Teh remained in Yenan and continued to
rule from there, the greater part of the administrative offices,

the University, the Art Academy, the Military College, and the Medical College made their way toward the Yellow River. Caravans of mules, ponies, and donkeys laden with books, beds, office files, and food wandered among the yellow hills of Shensi. For the second time since the Kiangsi Soviets the government was on the march.

In the early days of 1946 there was a breathing spell. General George Marshall had been sent to replace General Hurley. He was a man of an entirely different caliber. He made a serious effort to understand the opposing camps. He visited Yenan and commented favorably upon the Communists' social policies, and he detested the servility of most of the Kuomintang officers he met. Urbane, polished, sensitive to social forces, he refused to accept the claims of either side in the quarrel, his preferences remaining with the liberal groups in the center, though for the most part these had long ago despaired of the reactionary policies of the Kuomintang.

There was sufficient evidence to show that the reaction was in full swing. On February 22 the Kuomintang secret police raided the Communist newspaper offices in Chungking, reducing them to debris. The political programs of the People's Consultative Assembly were deliberately sabotaged by Chiang Kai-shek, who kept urging Kuomintang members to carry out "a decisive campaign" against the Communists. Increasingly, on the radios of both sides, there was to be heard only violent vituperation.

The Communists had more cause for their invective than the Kuomintang. Their armies were being attacked by Kuomintang troops armed with the latest American equipment, and a military advisory group of high American officers was established under the name of MAGIC (Military Advisory Group in China) in Kuomintang headquarters. There were battles outside Changchun, and a serious engagement, which reportedly cost 100,000 lives, at Shihpingchieh. The Communists possessed three ports, Weihaiwei, Chefoo, and Lungkow. Through all the other ports military aid to support the Kuomintang was arriving in huge quantities. It seemed, as summer came on, that civil war would be inevitable, and not even the diplomacy of General Marshall could prevent it.

The Communists had reported earlier that a million Kuomintang regular troops were being transferred for an offensive against their own areas, while seven Kuomintang armies were being transported to Manchuria by United States airplanes and warships. Suddenly, at the beginning of June, the tension quietened. A truce was announced. And to make sure that the truce was effective, General Marshall organized truce teams consisting of American, Kuomintang, and Communist officers. A hush came over China. It was as though quite suddenly history had grown silent and was holding its breath.

A JOURNEY TO YENAN

During the truce I flew from Peking to Yenan, determined to see Mao and to try to fathom the sources of Communist power in China. I was also anxious to discover more of Mao's poetry, for some poems of his were known to exist, and one of them had been printed in *Ta Kung Pao* in Chungking. I half expected to find a large, thriving city and had not guessed that I would find only a beautiful valley with the winter wheat growing on the loess hills. The beauty of the valley mocked the tragic summer. There was no great arsenal of power; instead, there were yellow hills, a few houses, a market place, a sluggish blue river, a crumbling old pagoda, date palms and apple orchards set in a strange wild desolate valley thick with dust, everything yellow except for the gay blankets covering the entrances to the caves. Yenan suggested the famous story of the Peach Blossom Fountain, which lies beyond the cliffs at the other end of the world.

There was no sign of Mao. There were rumors that he had suffered a kind of stroke a few months earlier when twelve of his closest friends, including Yeh Ting and Wang Jo-fei had been killed in an air accident as they returned from a conference in Chungking. There was time enough to take stock of Yenan. I spent an evening and half a night with Chu Teh in his garden among the date palms, while the wolves howled outside in the moonless valley. Peng Teh-huei talked of his campaigns. Ma Hei-teh talked of the cave hospital. Yang Shan-k'un talked about the Sian Incident. There were *yang-k'o* dances, and an admirable performance of the "Yellow River Cantata," and long walks in the valley, which had been inhabited since the birth of China. The printing-presses were in the caves beside the river: thousands of sculptured buddhas gazed down on the small rotary presses, many of the statues dissolving in the steam. I remember once coming upon a boy resting his foot idly on the head of a sculptured prince of the T'ang Dynasty so fresh and so delicately carved that even now, though the head had lain beside the road for countless years, the closed eyes seemed about to open; and there was something in the expression and the curling hair which showed the influence of Alexander's voyages.

Mao remained invisible. There were unaccountable difficulties in seeing him. They said he saw no one, he was displeased with foreigners, they even hinted that he refused to see any foreigners again. It sounded possible. From conversation with the people in Yenan, it became clear that there was a kind of remoteness about him. Intangible and aloof, from a small house in the shadow of the mountains, not far from the radio transmitter which derived its electricity from a foot-pedal, carefully tending a small garden of tobacco plants and tomatoes, he spent the nights pondering over the telegrams received from all parts of China, and every decision he made had incalculable consequences. The truce teams were marching out from Peking; there was the possibility of peace; but the final conclusions were known only to a few men in Nanking and Yenan.

Mao had not entirely disappeared. Once I caught a glimpse of him in a jeep—a cloud of dust, a red, sunburned face peering through, then the dust swallowed him. There was only time enough to observe that he looked amazingly fit and well, and the stories of the nervous prostration were probably unfounded. A few days later I saw him at a play. He sat directly in front of me, his face illuminated by the blinding blue light of the stage, a ruddy face which reflected almost childishly all the passing emotions of the actors. The play was a morality, based on one of the innumerable incidents in the novel *All Men Are Brothers*. There was the heavy, leonine head, with blue-black hair, very thick, muscular shoulders, a long, smooth forehead, the spectacles glinting and his hands braced against his knees. One can tell more about a man from the way he enjoys drama than from observing him elsewhere. What was strange was that he was wholly feminine, reflected all the gestures of the actors, pursed his lips when they sang, made his mouth into a square when they were roaring with anger, and gently waved his arms when the firecrackers exploded; and he glowed with the wildest joy when the armies of stage peasants, in beautiful embroidered costumes, at last overthrew their feudal lords in still more beautifully embroidered costumes. It was a medieval morality, and Mao enjoyed its medieval gusto. The peasant heroes wore the finest silks, the finest dragon-painted gowns; some of the evil princes wore ugly red and black masks which gave them the appearance of tigers. It was all impenitently romantic, with the fierce romanticism of the Chinese—that race which is permanently sustained by romanticism—and with the last flutes and the last drumbeats, while the saltpeter flames of the burning castles filled the stage, Mao clapped and cheered as Americans clap and cheer at a football game.

The play concerned the victory of armed peasants over their feudal lords, one of those legendary victories which occurred two thousand years ago; yet the same play, against the background of the whole of modern China, was being played elsewhere, far from Yenan, in a thousand hamlets and a million villages. I think it was at this moment, while we were all scrambling out of the theater, that I realized fully how certain the Chinese Communists were of their eventual victory. In the end the captains with their nodding plumes, their crowns of emeralds, their robes of flowing jade and red-gold watered silk stood out among the broken towers, and without the least shock one realized that at the core of the Chinese Communists there was the sense of a known victory. They knew that because they had the unnumbered peasants at their side, the diadems and the crowns would fall to them. Mao disappeared down the dark road, a half-smiling figure with heavy shoulders, a shadow against the starlight.

I began to think that this was the last I would ever see of him. He appeared at night and slept by day; he had the scholar's desire for solitude, and he was content to calculate and pore over the reports coming into this half-deserted village by radio and messenger. I would leave Yenan and never see him face to face. Meanwhile the winter wheat grew wild on the loess mountains, and sometimes, visiting an old ruin or coming down from a cliff dwelling, I would see in the dust a rider of the Eighth Route Army racing toward Chu Teh's date garden, and it was pleasant to see the Persian roses on the saddlecloth.

But if it was impossible to see Mao, it was at least possible to see his friends. Men spoke of him, as they spoke of all legends, quietly, without emphasis, relating how he had gone among the peasants of Hunan with no weapons, wearing a drab white cotton coat and white trousers, and the famous sun helmet, lean and youthful-looking. They had known him when he was in command of a peasant army less than a hundred strong; and now this solitary man possessed armies greater than any possessed by Napoleon, and seemed unaware of his great possessions. A man who could organize the Chinese peasants in this fashion is not to be despised. With his Hunanese fire, his addiction to scholarship, and his passion for the *lao pai hsing*, the peasants with their hundred names, he represented the potentiality of the people in much the same way that Leonardo da Vinci represented the potentiality of art. It was not only that he was new, but he possessed the flair for discovering unsuspected newness everywhere— it was he, and he almost alone, who had brought this movement into being, and at the same time his decisions were the result of popular forces he could hardly control. He guided and was guided, imitating in himself the classic theorem of Aristotle that freedom "is to govern and to be governed." He led the way—the way which had been made possible by the emergence of consciousness among the Chinese peasants.

For it had come at last, this last and greatest revolt from the

heart of Asia. Colonialism, imperialism, exploitation—those
tarnished words were losing their meaning, or rather they
were slips of burning paper and the flames were biting the
edges. We had thought too long that nations were permanent, and when we thought of the West as in decline, we imagined that it was declining from its own weakness and not
from the strength of others. There were places in China
where the West was not important. In the whole of Yenan
only the printing-presses, two jeeps, the radio, and the sculptured head of a T'ang Dynasty prince showed the influence
of the West. On the walls of the huts of the Communist
generals there were no maps of America or Europe; they
were content with China, content with the Chinese peasant.

I confess I preferred it like this. The scented valley, steam-
ing with the summer sun and crowned with mountains of
winter wheat, showed the beginnings of a new civilization.
In the same way, on the shores of the Euphrates, below Mount
Hymettus, and on the seven hills of Rome, and around the
Ile de la Cité, new civilizations had sprung from a simple
thesis; and now, while civilizations fade or gather strength
by desperate missions, we must set ourselves more than ever
to understand how the seed dies and is born again in a flower-
ing tree.

So I thought, wandering in Yenan, perplexed by the figure
of Mao, who seemed even then to be destined to fulfill the
role assumed by the Chinese emperors. Though I heard the
legends concerning him, the essential man escaped, as perhaps he will escape all historians in the future. I came to believe, on those days when the sunsets were bursts of gold on
golden mountains, that I would see only the ancient Shensi
earth, the solitary peasants, the generals in the caves, and
once again, for already it had become like the phrase of
Vinteuil, the haggard rider coming through the dust with
the blaze of a scarlet saddlecloth, a gun on his shoulder, and,
in his saddlebag, reports from the hundreds of scattered
armies directed from a cave.

One evening, just before the airplane was due to arrive
from Peking, a message came from Yang Shan-k'un, the
chief of staff, to say that Mao was giving a small party. The

day had been cloudy. Now the clouds lifted, and the violence of the sunset saturated in sand only increased the sense of violence which had been present all day. During the afternoon I had ridden in one of the two jeeps to the cave-hospital. On the way back we had stopped at the cave-university, and when the jeep turned up a steep incline, we climbed out, for the sand was slippery. A moment later, the jeep with its driver slipped over the edge of a small cliff. There were some black pigs in a sty at the bottom of a thirty-foot drop. The driver was still in the jeep. When we ran down he was not dead as we had expected, but covered in blood and oil, and groaning, and the jeep had broken the back of one of the pigs, which was screaming. It was some time before a peasant brought a knife and skewered its throat. The jeep axle was bent, probably broken. In the capital of the Chinese Communist empire, there now remained exactly one jeep.

I remember that I was almost afraid Mao would turn on me and say I was responsible for destroying half of his remaining vehicles. But nothing of the kind happened.

It was growing dark, and in the little enclosure of the "Foreign Office" the Chief of Staff was playing with his children among the wilting tomato plants. There was a high wall. An armed guard at the wicker gate was picking his nose and gazing down at the river and the plain. Beyond the tomatoes lay a small bare room with a stamped earth floor, three yellow home-made chairs, and a vast map of China disintegrating with age; and beyond a curtain dinner was being prepared with a clatter of bowls and chopsticks. There was Peng Teh-huei, vice-commander in chief of the Border Regions, thickset, with the face of an angry Buddha; there were some secretaries and soldiers in dusty gray uniforms; and there was a Chinese-American major who alone represented a foreign power.

Then Mao came into the room. He came so quietly that we were hardly aware of his presence. He wore a thick brown Sun Yat-sen uniform which seemed to have been woven of goats' hair, and as he stood beside the towering Peng Teh-huei he looked slighter and smaller than I had imagined him. I had suspected he was changeable when I saw him at the theater; now, once again, he assumed the appropriate disguise. There is hardly a photograph of him which resembles any other photograph, so strangely and so suddenly does he change. Today, he looked like a surprisingly young student, a candidate for a doctorate, and perhaps he played for the college: the shoulders were very heavy. The hair was very sleek and long, the eyes large, the lips pursed, and he had no mannerisms. There was about him a kind of quietness such as you will find among people who have lived much alone. But this quietness was delusory. It was true enough, and almost tangible, but it went oddly with the young student who seemed to be, not the giver of the party and the equal of Emperors, but a young man who had strayed by accident from a university campus. He was fifty-three and looked twenty.

Unaccountably, the room filled up. His wife came in, wearing black slacks and a sweater, and she said *"Nin hao?"* in greeting, with a classical Pekingese accent, and suddenly you realized that her long face possessed more beauty and expression than the face of the considerably more famous Mme. Chiang Kai-shek; also, she brought with her the scent of the flowers she had been gathering in the uplands. Chu Teh came in, limping a little, for the water in Yenan has a strange effect on the bones of the legs—I observed twenty to thirty peasants who limped in the same way. He had the face of a wise peasant and smiled broadly. God knows how many other generals there were at this time. It was like the opening scene of Tolstoy's *War and Peace*: you were continually expecting the princes and generals to enter, forgetting that they had entered a few minutes ago, disguised as university students and peasants.

The major-domo—a soldier in a faded gray tunic, wearing rice-straw sandals—announced that dinner was ready in the room behind the faded curtain. We sat down to the blackwood tables piled high with chicken soup, huge loaves of soft white unleavened bread, sweet rice, millet, and tomatoes which glowed like small fires in the darkening room. Behind us there were photographs on the wall of Mao, Chu Teh, Attlee, Truman, Stalin, and Chiang Kai-shek. All the photographs were thick with dust.

Mao began speaking in a surprisingly low voice, smiling at Chu Teh, whose harsher voice growled in reply. One by one the people in the room seemed to disappear in the thick wheeling shadows, until the electric light from the American generator on the other side of the river clicked on, blinding us all in its yellow glare. The sun sets quickly in North China. There is a final flash of sunset some minutes after the sun has gone down, then the valley is given over to the landscapes of the moon. Wolves howled, and sometimes, through the thin walls, we heard the gun butt of a soldier, or a distant command.

In embroidered blue gowns, two old scholars were sitting at the table. One of them had been Mao's teacher years before. This small man, whose forehead resembled a brown egg and whose eyes resembled black coals, with a small threadbare beard, was at least seventy: delicate, precise, attentive, speaking with a soft Peking drawl. He looked as though he belonged to a different race altogether. He had come in the same airplane that brought me to Yenan, and when we fell into air pockets over the Shensi mountains, he continued to fan himself as though nothing so irresponsible as an airplane would deflect him from the purpose of traveling in comfort. Now he asked Mao questions about the Long March, and shook his head in wonder. "Yes, yes, a strange journey—and the airplanes, what about the airplanes?" "We were afraid at first," Mao answered. "Then they no longer frightened us at all." Chu Teh was drinking an eggcupful of rice wine. Peng Teh-huei was eating cheesecurd—he was still troubled by ulcers. Mme. Mao smiled. The American major began to take photographs by flash-bulb. Mao went on talking about the Long March, lost among his own legends, his voice rising and becoming gradually more animated, losing its feminine quality, his long fingers making expressive gestures over the salad bowl.

"And what was the strangest thing of all?" The old professor leaned forward, a delightful expectancy written all over the delicate thin face.

Mao thought for a moment. "I suppose it was the fishes," he said. "We came to places where so few people had been before that if you waded into the river, the fishes would leap into your hands."

I said, with the hope of bringing him away from fishes: "Lao Tzu was of the opinion that government should be as easy as the cooking of little fishes. Do you agree?"

He answered: "There should be no government—the people should rule. And in the Communist areas you may be sure they rule themselves."

A little later he returned to the Long March. "There will be many Long Marches in the future."

"So the war goes on?"

"It must, unless the Kuomintang allows the people to rule." It was a strange statement, the first intimation that the peace talks were breaking down. Something in the way he said the words sounded like doom. A week earlier, talking to Chu Teh, it seemed that a vast hope of peace ruled in Yenan, that all problems might be solved, that soon enough there would be a coalition government, a government of the talents.

After dinner, when the generals and professors had departed and the last flash-bulb had exploded, I was left alone with him. He smiled, pushed his hands through his thick hair and sat down astraddle a small blackwood chair. I asked whether it would be possible to see more of his poems and told him how well received they had been in the South. Previously I had asked Yang Shan-k'un to make inquiries about them.

"I have been thinking," he answered, "and I have decided not to give them to you. They are *ma-ma-hu-hu*—so stupid. I only write poetry to amuse myself. Would you like me to write a poem on your visit to Yenan?"

"Yes, please."

"I shall see if I have time." After a while he said: "We are fighting tremendous battles now—it is not the time to write poetry." He was talking, I imagine, of battles which take place in the minds of people, for it was still the period of truce.

He talked about his poem called "The Snow." "Yes, it's a good poem. I wrote it in the airplane. It was the first time I had ever been in an airplane. I was astonished by the beauty of my country from the air—and there were other things."

"What other things?"

"So many. You must remember when the poem was written. It was when there was so much hope in the air, when we trusted the Generalissimo." A moment later he said: "My poems are so stupid—you mustn't take them seriously."

The light had gone out. A servant brought a rapeseed oil lamp, and in this light his face seemed to shine blood-red, heavy and drawn. I don't know why, but I had a feeling we were engaged in a kind of duel. He asked about the health of Wen Yi-tuo and Chang Shih-jo, two professors I knew in Kunming. "They are good men. If you see them, tell them how much we admire them." Then he asked about university life in the South, how the students lived, whether I thought they would be returning to Peking immediately, and then, because the conversation was running into generalities, I said something about the failure of the Spanish Republic in the civil war as it fought against the massed artillery of the Germans. I had been there. Once in the distance I had seen the guns. The Kuomintang possessed heavy artillery: could the Chinese Communists fight against such heavy weapons?

The softness of the face turned to darkness. Even in the blood-red light of the lamp (there were some chemicals in the oil which turned the flame scarlet), he resembled a student, with the gentleness of a student, but now the voice changed timbre, and there was a kind of inflexible sadness in the gaunt features: the lines had grown hard, and it was like a face of lead, as heavy as lead. He said: "Spain is not China. There were only 8,000,000 people fighting against Franco, but the Chinese liberated area numbers a population of 130,000,000. The Spanish Republic fought for three years. We have fought for twenty-one years. But from the beginning up to now we have desired peace and we do not want this war to be prolonged."

He went on: "There are some people abroad who are helping the Kuomintang to fight with their offer of ammunition. These supplies should be stopped, and the democratic people of other countries should oppose the sending of ammunition to the Kuomintang. There are people abroad who do not want and do not approve of democracy in this country. These people are acting with the consonance of the reactionaries in China. Let them know that whatever happens, if we are faced with mechanized war, we shall fight on if necessary with our hands and feet." At that moment he made a violent gesture, throwing out his clenched hands and feet, scowling at the invisible enemies across the seas who were responsible for the killing of his soldiers. Then he grew very quiet and said: "Have you any criticisms?"

"About what?"

"About Yenan."

I said there were two. In all the government offices I had seen there were maps of China, but no maps of the world; and the Yenan radio was still behaving with an extraordinary violence, the same kind of violence which had long ago betrayed the Kuomintang broadcasts from Nanking. "Why do you curse one another in a period of armistice?"

He said: "About the maps—we shall learn in time. Remember we are learning all the time. About the radio—it is mostly for internal consumption. Also, we have to scream at them because they scream at us. They are entirely hateful. That's why we are fighting. We can't have this endless corruption and the killing of soldiers who have surrendered." The last accusation had been made with great bitterness by Chu Teh. The Communists said they captured as many prisoners as possible, for they could use them; and there were sufficient reports that the Kuomintang simply murdered prisoners out of hand. It was this which hurt most.

I asked when there would be peace, for it was clear that the armistice could only survive by a miracle.

"When the people rule," he answered. He had a way of saying *ming-sheng*, the people's rule, which was like the sudden, startling pealing of a bell. He said quickly: "The people who are fighting against us don't want to realize democracy at all."

The duel became more intense later. "There seems," I said, "to be one—and only one—solution for the problem of civil war." This was that the leaders should retire from the scene. They were incrusted with legends. Mao himself, Chu Teh, Peng Teh-huei had almost ceased to be human beings. They were regarded with the awe generally reserved for gods. It was the same with Chiang Kai-shek and his immediate entourage. "The best, surely, is a government of the ordinary talents, without geniuses." I spoke of how in ancient Greece as soon as politicians became too popular they were exiled. Chu Teh had been responsive to the argument, saying with a kind of peasant gravity: "Perhaps you are right. If it would help China, and if legends are dangerous, I am prepared to go." He had, I learned later, discussed the strange suggestion with Mao by telephone. Now Mao answered quickly and almost angrily: "I am no one. Why should I go? What can one man do? If the Generalissimo died, it would make no difference: the rotten social system would go on." Being the politician he is, he could hardly have given any other answer.

It was the end of the road. The theory of "no one," which lies deep in Chinese history, had him in its toils. He asked about England, saying first (which pleased me) that he had read some of her poets in translation. I said there was a social revolution in England on a scale never achieved before, and it seemed to me that Chinese communism and English socialism had something in common: certainly the program announced in *The New Stage* and *Coalition Government* did not differ widely from English practice. The English were nationalizing their heavy industries, and there were vast programs of social reform.

"Yes," he answered, "but they are taking over the heavy industries only because they can then put into operation a firmer export drive."

"Is that the only reason?"

"Of course. They are not truly Socialist."

I insisted that they were, for the announced aims of the English Socialists were to share the wealth of the country more equitably—"the share wealth party" is also the name of the Chinese Communists.

"If they are really Socialist," he went on, "how do you explain their foreign policy? They are still imperialists. They will never let India free."

I said they would, sooner than he believed.

He looked incredulous, almost as though he was talking to

an ignorant child, and changed the subject of conversation to pronunciation, asking how the word "India" was pronounced and repeating it several times. I had observed that he listened intently to the translator, but he also listened to my words, and he was evidently comparing them. He knew much more English than he was prepared to admit. He said: "There is one good thing about the English—they are not helping to extend the war in China. We shall remember that." He spoke fiercely against the French in Indo-China and the Dutch in Indonesia, and all the time there was that heavy, moody look on his face, such a look as I had seen in Spain when General Modesto complained about the German guns. The rapeseed oil lamp was gutting, throwing up hard little sparks of silvery flame. He was looking tired. He was a man who threw his whole energy into conversation, unconscious of anything else, unconscious even of the soldier with the dispatch case who had come in some moments before. Now he read the dispatches quickly, then he said: "Have you any more questions to ask. I'm tired."

"One more. How long would it take for the Chinese Communists to conquer China if the armistice breaks down."

"A year and a half."

He said this very simply and slowly, but with absolute conviction. Occasionally he had used the word "correct," and it was clear that he regarded this judgment as a "correct" summary. Then he rose, standing like a great bear in the lamplight, and when making a handshake he lifted his elbow high, as though to avoid the impact of a Western handgrasp. I asked once more about the poems. He smiled, and said: "We shall see about them." I saw him wandering up the road, the heavy shoulders, the blue-black, glossy hair, a bowed figure whose shoulders seemed to be streaming with blood from the blood-red lamp of the soldier who walked behind him in the night.

I did not see him again until the day I flew back to Peking. The sky was gray. The whole of Yenan was a gray puddle, the rain falling in torrents. He came to the airfield, wearing a drab blue cotton coat, blue trousers, a woolen scarf tied round his throat, and a workman's cap on his head. He looked almost unrecognizable. He was hardly distinguishable from the peasants on the field. He said: "I have come to see you safely off." He laughed and joked.

I asked for the last time about the poems and told him I had found two more to add to the collection.

"That makes how many?"

"Three."

He laughed again, the rain coursing down his face. "How did you get them?"

"The editor of *Liberation Daily* gave them to me." The propeller was revolving. "No poems?"

"No more for a little while."

As the airplane streaked over the airfield in the pounding rain, to rise above the dark pagoda and the river now flowing in torrents, Mao disappeared among the small knot of peasants on the field. Four hours later we were flying over the gold roofs of Peking.

The truce was still on. There was time to examine the poems, and put together whatever else could be learned about Mao and the arts.

The Wind and the Sand

We understand men best through their poetry and their sensitivity to the arts: and of everything that Mao has written, nothing is more revealing than his poems and his attitude toward the developing culture of China.

Those who are close to him say that they can never remember a time when he did not write poetry. He wrote verses as a boy, and kept on writing poems throughout the revolutionary wars. At meetings of the Soviet government in Yenan, he would write poems as other men wrote "doodles," and after the meeting was over there was always a rush to pick up the poems he had thrown haphazardly on the floor. What is curious about these poems is that they are written in the strict meters of classical Chinese prosody. There are no innovations, no experiments. His classical mind seems to recoil from the dangerous temptations of free verse. Publicly, he inveighs against all poetry which does not possess a social content and is not written according to the modern idiom. Privately, he is the master of a kind of classical verse which will probably remain, because it possesses qualities free verse can never acquire, and because it is perfectly possible, as he has proved,

to write clasical poetry with modern feeling, in the same way
that it is possible to write sonnets with modern feeling.
Speaking in May 1942, he declared: "Our primary duty
is, not 'to add flowers to the embroidery,' but 'to send coal to
the snowbound.'" Art must be placed wholly at the service of
the revolution; it can have no other purpose than to extol
and educate the peasants and the workers. In effect, he was
stating once again the necessity of socialist realism.

It is doubtful, however, whether Mao entirely believes
that art is a state weapon, and nothing more. Like hundreds
of thousands of Chinese, he is known to admire the Ch'ing
Dynasty novel *The Dream of the Red Chamber*, which describes the innumerable love affairs of a young aristocrat who
eventually becomes a Buddhist monk—a book written with
a superb delicacy and understanding of the movements of the
human heart. Man is not wholly a political animal. In birth,
childhood, marriage, and death he removes himself almost
entirely from the political arena. Mao is half prepared to accept a divergence between art and politics, but he insists that
there must be a synthesis between motive and effect, and the
motive can only be political. There are even moments when
he gives the impression of believing that all the art of China,
except the songs of the peasants and the works of a few recent proletarian writers, are nothing more than bourgeois
propaganda. It is a strange and probably untenable position,
for his own poetry has been deeply influenced by a T'ang
Dynasty poet who celebrated the imperial splendors of a decadent court.

Ts'en Ts'an, one of the major poets of the reign of the
Emperor Su Tsung, was born about 720 A.D. in the province
of Ho-nei. He was the friend of the greatest of all Chinese
poets, Tu Fu, who called him his "younger brother," and
who accompanied him on many journeys. He climbed high
in court circles, becoming censor and eventually governor of
Chia-chou. There was no evidence that he was ever a soldier,
yet he described battles, usually battles which had occurred
hundreds of years previously in the Han Dynasty, with a remarkable sense of movement. He was one of the very rare
Chinese poets who rejoiced in the poetry of war. He wrote a

famous poem on a Taoist monk who lived among the unscalable cliffs of a mountain and kept a dragon in a jar under his bed, and there are some delightful songs dedicated to a certain General Chao, who kept many dancing girls and won a fur coat at dice from the Black Khan. But the two poems, which are his chief claim to fame, are concerned wholly with the pleasures of hunting down the enemy in winter. In these frozen, romantic landscapes, to the sound of the jingling of coats of mail, the poet is perfectly at home. Because Mao's furious imagination is also at home in them—he quotes from them often, and he echoes them in his own poems—they should be quoted in full. The first describes a visit to a general commanding a frontier post near Kokonor. It was from this poem that Mao quoted to Edgar Snow the phrase about the trees of Peking resembling "ten thousand peach trees blossoming." The second describes the preparations for an advance by the same general against the Huns.

A Poem of Farewell

The north wind sweeps over the land, twisting and break-
   ing off the hoary grass:
The barbarian weather brings the fluttering snow of early
   August.
As though overnight a small wind came to make thousands
   of pear trees blossom.
These snowflakes slip through pearl curtains and wet the
   screens,
The fox fur no longer warm and the silk coverlet too thin,
Benumbed with cold, the general can hardly draw his horn-
   bow.
But the border guards must still wear their freezing armor,
And icy pillars a thousand feet high pile on the northern
   ocean,
While overcast clouds hang curdled for ten thousand li.
Amid the booming of pipes and the squeaking of flutes,
The orderlies drink a toast in honor of the returning guest.
The evening snow whirls thick on the gates of the camp,
And the wind fails to move the frozen red flag.
Then, at the north gate of Lun-tai, I bade you farewell,

You who will go on the drifts of snow of Tien Shan.
I lost sight of you when you turned beyond the cliff,
Leaving only the footprints of your horse behind.

Horsemen of the Great Szechuan Road

Behold, the horsemen are galloping along the Szechuan road
*   beside the snow-white sea,*
Sand stretches like prairie grass, so vast, and the yellowness
*   meets the sky.*
Here at Lun-tai, in late autumn, the wind howls at night.
A riverbed of broken stones as large as kettledrums
Is thrown up by the wind, and everywhere the air is full of
*   stones.*
The Huns pasture their fat horses on the yellow grass.
Westward among the gold hills smoke and dust are flying.
The Han general collects his forces against the western enemy.
All night he has not removed his coat of mail.
All night the army marches, weapons touching:
The wind's muzzle is a knife slashing the sky.
The manes of the horses are icicles, strings of cash turned to
*   ice,*
Five-petal flowers among the smoke clouds of sweat.
In the tent the general dips his pen in ice.
Ah, if the Huns heard of it would not their courage fail?
We—we know that they have no love for our short swords.
We—we know that the army awaits tidings of victory.

Mao's own poetry reflects a similar excitement, a similar
atmosphere, and a similar assurance of victory. There is nothing ambiguous in the poetry of Ts'en Ts'an, and there is a complete absence of the self-pity which occasionally characterises
Tu Fu. It is poetry direct and swift as an icicle.

Only three of Mao's poems have been widely published.
Of the collection of about seventy poems brought together
under the title *Wind Sand Poems* (*Feng Chien Tze*) very
little is known except that it includes a long poem called
"Grass," written in memory of the journey through the Grasslands, and a poem on his dead wife. The collection is known
to his intimates, but Mao has sedulously refused to publish

it. He says that the poems are not well written and he is afraid that people would read them only because he is chairman of the government.

The first of the three poems I was able to find was written when the Long March was coming to an end.

The End of the Journey

The sky is high, the clouds are winnowing,
I gaze southwards at the wild geese disappearing over the horizon.
I count on my fingers, a distance of twenty thousand li.
I say we are not heroes if we do not reach the Great Wall.
Standing on the highest peak of Six Mountains,
The red flag streaming in the west wind,
Today with a long rope in my hand,
I wonder how soon before we can bind up the monster.

Mao has been careful to explain that by "monster" he did not mean Chiang Kai-shek only. "I meant all the evils—the Japanese, the Kuomintang, the terrible social system." Nor should the red flag be taken to mean only the Communist flag, for here there is a deliberate confusion between the red flag and the red banner carried by the ancient Chinese generals. Mao delighted in such confusions in the same way that T'ang Dynasty poets would deliberately write poems about the border warfare of their time, while pretending to be writing about wars a thousand years earlier.

The second poem appears to have been written in a mood of tranquil rejoicing some time after the Red Army was settled in Shensi.

The Long March

No one in the Red Army fears the hardships of the Long March.
We looked lightly on the thousand peaks and the ten thousand rivers.
The Five Mountains rose and fell like rippling waves,
The Wu Meng mountains were no more than small green pebbles.
Warm were the sheer precipices when Gold Sand River dashed into them,

Gold were the iron-chained bridges over the Tatu River.
Delighting in the thousand snowy folds of the Min
*   Mountains,*
The last pass vanquished, the Three Armies smiled.

The geography of the Long March provides the necessary commentary on the names of the mountains and rivers in the poem; it is unnecessary to discuss them here. What is remarkable is the use of phrases like "the Three Armies," which were the number of armies possessed by the Chou Dynasty emperors, the traditional poetic name for the armies of the empire. In fact, at least four armies had taken part in the Long March. The third and fourth lines of the poem are almost contemptuously traditional. The poetic imagination, so carefully based on archaic sources, rises slowly, and it is only in the last four lines that we are made conscious of the poet's imaginative powers.

The significance of this poem lies in its desperate invocation of the *whole* of the long epic march across China, and it is precisely here that modern Chinese poetry fails. The great innovators, Ai Ching and Tien Ch'ien, who have changed the direction of modern Chinese poetry, are entirely incapable of these effects. Ai Ching has described the death of a trumpeter in three hundred lines. A T'ang Dynasty poet would have described the same death in two lines and made them more memorable. It is partly, of course, the use of names whose resonance gives depth to the poem: for the Chinese the Min Mountains have the same kind of heraldic significance as the vast profusion of foreign names which Milton derived from the Near East. Mao is talking of great deserts and deliberately employing the corpus of Chinese legends. They hover like enormous statues seen through the mists—his poems seem nearer because the legends are farther away—there is depth and a kind of permanence in the juxtaposition of the legendary past and the present. Then, too, he uses numbers as the mystics use them, with a complete sense of definiteness: "the thousand snowy folds" are immediately made tangible to us, though a geographical survey would reveal concrete differences. By being mathematically inexact, the poem acquires an emotional accuracy; the strict verse form gives it substance; rhyme is a prison, but the poet needs to imprison his imagination for fear that he will spill himself grotesquely through all the countries of the mind. In Chinese, too, even a phrase like "the Red Army" has connotations which are completely absent in the English. In Chinese, as in Russian, red is the adjective for spring, courage, the beauty and health of adolescence, without any connotations of communism.[1]

In "The Snow," written in August, 1945, while flying in an airplane between Yenan and Chungking, at a time when there seemed to be some hope that the Kuomintang and the Communists would form a truce, he wrote the most famous of all his poems. It shows signs of having been written under the strain of intense excitement. But Mao says he simply wrote the poem to while away the time, and to give a present to a friend he had not seen since 1927, who would be waiting at the airport. The friend allowed a copy of the poem to pass into the hands of the editor of *Ta Kung Pao*, and from that moment hundreds of Chinese, particularly in the Universities, came to feel a real respect for Mao as a poet. The poem attempts something which had rarely, if ever, been attempted before. With a full consciousness of the whole weight of Chinese history, and of his own position in it,

1. Red is the proverbial color of joy in China. It is also the color which represents great dignity. The face of an emperor or a sacred personage is painted red on the Chinese stage, but so too is the face of the heroine. Red was the imperial color of the Chou dynasty. It is also the color associated with sex: the famous novel *The Dream of the Red Chamber* immediately suggests to a Chinese by its title a dream of sexual devotions. Usually, death is denoted by white, but the death of an old man who has many descendants is always celebrated with red. Oddly enough, red sometimes signifies death. On the Chinese stage death is denoted by a red flag or a red cloth thrown over the face. The particular value attached to the name "the Red Army" by the Chinese is something which should have been studied and elucidated. The Kuomintang armies never had a name comparable with this; and though it was Chiang Kai-shek who ordered that the Communist Army should be called the Eighth Route Army, his own armies never acquired the peculiar luster which the Communists succeeded in shedding over this name.

Mao had tried to write a poem which would embrace the whole of Chinese legend and Chinese history in a moment of time:

The Snow

In this north country in the flaming wind
A thousand acres are enclosed in ice,
And ten thousand acres in whirling snow.
Behold both sides of the Great Wall—
There is only a vast desolation left.
On the upper and lower reaches of the Yellow River
Only a great tumbling of waves.
The silver serpents are dancing on the mountains,
The winter elephants career on the plains:
We desire to compare our height with the skies.

O wait for the pure sky!
See how charming is the earth
Like a red-faced girl clothed in white!
Such is the charm of these mountains and rivers
Calling innumerable heroes to vie with each other in pursuing
    her.

The Emperors Shih Huang and Wu Ti were hardly lettered,
The Emperors T'ai Tsung and T'sai Tsu were barely
    chivalrous,
For a whole generation Genghis Khan was a favorite of
    Heaven,
But he knew only how to bend his bow at the eagles.
All have passed away—only today are there men of great
    feeling.

What is surprising is that the poem is almost a love poem addressed to the Chinese earth, and there is even a hint of sexuality in the description of the "red-faced girl clothed in white," for everything about the description is ambiguous, and the lines could be translated in many different ways. There is a further hint of sexuality in "the silver serpents dancing on the mountains," for the serpent has an obvious sexual meaning in Chinese, though here they may well be the mountains themselves or the smoke-wreaths seen from the airplane. As often happens in Chinese poetry, there are varying depths of meaning, yet these different meanings meet at a point of fusion, and the implication is clear—there is a compact with the past for the sake of a future inheritance, and a proud belief that the time has come when the Chinese will be masters of their own land. What is certain is that Mao deliberately attempted a poem which invokes the whole past history of his country, all its legends and all its landscapes, a poem comparable in its intensity with Hölderlin's "Patmos," where the whole of European history and legend is placed in the fire of poetry, seen through the flames and made to glow permanently in a moment of time. The poem is an astonishing achievement, for in the shortest number of words he had produced the most complete picture of the Chinese scene, and the method was peculiarly his own; for the poet had built up slowly the vivid portrait he desired to convey, and crowned it in the last line of all, and this method is something altogether new in Chinese poetry, which knows few climaxes comparable to these. Mao still refuses to publish his poetry, and it is sad to reflect that some of the best poetry now being written in China may well remain in manuscript.

There are probably deep-seated reasons for his refusal to publish the romantically entitled *Wind Sand Poems*. He knows, as all Chinese poets do, how much of a man's character is revealed in his poetry. He has always been secretive, always a little apart, exalted above the crowd. His insistence that the modern artist must mingle with the crowd and derive his roots from the broad masses of the people is perhaps only a measure of his own conscious distance from people. Though he talks with everyone quietly and naturally, no one is ever for a moment forgetful of that distance which always arises between those who have never wielded authority and those who wield it daily.

Meanwhile he has stated publicly that he regards all experiments in the old forms of Chinese poetry as doomed to failure; he has given his benediction to the new forms, which he cannot write and does not intend to write. At Yenan he showed a very real respect for the Yunnanese peasant-poet, K'e Chung-ping, who wrote, during a long imprisonment in

Shanghai, an immense epic called *Wind Fire Mountain*, describing a mysterious journey by the expropriated peasants and the Red Army to a mountain where all lived in safety—a poem curiously prophetic of the beginnings of the Red Army at Chingkanshan.[2]

"THE WHITE-HAIRED WOMAN"

Mao also immersed himself in the production of plays, devising new situations in the traditional drama and sometimes rewriting the old plays altogether. He is said to have suggested the story of the play *The White-Haired Woman* (*Pai Mao Nu*). He may even have been one of the six anonymous persons who wrote it. There were many variant passages, and some of these he is certainly responsible for. The play was by far the most popular of all the plays performed in the Communist territory during the war. The fact that his own name is part of the title is of some considerable significance.

The main outlines of *The White-Haired Woman* are exceedingly simple. Mostly, the story is one of unrelieved horror. Hsi-erh, the daughter of a farmer, is waylaid by the landlord's agent, Mo Jen-chih, and forced to enter a landlord's household as a maidservant in payment of her father's debts. The landlord's mother torments her. Dissatisfied with her cooking of lotus-seed soup, she flares into a temper and spikes the girl's tongue with a sharp metal pipe-cleaner. Hsi-erh is raped by the landlord's son. Fear of reprisal by the villagers makes the landlord decide to kill her. She is trussed up and hidden in a closet, from which she escapes with the help of another maidservant. Then she decides on flight. As soon as she has climbed over the wall, the dogs bark, her flight is discovered, and she is pursued by the landlord's agent. On the bank of a river they find her sandal and believe she has been drowned. The play takes place in the dead of winter, snow

2. Some translations of the poetry of K'e Chung-ping are given in my *China Awake*, New York, 1947.

falling and the river in flood. But the girl has not been drowned. Pregnant, she hides in a cave, where she lives on wild fruit, grass roots, and the sacrificial offerings from a nearby temple. She gives birth to her child, and her hair turns completely white. At this stage there comes rumors that the Eighth Route Army is approaching the village. The landlord is frightened. He makes a special pilgrimage to the temple to seek the advice of the gods. Will the village be spared? While he is kowtowing to the gods, he sees suddenly in the far distance a woman with white hair. He believes she is the Goddess of Mercy, and that she has come to him to predict that the village will not have to suffer the presence of the Eighth Route Army for long. Then the Red Army soldiers come on the scene. They adopt Hsi-erh, and tell her they are preparing to liberate her village. Thereupon she sings for them an astonishingly vibrant song of hope and rejoicing, just as previously she had sung the heart-rending songs of grief which make the play memorable. The landlord, the son, and the agent are all arrested by the Eighth Route Army, and their trial takes place before the whole village. The punishments differ according to different variants of the play. Generally, the landlord's son is sentenced to death and the agent is sentenced to imprisonment for ten years. Finally the village lands are divided up, and it is made quite clear that the landlord's family must receive its due apportionment.

The story is wildly melodramatic and is written with something of the fervor of *Uncle Tom's Cabin*; but it did reflect the behavior of the landlord class, and since China is essentially a country where melodrama is a commonplace of life, the story stated the peasants' relationship with the landlords in a way which could be immediately understood. The stroke of genius lay in the invention of the White-Haired Woman singing her wild songs of grief and hope, her face hidden behind her hair. Quickly, with a few heavy strokes, the authors of the play had invented a peculiarly Chinese symbol of oppression.

There are mysteries here, as elsewhere. Anyone reading the histories of Chinese revolutions is struck with the insistence upon "hair." The Taiping rebels called themselves "the long-haired ones" (*chang mao*). The queue was a sign of Manchu domination. Mao's name, and the drama which swept through Red China, giving impetus and symbolism to the revolution, employ the same character. It would be dangerous to believe that the choice is altogether fortuitous in every case. Probably the answer to the riddle lies in one of the classical Confucian axioms: "Not a hair of the head must be touched," where the word "hair" is simply a symbol serving for the whole human body. It is in this sense that the White-Haired Woman comes to symbolize all the sufferings of the human race.

This is dangerous ground, and *The White-Haired Woman* was a dangerous drama. Because it concentrated an extremely pathetic theme with an obscure mythology, it tapped powerful forces in the human soul, and those who watched it felt themselves in need of some violent, physical action which would resolve their own inner conflicts. Landowners, even when they were in good standing with the Communists, were in danger during performances of the play. In *China Shakes the World*, Jack Belden has related how, during a peculiarly moving incident of the drama, the audience would rise and scream the terrible word *"sha,"* meaning "Kill," as though nothing would satisfy them except the execution of the actor on the stage.[3]

Hundreds of other dramas were written in the Red areas, but none of them possessed the force or the validity of this drama, which Mao is said to have outlined after hearing the story of a girl who had taken to the hills when her whole family was wiped out by the Kuomintang.

THE NEW MYTHOLOGY

A new mythology was emerging. It was characteristic of Mao that he should attempt to canalize all the resources of mythology. He understood the enormous power of the story-tellers who wandered over the Shensi countryside, with their strange clappers and bells attached to their knees and elbows

3. Jack Belden, *China Shakes the World*, New York, 1949, p. 210.

—for they provided their own musical accompaniment. It was Mao who insisted that the ancient stories should be preserved, but all the heroes should be magically transformed into peasants and workers. The innumerable *chien-hsia*, the stories written about the ancient sword-wielding heroes, assumed their new dress, but the heroism of the stories remained. It was the same process which enabled the Anglo-Saxon monks to rewrite whole passages of *Beowulf*.

In the same way Mao concerned himself with even more primitive symbols. The *yang-k'o* were originally love songs sung at harvest to a simple dance, the men and women facing each other, then interweaving among one another. Mao suggested that this simple dance should be broadened to include a much wider range of experiences. Was it possible that the whole socialistic revolution might be represented by a dance? Experiments were made. They proved to be astonishingly successful. Within the framework of the dance, short plays were introduced. All these plays began with the dance and ended with the dance, but it was the central play itself which carried the message. There were hundreds of these plays. They rarely lasted more than twenty minutes. They were simple, highly colored; in human terms they said no more than the slogans of the time—"Be hygienic," "Learn to write," "The Eighth Route Army is our friend." But it was precisely the fact that the slogans could be interpreted in such simple terms which made them politically valuable.

Most of the credit for inventing the modern *yang-k'o* goes to Mao. His dramatic imagination was always seizing upon these dramatic simplifications: in slogans, in wall-newspapers, in the presentation of a political case, in the drama, and in the dance. Sometimes such simplifications are dangerous.

Essentially the aesthete, Mao set himself deliberately against aetheticism. He did not always succeed. In his speeches on art and literature delivered in Yenan in the spring of 1942, he urged upon writers the necessity of writing for the masses, and for the masses alone. Their heroes should be "the broad masses of the people, the Communist Party, New Democracy and Socialism." Fadeyev's *The Nineteen* was proposed as a universal model. It is a novel concerning a small band of anonymous guerrillas: there are no *persons*.

In the medieval Chinese novel the person is treated with all his individual characteristics revealed, and his individual fate becomes a matter of deep concern to the reader. Mao proposed an anonymous, universal novel—the novel produced by many people, like Gorky's celebrated attempt to include within two covers all the incidents which took place on a single day in Russia. He could point to the new dramas which were being performed in Yenan: twenty or thirty people had sometimes contributed to the writing of them. Surely there was a mass epic, a kind of novel which would present the people to the people? But he was more comprehensible when he spoke of the writers who are "heroes without a battlefield," striking attitudes, or when he objected violently to the "poster-and-slogan" style of so much contemporary Communist writing, though by deliberately encouraging the use of slogans, and inventing them—he invented thirty to celebrate the assumption of power in Peking—he was himself partly responsible for the new style.

Lenin shook his head and disapproved of the wild "slogan-poetry" of Mayakovsky. Something very similar happened in Yenan when Mao found himself at a loss to understand the poetry of the young Hopeh poet, Tien Ch'ien, who wrote with a harsh violence, making each word sound like a drumbeat. On this poet Wen Yi-tuo wrote his famous essay on "The Drummer of the new Age." But Mao preferred the peasant songs of K'e Chung-ping and the poems of Ai Ching, which were deeply influenced by the contemplation of the paintings of Van Gogh. Even in the theater, it was noticed that he attended the performances of the classical Chinese dramas in preference to the naturalistic dramas put on by the modernistic playwrites of the Lu Hsun Academy. He approved of waving peacock feathers and heavily embroidered silk costumes, the clanging of bells, the sudden explosions of saltpeter as the gaudy silken walls of stage fortresses fell down. It is possible that on the brightly lit stage of his imagination Mao sees the forces of the world at work as they appear on the Chinese stage: highly magnified, enormously colored, grotesquely beautiful. In China, stage villains are not simply villainous: they are terribly, remorselessly, despotically, and perpetually evil, beyond hope of grace. For him Chiang Kai-shek, American "militarists," the denizens of Wall Street must have something of the appearance of the huge, buskined, white-faced villains of the Chinese stage.

Though he has had an enormous influence on the developing culture of China, there are odd gaps in Mao's understanding of the arts. He is insensitive to music, and showed little interest in the amazing sculptures to be found all over Shensi. Hundreds of superbly beautiful stone Buddhas stood in the cave-temples at Yenan. He allowed them to melt away in the steam from the printing-presses installed in the caves, though it would have been a simple matter to direct the steam outside. Passionately excited by China's past glory, he thought of this glory in terms of poetry, history, philosophy, and the novels, and he saw it in those places which have been sanctified by "great events," but sculpture and painting are largely outside the field of his sensitivity.

His most aesthetic achievements lay in his guerrilla campaigns, the small armies under his command performing a dangerous and relentless dance around the enemy's divisions —a dance not unlike the sword-dances on the Chinese stage. Even his signature dances, the characters having a wild, curving ebullience, and perhaps it is no accident that part of his signature closely resembles the serpentine curve shown in the map of the Third Annihilation Campaign. His signature, based on T'ang Dynasty models, flows like water; Chiang Kai-shek's signature, based on the classic Han Dynasty script, is squat and square like a toad. A Chinese, comparing their signatures, would know which would conquer the other.

In Yenan, Mao was compelled to come to grips with the arts. To the cave-city there came many of the finest Chinese poets, musicians, and painters. It was characteristic of Mao that he should have praised most highly the engraver Ku Yuan, who had been deeply influenced by Käthe Kollwitz, and it was Mao who suggested that the artist should engrave new designs for the door gods, those fierce guardians who have been pasted since time immemorial on the doorposts of Chinese houses, with bearded faces and uplifted swords. "How shall I draw them?" Ku Yuan asked. "You know, I don't believe there really are any gods," Mao answered. "Make them like peasants."

Philosophers came to Yenan. Sometimes Mao attended discussions, saying that he wanted simply to listen, urging them to speak and promising there would be no punishments, all that was necessary was that these matters should be debated at length. What were the foundations of art? One of the professors at the university answered: "It must be—there can be no other foundation but love." "What kind of love?" Mao asked. "The love that springs from the heart. Communism is love." "No, comrade, it is not so simple," Mao answered. "Communism is not love. Communism is a hammer which we use to destroy the enemy." Some months later he returned to the subject again in the famous lectures on "Art and Literature." He said:

The love that we writers and artists with our intellectual background bear for the proletariat stems from the fact that society has forced on us the same destiny it has forced on the proletariat. Nowhere in the world does love exist without reason nor does hatred exist without reason. As for love of mankind, there has been no such all-embracing love since the human race was divided into classes. The ruling classes have preached universal love, as did Tolstoy. But no one has ever been able to practice it because it cannot be attained in a class society.

A true love of mankind is attainable, but only in the future when class distinctions will have been eliminated throughout the world. Classes serve to divide society: when classes have been eliminated, society will be united again. At that time the love of mankind will flourish, but it cannot flourish now. Today we cannot love the Fascists nor can we love our enemies. We cannot love all that is evil and ugly in the world. We must aim to eliminate them.[4]

At the same time he had no patience for the proletarian writers who only described the "dark side" of life. "We should lean to the side of the proletariat, help them and educate

4. Mao Tse-tung, *Art and Literature*, New York, 1950, p. 39.

them. Why should we not extol the people, who are the creators of history and civilization?" So he spoke of "the long and sometimes even painful tempering process" by which the writers, accustomed to intellectual comforts, gradually learn the necessary discomforts of writing about people as they really are.

Here and elsewhere there are insoluble problems. The precise duties of the artist remain unknown, and must be, as long as he is in touch with forces over which he has no control: the unconscious plays too great a part in the mind of the artist to allow him to be rigidly controlled. A novel like John Steinbeck's *The Grapes of Wrath* obeys none of the tenets of socialist realism, it gropes too fervently after the patterns of suffering; and it is with suffering that the artist is immediately concerned. The human soul with all its complexities may be forgotten in the contemplation of the abstractions called "the broad masses of the people" and "communism"; and the tendency of the Russian novelists to interpret types rather than people is only one of the misfortunes of bureaucracy.

But there are wise things in Mao's lectures on art and literature. When he says: "The cleanest people in the world are the workers and peasants: even though their hands are soiled, and their feet smeared with cow dung, they are cleaner than the bourgeoisie," he is saying something that needs to be said, something which might reasonably be written on all the walls of all the Hollywood studios. And again: "How can we possibly talk about creating literature and art unless we learn the language of the people?" This, too, might be carefully taken to heart in Hollywood, which continually presents an America that is only a shadow of the real, pulsating and magnificently energetic America we know.

Mao has observed American films, studying them carefully with an interpreter by his side, deducing from them an en-entirely erroneous picture of American capacities. During 1945 and 1946, between thirty and forty American films were flown to Yenan for the benefit of the Yenan Observation Group, a small nucleus of Americans who lived within a stone's throw of Mao's cave among the Shensi hills.

He delighted in *Grapes of Wrath,* shuddered at Betty Grable, and was particularly interested in a strange picture called *A Walk in the Sun,* which showed a small column of Americans wandering aimlessly over the Italian countryside until they found themselves attacking a farmhouse. He observed their weapons, their behavior, and the peculiar way in which they advanced upon the farmhouse. "Do Americans really fight like that?" he asked. It was not the first time that the showing of an American film had done incalculable harm to American interests.

Meanwhile, Mao holds all the arts of China in his hands. Lenin had neither the learning nor the inclination to assume the role of *transformer* of culture. Mao, far more widely read and with a comparable subtlety of mind, has clearly determined to accept the position thrust on him, and no one can foresee the changes in the basic structure of Chinese culture which will derive ultimately from his will. In 1942, in a short paper called "Correcting Unorthodox Tendencies in Learning," he summed up his opinions on the new kind of writing demanded by the times. He castigated those who pretended that writing was easy. No, it was immensely hard, it demanded all the resources of the writer, and it was the writer's duty to be humble before his art. "Think twice," he said. "Always think twice." The phrase, like so many other of his phrases, is purely Confucian. The greatest enemy was the empty phrase, the words without substance, the endless idiotic perorations, "like the foot-bindings of a lazy old woman, long and foul-smelling." It was perhaps characteristic of him that the next greatest enemy should be described as "he who makes a false show of authority in order to instill terror." He quoted from Lu Hsun: "Insult and threat are certainly not to be considered as fighting." The third enemy was "shooting without a target" or "playing the lute to the cow." So it goes on; and the extraordinary argument, with its dull and ambiguous title, becomes an ironical version of the famous "eight-legged essays" candidates in the ancient imperial examinations wrote in their examination cells.

Once, receiving some young soldiers who asked him for his favorite verses, he answered: "When Lu Hsun lay dying, he wrote some verses, and everything is there, all the revolution, all our turmoils. Listen:

> *O raise your head in utter defiance,*
> *Stare coldly at the thousand enemies.*
> *Remember to bow your head to the earth*
> *As the cow submits to the suckling child.*

The revolution is for the young—that's what we have been working for, and you are the suckling children." He seemed to be thinking of his student days in Peking, when he met Lu Hsun briefly, the time when Chen Tu-hsiu was editing the *New Youth* and the whole nation seemed on the verge of a youthful apocalypse. Now the apocalypse was coming.

The Conquest
of China

When the Japanese war with China was coming to an end in 1945, Generalissimo Chiang Kai-shek delivered a broadcast speech to the nation in which he made extraordinary claims for the party he represented. "The Kuomintang," he said, "is the historical party of national revolution. It overthrew the Manchu dynasty. It destroyed Yuan Shih-kai, who wanted to be emperor. It utterly defeated the militarists who followed Yuan Shih-kai. It brought about national unification. It achieved the removal of the unequal treaties. It led the country in the eight-year-old struggle with the Japanese. Finally, it is the party of liberation and progress."

If any one of these statements had been entirely correct, it is probable that the Kuomintang would have retained its

power. Unfortunately, none of them was correct. The Kuomintang did not overthrow the Manchus, or Yuan Shih-kai,
or the militarists who followed. All these had been overthrown
by popular movements which the Kuomintang had followed
rather than led. The removal of the unequal treaties was a
bribe offered by Great Britain and America to keep the Kuomintang from making a separate peace with Japan. Nor had
the Kuomintang led the nation throughout its eight-year old
war with Japan, for after the third battle of Changsha, early
in 1942, the Kuomintang completely failed to resist the
enemy. As the war progressed it had become so reactionary
and corrupt that any talk of liberation and progress was merely
ironical. By the end of the war the Kuomintang was an over-
ripe fruit on a tree, waiting to be plucked by the Communists.

Chiang Kai-shek's speech, delivered on a sweltering August day in Chungking, shortly before victory was announced,
was more interesting for its omissions than for its claims. It is
noteworthy that most of the claims related to military successes. He did not claim that he had freed the peasants from
excessive taxation or improved their social welfare, and he
made no reference to the perplexing increase in the number of
the Chinese Communists. He had decided long before the end
of the war to press on with his war against the Communists, and
in an incautious moment he had addressed his generals to the
effect that "now at last the time has come to destroy the Communists root and branch." He had hoped to accomplish the
conquest of China by the end of 1946. If he had read the
minutes of the Seventh Congress of the Chinese Communist
Party held in April 1945, the first since 1928 to be held on
Chinese soil, he might have paused. In 1937 there were
2,000,000 people in an area of 30,000 square miles living
under Communist rule. In 1945 there were 95,000,000 people
in an area of 300,000 square miles.

Chiang Kai-shek did not pause. There were reconnaissance
flights over Yenan by Kuomintang planes even during the
June truce. In the first week of July, Yenan was raided in
earnest by six P-47's and a B-24 Liberator. It was a month of
grim fighting. During the truce the armies had been held to

their fixed positions: now, like huge shadows racing across a sunlit landscape, they met and grappled, flung themselves upon one another in Manchuria, Kiangsu, and Anhwei, and General Marshall in despair could say: "We have done our best. There is almost nothing left that can be done." Now, as in 1919, when the Chinese students rose against the Treaty of Versailles, most of the blame was laid at the door of the Americans. Their popularity had once been great: now, when their popularity was in decline, they failed to take any remedial measures. Something was lacking, some fatal flaw was at work. Perhaps the reasons were not far to seek. It was simply that America had failed to assume its historical task, had failed to lead the Asiatic revolt. Too many of the soldiers and officers sent to China were ignorant of social forces. Coming from an artificial, complex, and industrial civilization, they had little but contempt for the slow-moving Chinese peasants, and they could not understand how these same peasants in battle captured so much American equipment. July was a month of horror. Slowly, dramatically, it announced the opening of an Attic tragedy.

All through his active life Chiang Kai-shek had been concerned to safeguard his rear. While the fighting between the Communist and Kuomintang armies continued, he struck out against the liberal elements in the country. Within a few days of each other Li Kung-po and Wen Yi-tuo were killed. Li Kung-po had been one of the famous "Seven Gentlemen" who stood out against Japanese demands in Shanghai in 1936, and had been imprisoned for his pains. Wen Yi-tuo, a professor of classics at Lienta University in Kunming, a poet and a born leader, had been elected to the Consultative Assembly which was to be held in Nanking in August. Others, like Kuo Mo-jo, had been attacked shortly before. Once again there was the promise of a reign of terror. When the Communists suggested that the only solution was the withdrawal by both sides to the lines held in January, Chiang Kai-shek answered with the oft-repeated claim that he was determined to smash the Communists within five months. The war was gathering momentum, and by January 1947 both Mao and

Chiang Kai-shek declared that there was no hope of further mediation: the war must be fought out to a solution.

The solution came much sooner than anyone had expected. From Nanking came orders that Yenan must be occupied. It was thought that the occupation of the Communist capital would demonstrate Kuomintang power to lay the Communist ghost. In fact, the ghost was never more alive. Yenan was occupied. Mao and Chu Teh simply saddled their ponies and wandered toward the Great Wall, to find a harbor later in the obscure railway center of Shihchiachuang. At the end of June the Red Army crossed the Yellow River, and in September new Communist laws concerning agrarian policy were passed. They had been written by Mao. Deliberately, as in his speech of December 15, 1944, he restated Communist policy toward the rich peasants. There was to be no feverish expropriation. "The peasant unions shall expropriate surplus animals, agricultural implements, houses, grain, and other property of the rich peasants. These shall be distributed to the peasants who are lacking and to other poor people, *and fur-thermore an equal share shall be distributed to the landlords."* It was a policy long hammered out in Yenan, and it was to re-main when the Communists had achieved power. Meanwhile, the Kuomintang wall was crumbling as though it was made of soft sand. By December, Mao could say: "Comrades, the turning-point has come."

It had come, indeed. No power on earth could now stop the flood. There was hardly any need to direct the war. Manchuria, once occupied by the Russians—who had played a devious game of removing industries existing there to Siberia while assisting the Chinese Communists by giving them captured Japanese rifles and machine guns—had become an arsenal; and Lin Piao's victories had become examples to be taught in textbooks.

Once again, for the third time, Mao retired almost com-pletely from the military direction of the Red armies. He was concerned with the political atmosphere, with a thousand problems of agrarian reform. At the Seventh Congress he had said: "Those comrades who have made mistakes, no matter how devious, grievous, and costly, if they admit their mistakes honestly and if they have analyzed their mistakes and learned from them, are better leaders than men who are untried." He was in a mood to forgive. The agrarian reforms were meeting unexpected obstacles. Minor cadres exceeded their powers. They had to be corrected, taught humility toward the people, shown that the revolution could only succeed, the armies could only make headway, if there was co-operation between the Red Army and the peasants. Again and again through his speeches of this year there are these simple, almost childlike warnings against pride, against exceeding "the proper attitude toward the peasants, which should always be one of brother-hood."

Yenan was recaptured a year after the Kuomintang drove down the empty valley. By June 1948 Mao was claiming that during the second year of the Liberation War—it had begun, according to the Communists, in July 1946—they had annihilated 1,520,000 Kuomintang troops and enlarged the liberated areas to nearly a quarter of the total area of China.

A People's Assembly was convened in Shihchiachuang. Once again, as previously in April, Mao was more concerned with the agrarian revolution than with the inevitable progress of the war. He had said in April:

We spend altogether too much time in seeking out the hidden wealth of the landlords. No, comrades, this is not the way. In this the masses are wrong. All the correct opinions of the masses we must carry out loyally, but sometimes they are incorrect. You must understand that some of the middle peasants must be allowed to obtain more land than the average of the poor peasants generally. We do not advocate absolute egalitarianism. Our aim is only to destroy feudal exploitation, and we must place special attention on the middle peasants, we must allow them to work freely. The whole area where agrarian reform is possible cannot exceed 8 per cent of the rural communities, or 10 per cent of the rural population. In the old and in the semiliberated areas this figure may be reduced even further. We must remember, comrades, that the development of agricultural production is also the most important aim of the agrarian revolution, and as long as the middle peasants, the independent laborers, the professional men, and the peasants who have newly acquired riches do not engage in exploitation, or engage only slightly in exploitation, then they must be allowed their freedom.

Much had happened since the Autumn Harvest Uprising in 1927. Squarely, Mao placed himself on the side of the middle peasants against the rest.

But a new enemy was taking the place of the Kuomintang. Mao's armies fought with captured American equipment. Huge spoils had been gathered, but bitterness remained. He thundered against what he called American imperialism, and he saw no excuse for the American blunder in supporting the one party in China which opposed revolution. On November 7, 1948, he placed American imperialism before the Kuomintang as the main enemy of the Chinese Communists. He said: "The particular task of the Chinese Communists is to unite all revolutionary forces within the whole country, to drive out American imperialism, overthrow the reactionary rule of the Kuomintang, and establish a unified democratic people's republic in alliance with the Soviet Union."

Now, as winter came on and the Red armies came in sight of Peiping and fought into the outskirts of Changchun, the whole theory upon which Chinese communism reposed was due for change. Soon they would occupy immense cities. The order went out for an entirely new orientation, a shift from a rural, agrarian revolution to an urban, industrial revolution. "The war of resistance is really a peasant war," Mao had said in 1942. Now he said: "We have it in our hands to use all the resources of industry."

THE DEBACLE OF THE KUOMINTANG

There occurred in 1949 a repetition of the revolution of 1911, when thousands of Manchus simply surrendered to the revolutionary armies without putting up a fight. This time it was the Kuomintang generals, long displeased with Chiang Kai-shek's organization of the war, who for the most part went over and calmly accepted the new dispensation. There was, however, one essential difference between the Manchus and the Kuomintang generals. The Manchus had possessed only cumbrous nineteenth-century weapons. The Kuomintang generals possessed the most modern equipment from America, and the spoils which the Chinese Communists had been waiting for were vastly more powerful than they had ever dared to hope.

During 1949, the Kuomintang lost its initiative beyond recovery. No one any longer believed in the star of Chiang Kai-shek. The dynamic which had brought the Kuomintang to power in the Northern March of 1927 had at last perished. Without loyal soldiers, without a strategy of defense, without will power, and without any sustaining belief in its own mission, it was slowly dying. A peripatetic government remained, continuing to exist like the branches of a fallen oak which put forth shreds of green without knowing that the tree is dead. The tree was hollow, and diseased; and few people in China could regret its passing.

The astonishing victories of 1949 were not wholly or essentially due to the brilliant military strategy of the Communists. Chiang Kai-shek defeated himself. His battle plans were unrealistic, and like Hitler he was disposed to order that towns should be held "to the last man," regardless of what the military situation demanded. As usual, he paid little attention to his foreign military advisers. He conceived an immense plan of defense in depth, and it was characteristic of him that he should resurrect the same strategy of retreat he had employed against the Japanese. He even thought he could hold his line indefinitely beyond the Ichang gorges, basing his command once again in Chungking. He never knew which way the wind would turn, and desperately attempted to retrieve a situation already lost.

One by one the provincial capitals fell. In the middle of January, Tientsin fell, to be followed a fortnight later, after prolonged negotiations, by Peking. Nanking fell on April 23. On the next day, five hundred miles away, fell Taiyuan, the capital of Shansi province. Hangchow fell a week later, to be followed in a few days by Hankow, Wuchang, and Hanyang, the three conjoined cities which had seen the birth of the 1911 revolution. Sian, the capital of Shensi, fell almost immediately afterward. The breathless pace continued. In five days, toward the end of May, Nanchang, which had seen the birth of the Red Army, and Shanghai, which had been the greatest industrial center of the whole of China, surrendered with only token fighting.

After the fall of Tsingtao, early in June, Chiang Kai-shek began to regroup his forces, and there were signs that he intended to launch a counteroffensive, but the desultory fighting in the summer ended only with retreats, which the Generalissimo excused on the grounds that he was once more buying time in exchange for space. In August, Fukien was overrun, and Lanchow, the capital of Kansu, at the other extremity of China, fell a few days after the capture of Fuchow. Sinkiang province surrendered in September, while most of Kwangtung, including Canton, was in the hands of the Communists by October. Kweiyang, the capital of Kweichow, and Kweilin, the capital of Kwangsi, fell in November, and on the last day of the same month fell the provisional capital, Chungking, though Chengtu was not to fall for nearly a month. Yunnan, Sikong, and Szechuan followed.

The series of uninterrupted victories read like a Napoleonic battle roll. The "soft underbelly" of south China split open, and generals who had sworn to die in defense of the Kuomintang saved their lives by leading their own troops to join the Red Army. Cheng Ch'en and Chen Ming-jen, who had fought against the Red Army in the annihilation campaigns, offered to lead their forces against Chiang Kai-shek. The redoubtable Ma Hung-kuei, whom they had fought in the Northwest, rode up to a Red outpost and surrendered almost as though he were making a journey to his private hunting-fields and desired to be accompanied by his new-found friends. General Lu Han, the Lolo tribesman, who had shared the rule over Yunnan with his half-brother for twenty years, surrendered almost as casually.

Almost alone the Kwangsi generals, who had possessed vast preserves in Central China, fought on stubbornly. Once again Mao had contrived that the initial battle should be the most damaging. The battle of Huai-hai, fought early in January, provided the break-through; the destruction of General

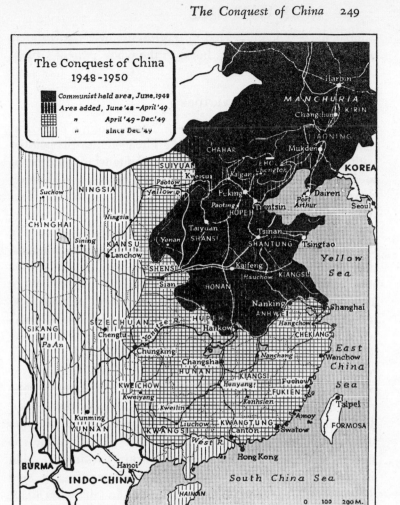

The Conquest of China
1948-1950

Communist held area, June,1948
Area added, June '48 –April '49
    "   April '49 – Dec.'49
    "   since Dec.'49

Pai Hsiung-hsi's forces in the middle of December by the New Fourth Army brought the campaign for the conquest of China to a virtual conclusion. At the beginning the Red Army was outnumbered five to one. For a brief while it fought large-scale guerrilla campaigns, but after the crossing of the Yangtse positional warfare was engaged in continually. It was not always necessary. A column of a hundred men entered Chungking and announced that it was in their hands at the same moment that the rear of the Kuomintang army left the city on its way to Chengtu. It was exactly as though the annihilation campaigns were being waged in reverse, not over the frontiers of Kiangsi and Kwangtung, but over the whole map of China.

THE PSYCHOLOGY OF VICTORY

Why had the victory come about? The Communists pointed with pride to their army and to the students who volunteered to do political work in the rear, to the twenty-year-old traditions of communism and to the military genius of Mao Tse-tung.

It is conceivable that the reasons were much simpler. The destinies of nations are not determined by military forces, they are determined by those undefined psychological forces which we know as legends: and now quite suddenly there arose the legend of Mao Tse-tung, the savior of China. "Do not suppose that Mao Tse-tung could be the 'savior' of China," wrote Edgar Snow shortly after his first meeting. "Nonsense. There will never be any one 'savior' of China." Edgar Snow's remark was perfectly understandable, and based on wide experience of the Chinese scene, but by 1949 it had lost its relevance. Suddenly there were portraits of Mao everywhere, even deep within Kuomintang territory. Sometimes the portraits stood together with a similar one of Chu Teh, but generally it stood alone. Soldiers went into battle with paintings of Mao on their red flags. Trains were provided with paintings of Mao thrown over the boilers like saddlecloths. In Shanghai there were portraits five stories high. Not all of them were prepared by the propaganda corps. They answered a psychological need of the people. Mao was shown with his head uplifted toward the rising sun, youthful and smiling. There had never been portraits of Chiang Kai-shek like this. Hitler scowled and accused from a million German walls; Chiang Kai-shek glared frostily; Stalin looked stern and demanding; only the portraits of Mao suggested a twenty-year-old youth awakening from a long dream, the new man, the savior.

In 1927 the playwright Tsao Yu produced a drama called *Peking Man*. It described the life of a decadent mandarin family caught up in interminable delicate quarrels in Peking.

Suddenly, bursting through the window, there comes the terrible, avenging image of the original owner of the Peking skull, a triumphant youth who is not in the least concerned with the problems of a declining mandarinate. He seizes the young daughter of the mandarin and disappears with her into the hills. The play, later banned by Chiang Kai-shek, achieved considerable success. It spoke of the new youthful China which had suffered sufficiently under the rule of senile warlords, and possessed an unappeased desire to escape from the ancient traditions. So it was now. With the arrival of Mao, there occurred an almost religious fervor, a recognition of religious resources, even a new religious ritual. The Communists had long employed the phrase *Fang Shen*, which occurs in Mencius and has the meaning of "renewing the body," though it meant more than this, for it included in its meaning a complete transvaluation, a total renewal of all the resurgent forces in China. Chiang Kai-shek had merely paid lip service to the idea of renewal; the Communists deliberately assumed new attitudes, deliberately invented new rituals, refused to make any compromise with the past, and turned their heads defiantly against the most sacrosanct customs. To misunderstand these psychological resources is to misunderstand the whole course of the Chinese revolution.

With the portraits of Mao as savior, there came the songs where he was openly greeted as "the savior." The most celebrated, sung to a lilting dance tune, begins with a line modeled on one of the most famous lines of the Confucian *Book of Songs*:

> Tung fang hung t'ai-yang sheng.
> Chung-kuo ch'u-lai i-go Mao Tse-tung.

> *The sun is rising red in the East.*
> *China has brought forth a Mao Tse-tung.*
> *He labors for the welfare of the people.*
> *Aiyayo, he is the people's great savior.*

> *The Communist Party shines like the sun,*
> *And wherever it shines there is light.*
> *Wherever there is the Communist Party,*
> *Aiyayo, there the people have freedom.*

Mao Tse-tung has a great love for the people:
He is the man who guides us along the pathway.
With him, we shall build a new China.
Aiyayo, he leads the people into the future.

Mao Tse-tung is a son of the Chinese earth:
He will lead us to fight the enemy.
There will come a time when we shall have mastery.
Aiyayo, all our enemies shall be beaten.

There were endless verses to this song. Every town or village added its quota of new lines. It was as though Mao was a living presence in places where he had never been, and which he may never have heard of. A wild and dangerous faith had been born: all problems could be solved by Mao. He would have been the first to reject such a claim, but the claim was seriously made by hundreds of thousands of people who saw in him "the people's savior." Such a faith may have conceivably been ill founded, but of its existence there is no doubt. Devotion had become as real as the air men breathed. In another song, nearly as popular as the one already quoted, he becomes the "victorious flag":

O, you are the bright sun and the flag of victory,
Long live our highly thought-of Mao Tse-tung.
We are happy to live in your age and learn from your example.
We will follow you and enter a new world,
Where there will be liberty and welfare for all.

Not only the songs but the names he received among the peasants reveal the peculiar quality of veneration in which he was held. Chiang Kai-shek was called *Ling Hsiu,* "the leader." Mao was called *Chiu Hsing,* "the saving star," a title which places him immediately among the legends, for three guardian stars protect the peasants from their high vantage point near the roof beams. It was out of such things: legends, the peasants' desire to own his land, "the broad masses of the people"—that phrase which was interminably repeated, acquiring an extraordinary resonance and depth of meaning —that Mao brought about the revolution.

It is important that the logic of the revolutionary process be understood. The tragic failure of the Kuomintang lay in the absence of any point of contact with the people. Like Henry Luce, who demanded that millions of dollars, hundreds of thousands of guns, and thousands of warplanes should be sent to China to aid the Kuomintang, the Kuomintang itself had come to live among shadows, where huge figures, fantastic dreams of power, took the place of actual power. The momentous figures became the reality, before which the people paled into insignificance. Mao did not forget the people. He based his strength upon the thousands of social groups in China, and he saw, very early in his career, that power in the modern world is not waged by guns, but by the agreement of the social groups to enforce their demands; *and there is no other ultimate power*. It is conceivable that the immense campaign fought in 1949 could have occurred without the use of a single weapon; and indeed, as it was fought out to its inevitable conclusion, it became a nonviolent resistance on the part of the Kuomintang, who fled in a rout.

The psychological forces which brought the revolution into being have long been known. They were known to Confucius. Asked the three things necessary to a ruler, he answered that there should be a sufficiency of food, a sufficiency of military power, and a sufficiency of faith in the people for their ruler. Asked what should be omitted if only two of these were possible, he answered: "Omit the military power." Asked further what should be omitted if only one of these was possible, he answered: "Let them lose their food, and keep their faith in you."

The faith had been provided. It was almost a personal trust in Mao's intentions. Mao might talk, as he did occasionally, in the strange unwieldy language of Marxist symbolism; but he could also talk in simple, communicable terms. He explained, in language that a child might understand, that there was absolutely nothing to fear. If the Kuomintang was armed with American weapons, their armaments should be regarded simply as part of a process of "blood transfusion"— the weapons would fall into the hands of the Chinese Communists. He repeated his old adage concerning reactionary rulers: "They are paper tigers, fierce to look at, but they melt in the rain." All through 1949 they kept on melting at a mounting pace, while the rain fell and the storm gathered strength. Sometimes, as victory followed victory, it was as though the Red Army resembled the monkey in one of Mao's favorite books who in one somersault could leap tens of thousands of miles.

But if he could talk simply, Mao could also talk dramatically. On April 21, 1949, when he ordered the crossing of the Yangtse River, the words of the order suggest his own dramatic instinct. He wrote: "Advance boldly, resolutely, thoroughly, cleanly. Completely annihilate all the Kuomintang reactionaries who dare to resist. Liberate the people of the whole country." On that day a million Red Army troops crossed over to the south bank of the Yangtse.

With the crossing of the Yangtse successfully accomplished, the end of Kuomintang rule was already in sight. The Red field armies swept through the southern and northwestern provinces, and by June 15, Mao could say that in three years the Red armies had destroyed 5,590,000 Kuomintang troops, with comparatively small losses to themselves. In a speech delivered to the People's Consultative Conference in Peking he was understandably jubilant, and once more he spoke of the victory as caused by the broad alliance of the laborers, peasants, the petty and national bourgeoisie—"an alliance so consolidated that it possesses the powerful will and inexhaustible capacity to vanquish all enemies and conquer all difficulties." He added: "We are now in an era in which the imperialist system is heading toward complete collapse. These imperialists are bogged down in an inescapable crisis, and no matter how they will want to continue to oppose the Chinese people, the Chinese people have the means to win ultimate victory." He concluded his speech with a peroration which subtly repeated the words of the song then sweeping over China. "Once the destiny of the people is in the hands of the people, the Chinese people will see a new China rising like the sun from the East, shining with brilliant rays. They will see her swiftly clearing away the debris left by the reactionary government, healing the scars of war and building a new, strong, prosperous People's Democratic Republic of China, which will be true to its name."

Now there remained little except to form the new republic. On October 1, 1949, in an astonishing ceremony held in the heart of Peking, the new republic was officially brought into being.

THE FOUNDING OF A REPUBLIC

Looking out over the immense square from the high balcony of the Tien An Men, or "Gate of Heavenly Peace," the scarlet, brass-studded gate through which the tribute-bearers came in the past to make their way, on their knees, to the yellow-lacquered throne of the Emperor, Mao watched the processions of people filing into the square. He was wearing the same drab cloth cap and the same worn clothes in which he entered Peking in March. He kept nodding vigorously, but he looked tired in the chill wind coming from the Gobi. Chu Teh and Chou En-lai stood beside him, but on an impulse they stepped back—it was Mao's name, not theirs, which echoed thunderously over the square: *"Mao Tse-tung wan shui! Mao Tse-tung wan shui!* "May Mao Tse-tung live ten thousand years!" He kept nodding, while the shouting echoed from the red-painted palace walls. And then there came a sudden hush, as the people saw the flag slowly sliding up the immense white flagpole in the square: a flag like a small bundle which cracked open at last to become the largest flag that anyone had ever seen, for it was at least thirty feet broad, blood-red, with its five yellow stars, and immediately afterward the guns roared a salute. Then the crowd thundered the words of the anthem which had been sung for fifteen years all over China, by the Kuomintang troops as well as by the Communists, the famous *Chi-lai* sung by schoolchildren, but also by soldiers entering battle:

Arise, you who refuse to be slaves,
Our very flesh and blood will build a new Great Wall
A savage indignation fills us now,
Arise, arise, arise!

At the end of the song, from all over the square, where only
recently there were trees and small, yellow-roofed palaces isolated behind high walls, now leveled to provide a parade
ground and a meeting-place for the people, there came more
cries of *"Mao Tse-tung wan shui!"* until at last, over the
microphones in the square, there could be heard a low Hunanese voice saying: "The Central Governing Council of the
People's Government of China today assumes power in
Peking. . . ." There was some significance in the fact that
Mao used the imperial name meaning "Northern Capital"
rather than Peiping, meaning "Northern Peace," the name
bestowed upon the city at the end of the Kuomintang northern march in 1927. Shortly after the declaration of the new
government, the tanks rumbled across the square with their
red-painted stars glittering in the low sun which came through
the low clouds. They were followed by the mechanized troops
in armored trucks, and after these came the captured cannon,
sailors with fixed bayonets, Red Guards with automatic rifles,
a detachment of peasant guerrillas, and at the end, in their
traditional white costumes, the *yang-k'o* dancers. It was almost
exactly twenty two years since an armed rabble of a thousand
men climbed through the wooded, ice-cold slopes of Chingkanshan.

Looking down at the people waving madly in the square,
calling his name, Mao may have reflected that it had happened
much sooner than he had dared to expect. External forces had
been at work, making the victory easier. The tanks, the armored lorries, the automatic rifles, even the machine guns in
the parade, had all been captured; only the red-tasseled spears
carried by the guerrillas were made in China. Even the uniforms were captured. "Above all," he had said in *Strategic
Problems,* "we must concern ourself with the spoils of war."
Now the spoils were paraded in the harsh October sunshine;
and soon the fireworks rose over the yellow roofs of the palaces,

and red lanterns, shaped to resemble red stars, twined through the city streets with the coming of dusk, and late into the night.

A new dynasty had come into being. There had occurred one of those events which happen only at long intervals in the history of China. Though on this same day it had been agreed that the Christian calendar would be employed, "since this is the calendar universally recognized throughout the world," in fact, a new element of time was involved, and people would date events from this strange parade of foreign weapons, and the stranger speech heard in the square, its concluding words echoing the pronunciamentos of the emperors and the Manifesto to the Orient written by Lenin in 1917: "Let the world tremble."

The world did tremble. A huge, convulsive movement had been brought into being, breaking through the crusts of feudalism and corruption, exploding in violence across the length and breadth of China. Only a few had foreseen it. Mao himself in 1946 seemed to think that the Communist revolution in China would take twenty or thirty years to accomplish. Only Chen Tu-hsiu, who founded the movement, saw into the future with elaborate accuracy. One day in March 1927, before the Shanghai massacres in April had shown the extent of the cleavage between the two wings of the Kuomintang, Chen Tu-hsiu was talking to the patriarchal old Kuomintang member, Wu Chih-hui, who had founded in 1902 one of the many revolutionary societies which sprang to birth under the monarchy. Wu Chih-hui was commenting on the long period it had taken for the Kuomintang to come to power. Had not Sun Yat-sen said it would take thirty years for the Kuomintang to achieve the conquest of China? "What about the Communist party?" Wu Chih-hui asked. "Oh, in twenty years the Communists will completely control the country," Chen Tu-hsiu answered. "I suppose that means we have only got nineteen years to live," the old man said, shivering a little. There was no answer, only a quiet laugh from the man who had founded the Communist party, and who, a few months later, was expelled from it because he had failed to understand the forces at work.

Chen Tu-hsiu's twenty years were very nearly accurate, for by 1947 the wheel was beginning to turn full circle, and the defeat of the Kuomintang was certain. It could hardly be otherwise. Chiang Kai-shek had proved his incompetence on the field and in his knowledge of social affairs. Not he, but Mao, was being greeted with the traditional acclamation reserved in the past only for the Chinese emperors.

A JOURNEY TO MOSCOW AND A REPORT

The new republic came into being in October. By December, Mao was planning a journey to Soviet Russia—an unusual venture for the head of a new state. There were, however, sufficient reasons. If Stalin's seventieth birthday was the excuse offered publicly, there were other excuses closer at hand. For the first time there existed two large Communist states, and it had become immediately necessary to form long-range plans for their co-operation. Increasingly after 1939 Mao had read Stalin's works. There had been waverings in Stalin's attitude toward the Chinese Communists, but some clear principles could be seen; and consciously or unconsciously Stalin had supported the revolution Mao had brought into being, without sending more than token aid. Mao believed that the time had come for a complete understanding between them. There were now two poles to the Communist empire; and Mao himself ranked as the leading theoretician after Stalin, with all the extraordinary powers which theoreticians possess in Communist countries. At Potsdam, Stalin had disavowed the Chinese Communists, saying, as he had said many times before, that the Kuomintang was the only political force capable of ruling China. Mao's visit to Moscow was a demonstration that the Chinese Communist revolution was a complete success.

There were many things to discuss. The treaty signed by Molotov and T. V. Soong in 1945 had something of the appearance of one of the "unequal treaties" which China had been compelled to sign as a result of an inherent weakness. It was necessary to obtain a loan, to bring the Chinese Eastern Railway into Chinese hands, and to revise the treaty. It was also necessary to put Sino-Soviet relations on a firm theoretical basis and to discuss the implications of the inevitable alliance. These matters were presumably discussed during Mao's visit to Stalin on January 8, 1950, the longest of all his visits to the inner sanctuary of the Kremlin:—he had been received previously by Stalin immediately after his arrival on December 16. The photographs show him looking worn and tired after the journey, wearing a heavy fur coat and a fur cap. He attended a meeting held at the Bolshoi Theater in celebration of Stalin's seventieth birthday, standing immediately on Stalin's right. He visited factories, attended a performance of *Swan Lake,* and made a prolonged study of the Soviet Union's economic development; and he laid some Chinese flowers on Lenin's tomb within the Kremlin wall. The long visit, so long indeed that rumors were spread that he had been arrested, could be easily accounted for. He realized that the problem of Chinese recovery depended upon a spurt in industrial development, and he had comparatively little knowledge of the technical accomplishments of a modern industrial society. A day-by-day summary of his movements in Russia reveals an endless peregrination among factories in Moscow, Leningrad, and all the surrounding territory.

The minutes of the meetings between Mao and Stalin were never revealed. The text of the treaty was, however, published, and it contained few surprises. The Soviet Union promised a loan to China—a loan that was strangely small and bore little relation to the vast needs of a country shaken to its roots by a prolonged civil war. But if the $300,000,000 purchasing credit was inadequate to fulfill the immediate needs, the Soviet Union also promised to send large numbers of technical assistants to supplement the financial aid.

The incursion of thousands of Soviet Russian technicians was a calculated risk that had to be taken. The loan of $300,-000,000 was considerably larger than the loan of $20,000 which, according to the American White Paper, Chu Teh had asked for in 1942 from the United States. The American loan had been refused. Now, with a three-year economic plan, with the promise of Soviet Russian support, and with the knowledge that an entirely new adaptation to world conditions had become necessary, Mao prepared to return to China, having seen more collective farms and aircraft factories than he could conceivably have digested. More important than his survey of Soviet Russian industry was the knowledge that an alliance was on firm grounds. He might view Russian concessions in Sinkiang with alarm, and he shared the Chinese distrust of all foreigners, but the importance he attached to the alliance should not be underestimated. Addressing "the peoples of the East" on June 4, 1920, Lenin had emphasized that "for the time being actual communism can be crowned with success only in the West." In the colonial and semi-colonial countries "the bourgeois-democratic movements must play the leading role." The times had changed. Lenin had been proved wrong. The revolution in China had come about as the result of an agrarian peasant revolt, and only in its last phases had there been any reliance on the proletariat.

As he left for China, Mao declared at the Yaroslav station that he was content with his long stay; he praised Stalin; he said that it had been his life's ambition to enter "the country of Lenin"; and as he stepped onto the train he added: "The new alliance between our two nations will inevitably influence not only the development of the great powers, China and the Soviet Union, but the future of all humanity all over the world." It seemed, at that moment, extremely likely.

There followed a long silence. Living in a palace in Peking, working on administrative affairs, Mao spoke more and more rarely. For a short period after the journey to Moscow he was ill. He had aged considerably during the years of conquest. He had hoped to announce the complete conquest of Chinese territory on his return, but Formosa still held out. It was not until June that he delivered his first report on the state of the nation. As so often before, he spoke cautiously, succinctly, warning against dangers, against dogmatism, against every manner of foolhardy action. He said:

Since the decisive victory in the campaigns of Liaosi and Mukden, Hsuchow, Pengpu, Peiping, and Tientsin in the winter of 1948, the People's Liberation Army has occupied all the territory of China except Tibet, Formosa, and a few islands. In the thirteen and a half months since the crossing of the Yangtse on April 20, 1949, we have annihilated 1,830,000 Kuomintang troops and 980,000 guerrilla bandits. At the same time the people's security organs have discovered large numbers of secret service organizations and special agents; and we still have the task of rooting out remnants of guerrilla forces in the newly liberated areas.

In this past year, too, we have suffered widespread calamities. Eight million hectares of farm land and forty million people have to a greater or lesser degree been affected by flood and drought . . . So it is that we must carry forward the work of agricultural reform step by step, and in an orderly manner. The war has been fundamentally ended: the situation is entirely different from that which existed between 1946 and 1948. Now the government is in a position to help the poor peasants through their difficulties by means of loans. There must be a change in our attitude toward the rich peasants. We must no longer requisition surplus land and the property of the rich peasants: we must preserve our rich peasant economy, for nothing matters so much as the restoration of production in the rural areas.

Most of this he had said before; now he stated it with absolute authority. He outlined briefly a three-year plan of agrarian reform, industrial development, and large reductions in expenditure by government organizations. He warned against an excessive bureaucracy. Finally, he developed another "eight-legged essay," calling first for more production, then for an end to "blindness and anarchy" in the economic field, and then for a large-scale demobilization of the Army. He urged reform in education, relief for the unemployed, and once again he denounced those who refuse to allow free speech. "All delegates," he said, "must have the full and entire right to speak what is on their mind: any action which suppresses the people's representatives from speaking is wrong." Finally, he urged the suppression of all bandits and counterrevolutionaries, and the resolute carrying out of the party program in the summer, autumn, and winter of 1950. The peroration was brief. He said: "We must regard bureaucracy and authoritarianism as enemies. At the same time we must train ourselves, by reading certain set books, to understand the revolutionary process. Above all, we must conquer all sentiments of complacency and pride, all that makes us believe that we are heroes."

Pride was the enemy. Caught in pride's toils, incalculable harm could be done by the Communists if they felt disposed. Mao had spoken in June 1950 about the old problems—the whole speech followed the speech made in December, 1944, with comparatively few changes—and the old problems remained. He was still the peasant intellectual, wary, cautious, precise. As he said then, so he said now: "If we are proud, comrades, we shall fall."

The Shape of the Future

In our own day no man has reached power so quickly or so dramatically as Mao Tse-tung. Two years before he achieved supreme power he was hiding among the loess caves of Shensi. Today, he is the undisputed master of China, with an effective power greater than that possessed by any of the Chinese emperors. Never in history has any man possessed so much direct power over so many people. For good or evil the power represented by him has come to stay, and from now on the destiny of the world will be intimately, and perhaps violently, affected by the decisions made by him and by the people he leads.

Today, stoop-shouldered and sunburned, looking every day more and more like the portraits of Sun Yat-sen taken in his old age, Mao Tse-tung can look out from the ruined temple near Peking where he occasionally lives, upon an empire he has conquered almost singlehanded. He knows that without him the Chinese Communists would not have succeeded in capturing China, just as it is inconceivable that the Communists would have captured Russia without Lenin. No one else possessed the peculiar talents he had: the patience, the foresight, the astonishing capacity to learn thoroughly from his mistakes, the knowledge of military science, and the capacity to think in broad, strenuous outlines—all these were predominantly his contributions to the Chinese Communists. He was not simply a political figure: he was the novelist whose novel had become suddenly true, or the poet whose words have suddenly become people.

"Those who do great things have done them because they are in a difficulty, in a *cul de sac*," wrote Henri Michaux. The statement, which is so true of many great leaders, is probably untrue of Mao. It would be unwise to seek the causes of his rise to power in his hatred of his father or his love for his mother, even though rejection by the father plays a peculiarly characteristic role in the rise of nearly all the men who have made a name in history. The chief reason for his rise to power lies almost certainly in the failure of the three Chinese revolutions, beginning with the Taiping rebellion and ending with the revolution of 1927. Mao was one of the few who realized how and why they had failed. By sheer will power he made himself the technician of revolt. Carefully, over a long period of years, he prepared himself for the role he desired to play; and from 1924, when he first set eyes on Chiang Kai-shek, he realized that he possessed qualities his adversary could never acquire. In time, the history of China could be summarized as a duel fought to a finish between Mao and Chiang Kai-shek.

No duelists could have been more dissimilar. Chiang Kai-shek admitted to his close friends that he traced his descent directly to Duke Wen, the father of the founder of the Chou dynasty. This claim, which could only be compared with a Jew's claim to be a direct descendant of Moses or a Christian's to be a direct descendant of Christ, provides one clue to his downfall. Proud and intolerant, regarding himself as the secret possessor of the imperial mantle, conscious of belonging to a family even more ancient and honorable than that of his brother-in-law, H. H. Kung, who implausibly claimed direct descent from Confucius, Chiang Kai-shek was apt to treat people with a contempt which he took no pains to hide. When Mao flew to Chungking in 1945, Chiang Kai-shek's intolerance and contempt was only too evident. "He treated me like a peasant," Mao complained. It was probably the gravest mistake the Generalissimo had ever made. Incapable of understanding his opponent, capable only of hating him, the Generalissimo never fully realized the resources of his enemy, and he continued to underestimate the enemy until it was too late. In a very real sense the pattern of the Chinese civil war followed the pattern of ancient Greek tragedy: overweening pride produced its own Nemesis.

These conceptions of pride and humility must be faced. In China, where personal relations acquire a complexity unknown to the West, the duel between Mao and Chiang was essentially personal, but at the same time it was a duel between two opposed facets of the Chinese mind. Chiang claimed to be a Confucian and a Methodist, though he never explained how these two dissimilar faiths could be merged together. In fact he was an anarchist, an opportunist without principles, with an overriding ambition to make, as he said, a name in history. His faith in his own stubborn powers and in his almost divine ancestry were the chief motivating factors in his rise to power. Mao, with far greater subtlety of mind, a pure scholar and an excellent poet, found his resources in Confucianism and in a theory of revolution which derived partly from the Confucian classics and partly from the Marxist belief in the inevitability of the class conflict and the final victory of the proletariat. For the proletariat, in defiance of the *Communist Manifesto,* he substituted the peasants. Chiang never understood the peasants, had never been one, and never made credible advances to them. Mao did understand them, because he came from them, and he was under no illusions about his ancestry. Yet he was not humble in any ordinary sense, perhaps because no Hunanese is ever humble. He had modeled himself on the Confucian hero, who is scholar and man of action at the same time; and from his youth he had said very simply, and with a full consciousness of what he was about: "I shall overthrow the dynasty."

In *The 18th Brumaire of Louis Buonaparte,* a book of considerably more wisdom than *Capital,* Karl Marx sought for the causes of revolution. He did not find them in economic factors or in the waywardness of despotic rulers; he found them to be part of an inevitable evolution, the same kind of evolution which is present when a serpent sloughs off its skin. A revolution arises, he says, when the dead weight of the past becomes an insufferable torment to the present:

Men make their own history, but they do not make it just as they please; they do not make it under circumstances chosen by themselves, but under circumstances directly found, and given and transmitted from the past. The tradition of all the dead generations weighs like a nightmare on the living. And just when they seem engaged in revolutionizing themselves and things, in creating something entirely new, precisely in such epochs of revolutionary crisis they conjure up the spirits of the past to their service and borrow from them names, battle slogans, and costumes in order to present the new scene of world history in time-honored disguise and this borrowed language.

In effect, both Mao and Chiang had summoned up the past in order to help them wage their war in the present; but they had conjured up different pasts. Chiang saw himself as a Chou dynasty prince leading his feudal armies to battle, like any one of the princes described so brilliantly in the *Tso Chuan*. Mao saw himself as one of the heroes of *All Men Are Brothers*. Both employed ancient rituals, Chiang Kai-shek even going so far as to encourage his lieutenants to present him with copies of the ancient bronze tripods traditionally presented to victorious emperors. When the bronzes were already made, he professed to be unworthy of the honor, but even his profession of unworthiness followed a classic pattern. Mao resurrected the ancient peasant brotherhoods who took to the woods and defied the Emperor on the grounds that the Mandate of Heaven had lapsed, and he was never so innocent as to believe that the Chinese peasants were powerless. Mistakenly, he believed that Chiang Kai-shek and the small group of incompetent and anarchic advisers around him represented the bourgeoisie determined to crush the peasantry, and he saw the struggle in terms of the class war. In fact, it was only by an accident that Chiang Kai-shek represented the bourgeoisie: he represented only himself, or rather he represented the prodigious power of ancient ritual to survive. He was a nightmare wedded to a machine gun. He never knew where he was going. He was an emperor who had achieved the throne by violence and then never knew what to do with his royal powers. Because he was a vestigial remnant of ancient feudal traditions, the last wave thrown up by the expiring Manchu dynasty, he had no attachment to the present, and never knew where the present was going; and more than anyone else except Mao he was responsible for the growth of the Communist party, by confirming the other remnants of feudalism, the large landlords and the militarist dictators of whole provinces, in their powers. All except one of his prophecies were wrong. That one was revealing. At a conference in Kuling, just before the Japanese war, he prophesied that the war would be fought on the earth, on the seas, in the air, and *under the earth*. But it was not the Kuomintang armies which fought under the earth: this was left to the Communist guerrillas who fought the Japanese in tunnels scooped out of the loess soil of Shensi.

In the end it was Mao who represented the Confucian tradition of northern China, and Chiang Kai-shek who represented, ignobly and murderously, the anarchist tradition of the South. It was the tradition of the Confucian scholar that he should studiously examine the road he was traveling. Mao knew the road he was traveling because it was the simplest road of all. His road consisted of the innumerable small pathways trodden by the peasants. He obeyed almost all the classic injunctions of the Confucians. Chiang Kai-shek professed to have a peculiar affection for Tseng Kuo-fan, and in many ways he attempted to model himself on this Hunanese scholar who destroyed the Taipings, seeing himself as the inevitable and providential destroyer of the Communist rebels.

One of Tseng Kuo-fan's most famous phrases, constantly repeated by Chiang Kai-shek, was: "Things should be done soundlessly, and, as it were, odorously, with precision and economy of effort." In the small matters of murder and corruption, Chiang Kai-shek obeyed this injunction; in all larger matters he disobeyed it completely, and he never came to know the meaning of "economy of effort." He was a man who thought in terms of the small unimportant details of things, forever interfering with minutiae, apt to break into a torrent of abuse if a soldier did not obey him implicitly, or if a button was undone. He confused his generals by interfering by radio at the height of a battle, when it must have been perfectly clear that the general was preoccupied and in no position to give him a complete picture of the state of affairs. He did not live in a real world; he was like Marianne Moore's imaginary toad wandering about in a real garden. He lacked completely the ability to make cool, objective judgments and to distinguish between what was desirable and what was possible. His military judgment was warped by wishful thinking; and as a strategist he failed continually, long after the Chinese had lost patience with him, because he always wanted to satisfy his own whims. He ruled on the principle of *divide et impera,* and he denied to individuals all power of individual initiative. He insisted that all power should stem directly from him, with the result that overcentralization and overorganization led to confusion.

In all this, Mao was his direct opposite. During the civil wars and the Japanese war, power was decentralized, strategy and tactics were conceived in broad strokes with almost no insistence on details, and the Communist leaders in Yenan distinguished clearly between what was desirable and what was possible. They lived in a real world, and their judgments were based on an exhaustive knowledge of human psychology.

In *China's Destiny,* Chiang Kai-shek outlined a fantastic plan for China's recovery, enumerating the number of kilometers of railroad and the number of pounds of bitumen which would be available in five years, in ten years, in fifteen years, finding in the vast profusion of imaginary numbers the solace which was denied to him in contemplating the vast resources of the Chinese peasants. The greatest tragedy of all was that he never understood his own people, never understood the desire of the peasants for a place in the sun. "I am the government," he said once. "In assuming this power, my action is that of a revolutionary." He failed to understand that the real governors and the real revolutionaries were the peasants, for the spirit of the time demanded that the majority should rule. It is inconceivable that he ever read Herder. If he had, he might have come upon a curious reference to the *Zeitgeist*: "Lock it in cloisters, towers, and caves, nevertheless it will escape." From the caves of northern Shensi, in less than a year, the Chinese Communists swept him from Peking across the whole length of China until he found a small foothold on the island of Formosa. For such victories the *Zeitgeist* must always be at least partly responsible.

Today, Mao has reached the summit of power. He walks along a dangerous eminence. Few Chinese rulers have survived intact on these heights. Yuan Shih-kai, though he never possessed a tithe of Mao's effective power, aspired to the throne, went mad, and killed his mistresses with a meathook shortly before his own death. The Empress-Dowager also went mad, and killed the young Emperor Kwang Hsu on the day before her own death. The leaders of the Taiping rebellion seem to have gone mad quite early, and when the Manchus closed around Nanking, they set fire to their palaces and murdered one another. There is no reason to believe that Mao will succumb under the inevitable strains. Like many previous rulers of China, he has been moved by what Thomas Hobbes has called "the perpetuall and restlesse desire of Power after Power, which ceaseth onely in Death"; but unlike most previous rulers of China he is a peasant who has wandered through most of China and kept close to the earth and to the peasants.

Perhaps the danger lies here. Antaeus lost his strength when he left the earth: Mao will lose his whenever he removes himself from the Chinese peasants and the Chinese earth. It is possible that the complexities of the international scene may in the end confound him. He knows well only the peasants of Hunan, Kiangsi, and Shensi, though he has traveled over the whole length and breadth of China: he still remains remarkably ignorant of the world outside.

All through the period in Yenan, he received daily copies of reports from the monitoring service, and he seems to have trusted only the reports received from Soviet Russia. He has few advisers on international politics he can trust. He is sustained by the simple thesis of the class war and the inevitability of the dictatorship of the proletariat; in fact, the dictatorship of the proletariat is a physical impossibility in China, where 85 per cent of the people are peasants. Nor would the peasants of their own accord assent to the justice of such a dictatorship. He has realized this perfectly. For long periods he has fought against the instructions of the Comintern: none of the representatives of the Comintern sent to instruct the Chinese revolutionaries have ever possessed a fraction of his knowledge of the actual circumstances of the peasantry. Borodin was responsible for the debacle in Hankow. Li Teh was responsible for the debacle of the Fifth Annihilation Campaign. When Mao becomes dogmatic, he is always on unsure ground. He was on safer ground when he declared: "There are people who think that Marxism is a kind of magic truth with which one can cure any disease. We should tell them that dogmas are more useless than cow dung. Dung can be used as fertilizer."

But the perturbing element of dogma remains. His widescaling mind, which thinks in terms of wholes, sometimes overleaps itself: he will allow himself to generalize on insufficient evidence. Sometimes he generalizes with remarkable accuracy. Occasionally he fails, as when, during a long argument with him, he insisted to me that the British would never under any conditions give up India. I told him about Major General Christison's remark when he landed at Batavia in 1945: "I have not come to give this country back to the Dutch." Mao then explained at some length that the imperialists could never cease from being imperialists, and such a remark from an invading general was quite impossible. He refused to believe that Great Britain was truly socialistic: the imperialists were simply nationalizing industry in order to wage a greater war against the colonies.

He tends to simplify all problems, seeing everything in black and white, whereas most things are shaded between the two extremes. He was convinced, as he wrote in *The New Democracy*, that "without the assistance of the Soviet Union, final victory in China against Japan is impossible." It happened that his prophecy came true, but it might very well have happened otherwise, and indeed there was little ground for the belief, for the Soviet Union appeared to have no intention of entering into the war against Germany or against Japan at that time. Because Mao intends to simplify, there is always the danger that he may become one of the "Great Simplifiers," whose existence in the twentieth century Jacob Burckhardt prophesied in the nineteenth. Once he told Edgar Snow that he never took any interest in drawing. Asked to draw a picture representing Li Po's famous description of a scene which is "half sun and half rock," he simply drew a straight line with a semicircle over it. The danger point comes when the "Great Simplifiers" draw up innumerable lists of people and then strike lines through them.

But it is not in the least necessary to imagine that Mao represents wholly or partly the strange, murderous race of the Simplifiers. He has nothing in common with Hitler, and little enough with Stalin. He has read widely and learnedly and with great humility. Under another dispensation Mao would have become a *han-lin* scholar and risen high in the imperial government, and like his fellow Hunanese, Hsiung Hsi-ling, the last of the great *han-lin* scholars who achieved power, he would have retired baffled before the intricacies of Chinese ritual. His sturdiness and his energy—he uses the last word often and once wrote an essay in his youth called "The Energy of the Mind"—have saved him from committing the errors of indecision; and because in himself he represents so many of the conflicting elements of Asia, now almost completely emancipated from foreign rule, he is a portent of the future. In time there will be other Asiatic leaders like him, with the same subtlety and the same forthrightness, the same hard determination to bring Asia into its place in the sun.

At this point a word of warning should be uttered. Edgar Snow has suggested that Mao would never command great respect from the intellectual elite of China, chiefly because of his nonchalant habits and the slovenliness of his dress. In fact, nothing could be more mistaken: the great Chinese scholars have always been traditionally ill dressed and possessed of abrupt manners, and even Confucius thought it ill fitting of a scholar to take pride in his dress. The intellectual elite of China may conceivably disagree with him for intellectual reasons, but not for the manner of man that he is. Edgar Snow wrote when Mao was still developing. He emphasized the earthiness of the man who could casually enter a cave, take off his trousers, and lie down on a bed in front of strangers, while still deliberating on military strategy, forgetting that Mao was wholly dedicated to the tradition of the scholar-soldier and had trained himself to an intellectual eminence rare among politicians. We tend to underestimate those who oppose us: we underestimate Mao at our extreme peril. He belongs to the new type of Asiatic leader—Nehru and Shjahrir are others—who combine an extraordinary penetration and understanding of theoretical forces with a sense of reality, of a real world inhabited by real people who behave in real ways. By backing Chiang Kai-shek, the Americans made a fatal mistake: they backed an unreal and fictitious force which represented nothing at all except a continuing neurosis, while the real force, toughened by experience, lay secretly hidden among the hill caves of Yenan. Yet the secret was widely known, and twice at least an understanding could have been concluded between the Americans and the Chinese Communists.

If we are to understand the workings of Mao Tse-tung's brilliant, cautious, and subtle mind, we should go to the only other man of comparable peasant origins who shaped the destinies of a nation—Martin Luther. Luther was a heretic of the established church, and in his struggle for power he deliberately set himself against the peasants. He wrote in 1525, in a pamphlet entitled *Against the Robbing and Murderous Gangs of Peasants*: "Whoever can should smite, strangle, and stab, secretly or publicly. Therefore, dear gentlefolk, hearken here, save there, smite, stab, strangle at will these murderous and rebellious peasants." In everything that Mao stood for, and nowhere more than in his attitude to the peasants, he was poles apart from Luther; but there are large areas where they tread common ground. Both were poets and translators, both recoiled from traditional concepts, both were profoundly dogmatic, and both lived at a high pitch of intellectual energy. The Reformation did not reform, it revo-

lutionized. Mao's early attachment to the Reform party under
Kang Yu-wei and Liang Chih-chao corresponds to Luther's
early attachment to the humanists; and he became a revolutionary for the same reason that Luther became a revolutionary, because he saw the seeds of corruption in the established order. "I am a peasant's son; my father, my grand-
father, and my great-grandfather were all genuine peasants,"
Luther was accustomed to say, and Mao has said the same
more times than he can remember. Both delight in maxims.
Like Luther, Mao mingles scriptural quotations with the
rough language of the common people, quoting Mencius
when he describes the Red Army as being "unconquerable
under Heaven," and in the next breath describing the Kuomintang as "those people who take everything and give nothing, and ought to be cleansed in a basin of hot water," where
the reference is to scalding pigs. I suspect that this reliance
on maxims is absolutely deliberate, and at the same time he
has a very real belief in their effectiveness and truth. He
said in a talk to some labor heroes in 1943:

The maxim "Three common men will make a genius" tells us that
there is a great creative power among the people, and that there
are thousands and thousands of geniuses among them. There are
geniuses in every village, every town, every city. We must penetrate among these masses, learn from them, organize their experiences into systematic principles and methods, and then we should
teach them these principles and methods, and urge them to practice them in order that they may solve their own problems and
enjoy freedom and felicity.

Mao can look every inch the peasant: he can also look like
a Chinese Emperor, with a powerful sense of his own dignity
and intellectual eminence. An uncommon subtlety lurks in
him. His prose is marked by the repetition of the occasionally
empty phrases of a Marxist vocabulary, but sometimes, and
more often than one expects, there is a passage of cunning
illumination. He is at his best in *Strategic Problems,* where
the dry, cautious style invites a slow-burning wit. Sometimes,
too, the authoritarian temper leaps out of the prose, and then
there is menace in his voice. Too often, he uses the words

"annihilation" and "the evil of the world," those marks of the nihilist conscience, but he has more excuse than most: his enemies tried again and again to annihilate his armies, and the evil of poverty in China demanded violent solutions.

I have compared him to Luther in his private temper, but Luther fought no battles. In recent history there has only been one other scholar-soldier who fought and won extensive guerrilla campaigns—T. E. Lawrence. When the Chinese Communists were told of his exploits, they were tempted to disbelieve their informant, as though guerrilla warfare was their own invention, the legacy of the 222 wars fought in the "Spring and Autumn Period" and the countless Chinese wars which followed. But sometimes Lawrence seems to be talking with the authentic voice of the Chinese Communists, as when, after hammering out a diathetical theory of war in his tent at Abu Marqua, Lawrence said:

It seemed to me proven that our rebellion had an unassailable base, guarded not only from attack, but from the fear of attack. It had a sophisticated alien enemy, disposed as an army of occupation in an area greater than could be dominated effectively from fortified posts. It had a friendly population in which some two in a hundred were active, and the rest quietly sympathetic to the point of not betraying the movements of the minority. The active rebels had the virtues of secrecy and self-control, and the qualities of speed, endurance and independence of arteries of supply. They had technical equipment enough to paralyse the enemy's communications. A province would be won when we had taught the civilians in it to die for our ideal of freedom. The presence of the enemy was secondary. Final victory seemed certain, if the war lasted long enough for us to work it out.[1]

If the war lasted long enough. . . . Exactly the same problem faced the Chinese Communists, who confessed openly that only a long war could bring them to power.

Again and again, and most expecially in the concentrated thirty-third chapter of *Seven Pillars of Wisdom*, Lawrence suggests parallels with Mao's practice. Mao's complete and overriding belief in fluidity, constantly repeated, is equaled

1. T. E. Lawrence, *Seven Pillars of Wisdom*, New York, 1938, p. 192.

only by Lawrence's. "Armies are like plants," wrote Lawrence, "immobile, firm-rooted, nourished through long stems to the head. We might be a vapour, blowing where we listed."

It is unlikely that Mao would recognize himself in the portraits of Luther and T. E. Lawrence. If he wanted to compare himself with anyone, it would probably be the young and princely scholar Yen Huei, whose birthplace he visited. About Yen Huei, Confucius said: "Incomparable indeed was Huei. A handful of rice to eat, a gourdful of water to drink, and living in a mean street: these, others would have found unbearably depressing, but for Huei's happiness they made no difference at all. Incomparable indeed was Huei."

Mao was born at a time when the fifty-six imperial censors, known as the *erh mo kuan*, "the eyes and the ears," still reported to the central government and all the vast panoply of the imperial court was still being displayed as a sign of Manchu domination. He lived to see the imperial buildings with the marble walls and the yellow-tiled roofs taken over by armies of peasant rebels. A new dynasty has appeared, which deliberately employs imperial symbols, for the symbol of Communist domination over China is now the Forbidden City of the emperors, and the great square in front of the Tien An Men has become the Red Square of the Chinese Communists. He had done what he set out to do, step by step. He had admired the Reformers; then he admired the anarchists; then he admired the Communists; but in a sense nothing had changed. As the poem "The Snow" shows demonstrably, he had from the beginning worked with a prodigious sense of the glory of the Chinese people.

One day in Fontainebleau, Napoleon was turning the globe of the world. He said: "China? There lies a sleeping giant. Let him sleep, for when he wakes he will move the world." Now at last, and for the first time, the lion awoke from its long sleep, and stretched its claws.

No one can tell for certain in which direction the Chinese
revolution will go, but some things are certain: Mao's dominance will remain unchallenged while he is alive, and his
will will be written over China until he dies. The programs
he has outlined, the absolute determination to destroy the
class system, the philosophy he inherited from the West, the
belief in the infinite potentialities of the Chinese people—
these will remain. He has faced every kind of danger before,
and it is unlikely that he will be dissuaded from any course
of action by the danger involved. He is no Tito. Wherever he
can, he will work for the world revolution in the belief that
only in this way can the "Great Unity" be achieved. There
are evident dangers to the rest of the world in his attitude: the
habit of simplification is not easily lost, and the victor is always the prisoner of his spoils.

But it should be remembered that Mao is among the most
intelligent of living political leaders. He has always meant
precisely what he says. He knows exactly where he is going.
He has advantages over most political leaders because he has
been a guerrilla general for twenty years, and in the modern
world, diplomacy must increasingly take on the aspect of a
kind of guerrilla warfare. Because he is the scholar first, the
soldier afterward, he will always be able to defeat soldiers.
Without him, it is almost unthinkable that China would ever
have become Communist, and through him Admiral Mahan's
nightmare that the United States, in losing Asia, will forfeit
its status as a world power, may be confirmed.

These consequences are not pleasant to contemplate, but
they must be contemplated. Extraordinary mistakes have
been made, and are still being made, because Americans
in high places have failed dismally to understand the revolutionary changes in Asia, even though they were warned.
When the tattered rabble of Chinese Communist soldiers
walked into Shanghai, they were often barefoot, and they
carried the latest American weapons. They were behaving

precisely as the Americans had behaved at Concord Bridge, but their battle was waged over a fantastically larger battleground. A rebellion against the West, of vast and incalculable consequences, had succeeded, and it succeeded only because the West offered hostages to fortune. Without captured American equipment, the conquest of China might have taken at least three more years, or not come at all. That conquest was but one facet of the Asiatic victory, gained by weight of numbers and by the folly of Western diplomacy, which seemed to be fatally dedicated to error, as though, in all their relations with Asia, the Western powers had decided quite quietly upon suicide. There were obvious exceptions. The friendship between India and Great Britain began on the day when the British Army set sail for its home ports, and the Americans, by helping to bring to birth the United States of Indonesia, performed one of their rare acts of understanding in Asia. By sending military supplies to the Kuomintang while publicly accepting the role of mediation, they earned the hostility of the Chinese Communists, who were enabled to rage against American imperialism with a clear conscience—had they not won their battles with American guns? There were many opportunities between 1943 and 1946 for an entente between the Chinese Communists and the Americans. Was America to be fatally dedicated to the repudiation of all social change? The times were ripe for change. The atomic bomb showed revolutionary changes in our understanding of physical forces; the whole world was changing at a vastly increasing tempo; only America, once the home of revolution, attempted to stem the tide. She could have led the Asiatic revolt: instead, she lagged behind.

Working with the simplest means, basing his whole success on the Chinese peasant, Mao had sensed the prodigious strength which lies in ordinary people. He had breathed upon the peasants, and suddenly, as though they were clay before, they had become alive, determined to find their place in the sun. He still regarded himself as an old teacher, but one who demanded obedience: he was the pedagogue to the end, warning against pride, against bureaucracy, against authoritarianism.

There were dangers, of course. It was hardly possible at so momentous a period that they could be altogether avoided. In his youth Mao read Liang Chih-chao approvingly, and he may have remembered, when he came to power, Liang Chih-chao's favorite quotation from Montesquieu: "All autocratic rulers mislead when they say they unify the people. This is impossible: they do not rule the people with gentleness, but steal the people's right to liberty and make them afraid. What is called the Great Peace in an autocracy always contains in it the seeds of decay."

So it might be. None could tell in which direction the Chinese revolution would go. One thing, however, seemed certain. For the first time there had appeared a people's dictatorship in China, a strange political entity without foundations in previous Chinese history; and the experiment would be carried out to its inevitable conclusions under the leadership of a Hunanese peasant. Immersed in our own dangerous thoughts of the future, it would be a pity if we should ever for a moment minimize the extraordinary power wielded by this man who has the sensitivity of a poet and the intransigence of the ancient Chinese emperors.

Chronological Table

1850–65 Taiping rebellion.

1853   Yen Fu born.

1858   Kang Yu-wei born.

1866   Sun Yat-sen born.

1893   Mao Tse-tung born.

1894   Sino-Japanese War begins.

1895   Sun Yat-sen organizes his first insurrection.

1900   Boxer uprising. Sun Yat-sen's second insurrection.

1906   Hwang Hsing's second uprising in Hunan.

1910   Ninth unsuccessful revolt organized by Kuomintang at Canton.

1911   October 10. The revolution breaks out at Wuchang.

1915   Yuan Shih-kai accepts the Twenty-One Demands presented by Japan.

1917   Sun Yat-sen elected generalissimo of military junta in Canton.

1919   May 4. Student revolt breaks out.

1920   Civil war in Kwangtung between the armies of Sun Yat-sen and Chen Chiung-ming.

September. Congress of Oriental Nations held at Baku.

1921   June 30. The First Congress of the Chinese Communist Party held in Shanghai.

1922   May 6. Sun Yat-sen resumes northern punitive expedition.

The first All-China Labor Congress, and the First Congress of the China Socialist Youth League held in Canton in May.

The Second Congress of the Chinese Communist Party held at Hangchow, in July.

1923   February Seventh Incident—39 workmen in Wuhan, Chengchow, and Changshintien killed, by orders of Marshal Wu Pei-fu, while on strike.

Third Congress of the Chinese Communist Party held in Canton, in June, authorizing co-operation between the Communists and the Kuomintang.

During the summer Chiang Kai-shek sent to Moscow by Sun Yat-sen.

November. Reorganization of the Kuomintang.

1924   January 20–30. First National Congress of the Kuomintang. Complete reorganization of party, the Communists being permitted to become members.

June 16. Whampoa Military Academy opened near Canton.

In September civil war breaks out between Chekiang and Kiangsu, to be followed in October by another civil war between the Fengtien and Chihli factions.

October 15. Revolt of the Merchant Volunteers in Canton suppressed.

October 18. Sun Yat-sen launches unsuccessful northern expedition.

November. Chinese Communist party, in *The Fourth Statement on the Present Position,* urges convocation of a National Assembly in Peking, in agreement with Sun Yat-sen.

1925   January 22. The Fourth Congress of the Chinese Communist Party meets in Shanghai, speedy convocation of a National Assembly is urged.

March 12. Sun Yat-sen dies.

May 30. Workers in Shanghai fired upon by Sikhs under British command, causing a wave of strikes and protests against foreign influence.

1926   July 9. Beginning of the northern expedition against warlords. Hunan, Hupeh, Kiangsi, Anhwei and Kiangsu occupied within three months.

November 10. Formation of the Wuhan government.

1927   March 22. Capture of Shanghai by workers led by Communists in three separate uprisings.

April 12. Formation of Nanking government. Massacre in Shanghai.

May. Fifth Congress of the Chinese Communist Party meets in Wuhan.

May 21. Hsu Ko-chang orders massacre at Changsha. Chiang Kai-shek orders destruction of peasant and workers unions.

July. Borodin leaves for Moscow.

August 1. Nanchang uprising, following the "split" between the Chinese Communists and the Kuomintang.

August 7. Chen Tu-hsiu deposed at a secret meeting of the Central Committee of the Chinese Communist Party.

August 17. First Chinese soviet organized at Hailofeng.

September 12. Autumn Harvest Uprising organized by Mao Tse-tung in Hunan.

October. Mao leads three regiments to Chingkanshan, and holes in for the winter.

December 11. Canton Commune. Canton held by the Communists for three days.

1928   January 1. Uprising in southern Hunan led by Chu Teh.

February 29. Hailofeng Soviet destroyed.

May. Arrival of Chu Teh at Chingkanhan.

July. Peng Teh-huei leads a revolt in Pingkiang, joins Mao at Chingkanshan.

July–August. Sixth Congress of the Chinese Communist Party, held in a suburb of Moscow.

1929   April. Chiang Kai-shek finally wins the struggle for power between himself and the Kwangsi militarists.

August. Kian uprising led by Lo Ping-hui.

December. Military conference at Kutien: Mao formulates the basic principles of guerrilla warfare.

1930   July 27. Peng Teh-huei captures Changsha.

June. Li Li-san advocates attacks on Wuhan and Changsha.

December–January. First Annihilation Campaign.

1931   May–June. Second Annihilation Campaign.

July–October. Third Annihilation Campaign.

November 7. First All-China Soviet Congress held at Juichin. Mao Tse-tung elected party chairman.

September 18. Mukden Incident.

December 14. Uprising in Ningtu.

1933   April–October. Fourth Annihilation Campaign.

May. Formation of Tungkiang-Nanchang-Pachou Soviet.

October. Beginning of Fifth Annihilation Campaign.

1934 January 22. Second All-China Soviet Congress held at Juichin.

October 16. First Front Red Army begins the Long March.

1935 January 4. Conference held in Tsunyi, Kweichow, leading to new developments in strategy.

May 30. Crossing of Tatu River.

June. The First Front Red Army contacts the Fourth Front Red Army under Hsu Hsiang-chien at Tawei, Szechuan.

1936 July–October. The various Red armies drive through Sikang and Kansu to northern Shensi.

December 12. Chiang Kai-shek arrested by Chang Hsueh-liang.

1937 February. Battle between the Mohammedans and the Fourth Front Red Army.

July 7. Japan invades North China.

July–October. Elections in Soviet territory, followed by establishment of the Shensi-Kansu-Ningsia Border government.

August. Communist armies invade Shansi.

September 22. End of the ten-year-old civil war, establishment of the united front, and reorganization of the Red armies as the Eighth Route Army.

September 24. Lin Piao's victory at Pinghsinkuan.

1938 February. Red Army guerrillas in Central China reorganized as Fourth Route Army.

Mao Tse-tung's *On a Prolonged War* and *The New Stage* published.

March. Wang Ching-wei forms puppet government in Nanking.

1939   December 15. Mao Tse-tung's *The Chinese Revolution and the Communist Party of China* published.

1940   January 19. Mao Tse-tung's *The New Democracy* published.

August 20–December 5. Hundred-Regiment Campaign launched against the Japanese.

1941   January 7. New Fourth Army Incident.

February. Publication of Mao Tse-tung's *The Strategic Problems of China's Revolutionary Wars*.

December 6. Attack on Singapore and Pearl Harbor.

1945   April 24. Mao Tse-tung delivers a report "On Coalition Government" before the Seventh Congress of the Chinese Communist Party.

August 10. Japanese government accepts terms of surrender.

August 28. Mao Tse-tung flies to Chungking.

1946   January 10. Truce orders issued by the Military Executive Headquarters based on Peiping.

July. Assassination of Wen Yi-tuo and Li Kung-po.

December 28. Denunciation by the Chinese Communist party of the Kuomintang constitution.

1947   March 19. Kuomintang troops occupy Yenan.

July. The Eighth Route Army crosses the Yellow River.

October 10. Chinese Communist party issues the Basic Program of Chinese Agrarian Law.

December 25. Mao Tse-tung reports that the revolutionary war has changed from defensive to offensive.

1948   April 1. Mao Tse-tung delivers a speech on agrarian

policy before a meeting of party members of the Shansi-Suiyuan Liberated Area.

April 21. Yenan recaptured.

November. Winter offensive in Manchuria comes to an end.

1949   January 10. Hsuchow-Pengpu campaign comes to an end.

January 31. Peiping occupied by Chinese Communists.

March 25. Mao Tse-tung enters Peiping.

April 21. Mao Tse-tung and Chu Teh issue orders to Communist troops to cross the Yangtse.

April 23. Nanking and Taiyuan captured.

May 3. Hangchow captured.

May 22. Nanchang captured.

May 27. Shanghai captured.

June 2. Tsingtao captured.

August 7. Fuchow captured.

August 26. Lanchow captured.

September 30. Mao elected chairman of the Central People's government.

October 1. Proclamation of the People's Republic of China by Mao Tse-tung in Peking.

October 14. Canton captured.

November 15. Kweiyang captured.

November 22. Kweilin captured.

November 30. Chungking captured.

December 16. Mao visits Moscow.

December 27. Chengtu captured.

1950   February. Mao returns from Moscow.

June 6. Mao issues a general report on the Chinese situation.

June 24. Outbreak of Korean war.

Bibliography

AND

Index

SELECT BIBLIOGRAPHY

CLAIRE and WILLIAM BAND, *Two Years with the Chinese Communists*, (Yale University Press, New Haven, 1948)

JACK BELDEN, *China Shakes the World*, (Harper, New York, 1949)

CHIANG WEN-HAN, *The Chinese Student Movement*, (King's Cross Press, New York, 1948)

China Digest: all issues. (Hongkong-Peking, 1947–1950)

China Handbook 1937–1945, (Macmillan, New York, 1947)

DAVID J. DALLIN, *Soviet Russia and the Far East*, (Yale University Press, New Haven, 1948)

TYLER DENNETT, *Americans in Eastern Asia*, (Barnes and Noble, New York, 1941)

STUART GELDER, *The Chinese Communists*, (Victor Gollancz, London, 1946)

HALDORE HANSON, *Humane Endeavour*, (Farrar & Rhinehart, New York, 1939)

EMI SIAO, *Khunanskaya Fleita (The Hunanese Flute)*, (Moscow, Government Printing Press, 1940)

E. R. HUGHES, *The Invasion of China by the Western World*, (Macmillan, New York, 1938)

ARTHUR W. HUMMEL, *Eminent Chinese of the Ch'ing Period*, (U.S. Government Printing Office, Washington, 1943)

HAROLD ISAACS, *The Tragedy of the Chinese Revolution*, (S. J. R. Saunders, 1938)

ELIZABETH KENDALL, *A Wayfarer in China*, (Atlantic Monthly Press, Boston, 1913)

T. E. LAWRENCE, *Seven Pillars of Wisdom*, (Doubleday, Doran, New York, 1938)

PENG TEH-HUEI, *Unity and Defence in North China*, (New China Information Committee, Chungking, 1940)

M. N. ROY, *My Experience in China*, (Privately printed, Calcutta, 1945)

AGNES SMEDLEY, *Red China Marches*, (Vanguard Press, New York, 1934)

EDGAR SNOW, *Red Star over China*, (Random House, New York, 1937)

GUNTHER STEIN, *The Challenge of Red China*, (McGraw Hill, New York, 1945)

TENG SSU-YU, *New Light on the History of the Taiping Rebellion*, (Institute of Pacific Affairs, Cambridge, 1950)

TSOU LOU, *Reminiscences*, (Government Printing Office, Chungking, 1943)

NYM WALES, *Inside Red China*, (Doubleday, New York, 1939)

TSI C. WANG, *The Youth Movement in China*, (New Republic, New York, 1927)

VICTOR A. YAKHONTOFF, *The Chinese Soviets*, (Coward McCann, New York, 1934)

The sources of the translations of the more important documents written by Mao Tse-tung are:

The speeches delivered during the Kiangsi period are based on translations from Victor A. Yakhontoff, *The Chinese Soviets,* who obtained the documents from Miss Agnes Smedley.

The translations from *On a Prolonged War* I owe to the great kindness of Mr. L. A. Rossinger, of the Institute of Pacific Relations.

The translations from *Coalition Government* are based on the English mimeographed version published in Yenan, checked against the version given by Stuart Gelder, *The Chinese Communists.*

Complete translations of *The Strategic Problems of China's Revolutionary Wars* and *The Chinese Revolution and the Communist Party of China* are given in *China Digest.*

The translations from *The New Democracy* are based on the official version published by the U.S. State Department.

Our Task in 1945 is taken from the mimeographed version published in Yenan in 1945.

INDEX

A-B (Anti-Bolshevik) groups, 114, 119
Ah, Prince, 162
Ai Ching, 227, 235
Alexander the Great, 209
All-China Congress of Soviets, First, 126-130; Second, 130-135
All-China Federation of Labor, 160
All-China Labor Congress, First, 76
All-China Trade Union Federation, 95
All Men Are Brothers, 31, 101, 102, 146, 154, 166, 191, 210, 266
Americans in Eastern Asia, 15n.
Analects, The, 30, 61, 90, 158
Anhwei, 60, 85, 129, 130, 152, 159, 165, 243
Annihilation campaign, 145, 155, 170, 191, 198, 200, 205; first, 112-117, 119; second, 117-121; third, 121-125, 126, 236; fourth, 130; fifth, 104n., 130, 132, 137, 139, 154, 163, 192n., 270
Anshunch'ang, 148, 149, 150
Antaeus, 269
Anti-Comintern Pact, 161
Aristotle, 211
Art and Literature, 237
Attlee, Clement, 214
Autumn Harvest Uprising, 101, 102, 113, 246
"Awakening of the World, The," 8

Bakhunin, Mikhail, 13n., 55
Belden, Jack, 233

Bentham, Jeremy, 39
Beresford, Henry, 75
Bible, 6
Bonham, George, 12
Book of Celestial Decrees, 7
Book of Changes, The, 175
Book of Rites, 16, 18, 19
Borodin, Mikhail, 77, 78, 84, 87, 96, 97, 98, 100, 270
Browder, Earl, 87
Buddhism, 6, 10, 18, 25, 26, 27, 29, 31-32, 58, 101, 102
Bukharin, 68
Burckhardt, Jacob, 271

Caesar, Julius, 80
Canton, 4, 18, 22, 30, 42, 52, 53, 73, 76, 77, 78, 79, 80, 81, 82, 83, 86, 87n., 89, 90, 105, 106, 107, 127, 173, 248
Catherine the Great, 35
Challenge of Red China, The, 167n.
Chang Chih-tung, 36n.
Chang Chin-yao, 63, 70
Chang Chio, 8n.
Chang Hsien-chung, 6-7
Chang Hsueh-liang, 162-165
Chang Hui-chang, 115, 116
Chang Kuo-t'ao, 57, 72, 98, 102, 126, 128, 151, 152, 159, 164
Chang Shih-jo, 217
Chang Tai-lei, 98
Chang Tao-ling, 110
Chang Tso-lin, 72, 88

Changchow, 98n., 129
Changchun, 207
Changsha, 10, 11, 28, 29, 41, 42, 43, 50, 62, 71, 89, 90, 94, 95, 97, 98, 99, 101, 105, 106, 107, 123, 143, 144, 147, 242; battles of, 111, 112
Chao Heng-ti, 70
Chapei, 129
Chefoo, 207
Chekiang, 140
Chekuo, battle of, 200
Chen, Eugene, 97
Chen Li-fu, 169
Chen Ming-jen, 248
Chen Tu-hsiu, 56-60, 63, 64, 67, 68, 70, 71, 72, 76, 81, 83, 84-85, 87, 88, 91, 97, 98, 160, 240, 257, 258
Cheng Ch'en, 88, 248
Cheng Kung-po, 57, 72, 87n.
Chengtu, 21, 249
Chi-lai, 255-256
Chiang Kai-shek, 16, 23, 33, 45, 57, 72, 77, 78, 83, 84, 85-86, 88, 92, 95, 96, 97, 99, 112, 117, 119, 122, 129, 135, 141-142, 145, 157, 158, 162-165, 167, 169, 177, 180, 181, 183, 193, 199, 201, 203, 207, 214, 219, 226, 228n., 236, 264-269, 272; meeting of with Mao, 205-206; defeat of forces of, 241-262
Chiang Kai-shek, Mme., 214
Chiang Kan-fu, 46
Chiang Ting-wen, 123
Chieh-fang, 173
Chihli, 63
China Awake, 231n.
China Shakes the World, 233
China Socialist Youth League, First Congress of, 76
China's Destiny, 183, 268
Chinese Revolution and the Communist Party of China, The, 173, 184-190
Ch'ing dynasty, 223
Chingkanshan, 101-108, 109, 111, 113, 125, 140, 193, 231, 256
Chinwangtao, 206
Chiu Chiu-pei, 98
Chou dynasty, 32, 227, 228n., 264, 266

Chou En-lai, 74, 98, 99, 163, 167, 168, 205, 206, 255
Chou Fu-hai, 72
Chouping, 146
Christison, Charles, 270
Chu Kiu-t'ao, 9-11, 14, 16
Chu Shao-liang, 119
Chu Teh, 74, 99, 105-106, 108, 111, 113, 118, 129, 138, 139, 140, 145, 148, 152, 153, 154, 159, 161, 171, 194, 201, 204, 205, 206, 208, 211, 214, 215, 216, 218, 244, 250, 255, 259
Chu Yuan, 185
Chufu, 61
Chung-Fa (Chinese-French University), 53
Chung Wang (*see* Li Hsin-cheng)
Chungking, 21, 141, 160, 185, 190, 205, 207, 208, 228, 242, 247, 248, 249, 264
Coalition Government, 173, 194-199, 219
Comintern, 71, 73, 78, 82, 87, 92, 93, 96, 98, 100, 165, 270
Communist Party, Chinese, 54, 57, 64, 71, 76, 77, 78, 80, 81, 83, 86, 87, 91, 97, 98-99, 108, 144, 163, 177, 195, 234, 257; founding of, 71-74; First Congress of, 71-74; Second Congress of, 76; Third Congress of, 77; Fourth Congress of, 87; Fifth Congress of, 88; Sixth Congress of, 107, 194; Seventh Congress of, 194, 204, 242, 244
Communist Manifesto, 14, 47, 184, 265
Confucius, 6, 7, 16, 17, 18, 19, 20, 25, 27, 30-31, 32, 33, 39, 57, 58, 61-62, 90, 158, 171, 172, 175, 191, 233, 239, 251, 264, 265, 267, 271, 275
"Correcting Unorthodox Tendencies in Literature," 239

Darwin, Charles, 17, 37
De l'Esprit des Lois, 17, 35
Democracy and Narodism in China, 22

Dennet, Tyler, 13n.
Dewey, John, 69
Diligence - Labor - Simplicity - Educational - Society, 50
Doriot, Jacques, 87
Dream of the Red Chamber, The, 31, 34, 223, 228

Eighteenth Brumaire of Louis Buonaparte, The, 265
Emi Siao (*see* Hsiao Chu-chang)
"End of the Journey, The," 226
Evolution and Ethics, 17
"Evolution of Rites, The," 19

Fadeyev, Constantin, 234
Falkenhausen, General von, 131, 135
Fang Chih-min, 140
Fathers and Sons, 36
Feng Chien Tze (*see Wind Sand Poems*)
Feng Yu-hsiang, 27, 81, 154
Feng Yun-shan, 7, 14
"Fiery wall," 131, 135
"First engagement," 114, 120, 124
Five Objects of Knowledge, 36n.
Formosa, 269
Four Classics, 30, 34
French Indo-China, 21, 29, 220
Fu Ssu-nien, 54
Fuchow, 131, 248
Fukien, 11, 98n., 111, 113, 118, 119, 122, 125, 129, 131, 134, 136, 139, 140, 165, 191, 248
Futien, 114, 116, 119, 120, 123

Galliéni, Joseph, 48
Gladstone, William, 35
Gold Sand River (*see* Yangtse River)
Good Words Exhorting the Age, 5
Gordon, George, 15
Grable, Betty, 239
Grapes of Wrath, The, 238, 239
"Grass," 154, 225
Grasslands, 152-156
Great Heroes of the World, 35
Great Learning, The, 39

Great Revolution, 85-88
Great Snow Mountain, 151, 152
Great Wall, 160, 163, 166, 244
Guerrilla warfare, 103-105, 112-113, 120, 121, 123, 128, 139, 143, 155, 175, 190-194, 201, 202, 274

Hailofeng, 99, 102, 105
Hakka race, 4, 5
Han dynasty, 8n., 51, 61-62, 191, 223, 236
Han Teh-chin, 123
Han Ying, 126, 140, 170
Han Yu, 31-32, 56, 172
Hangchow, 76, 247
Hankow, 11, 43, 44, 51, 65, 87, 88, 90, 97, 100, 159, 173, 247, 270
Hanyang, 11, 192, 247
Hao Men-ling, 119
Hegel, G. W. F., 74
Henyang, 93, 100, 114
Herder, J. G. von, 269
Hindenburg, Paul von, 48
Hitler, Adolf, 45, 250, 271
Ho Chien, 95, 108, 111
Ho Lung, 102, 153
Ho Tzu-ch'un (*see* Mao Tse-tung, Mme., second wife of Mao)
Ho Ying-ching, 118-119, 123, 163, 164
Hobbes, Thomas, 39, 269
Hölderlin, Friedrich, 230
Honan, 63, 129, 130, 152, 159
Hong Kong, 21, 50, 76
"Horsemen of the Great Szechuan Road," 225
Hsi hsueh ("Western learning"), 39
Hsiang River, 10, 24, 41, 44, 85
Hsiang River Monthly Review, 63, 70
Hsiang T'an, 25, 28, 42, 89
Hsianghsiang, 33, 34, 42, 46, 89, 93
Hsiao Chu-chang (Hsiao San), 34-36, 41-42, 45, 46, 47, 49, 50, 53
Hsiao K'eh, 136, 141
Hsiao San (*see* Hsiao Chu-chang)
Hsien Tsung, 31
Hsin hsueh ("new learning"), 39
Hsin min ("new people"), 39

Hsin Min Chung Pao (*The New People's Journal*), 38-39, 40
Hsin Min Hsueh Hui ("New People's Study Organization"), 48, 49, 50, 63, 70, 100
Hsingkuo, 108, 110, 111, 112, 114, 116, 123, 125, 136, 137
Hsipei, 164, 165
Hsiung Hsi-ling, 21, 47, 271
Hsu Hsiang-ch'ien, 102, 141, 151, 154
Hsu Ko-chang, 94, 95, 116, 123
Hsu Teh-li, 50
Hsuan T'ung, 35
Hsueh Yueh, 147
Hu Han-min, 29, 40, 78-79, 80, 82, 84, 87n.
Hu Shih, 39, 55
Hu Tsung-nan, 162, 165
Huai-hai, battle of, 248
Huai Nan-tzu, 191
Huai River, 61
Hughes, E. R., 38n.
Hunan, 6, 9, 21, 24, 26, 28, 29, 30, 31, 42, 43, 51, 53, 55, 62-63, 70, 73, 76, 77, 79, 82, 85, 101, 106, 108, 112, 129, 132, 141, 154, 165, 211, 269; uprisings in, 88-101
"Hundred Regiment Campaign," 200
Hung Hsu-ch'uan, 4-16, 18
Hung Shan, 42, 89
Huns, 166, 224
Hupeh, 29, 85, 88, 102, 129, 130, 152, 159, 165
Hurley, Patrick, 206, 207
Huxley, T. H., 17, 37
Hwang Hsing, 28-29, 42, 43
Hwangpi, 123, 130

Ichang gorges, 169, 247
Indonesia, 220, 277
Inner History of the Chinese Revolution, 94n., 96n., 97n.
Inside Red China, 130n.
Interprovincial Peasant Union, 89
Invasion of China by the Western World, The, 38n.
Isaacs, Harold, 93n., 95n.

Journey to the West, The, 31, 154
Ju River, 117, 129
Juichin, 125, 130, 132, 140, 143, 147, 192n.

Kalgan, 36, 206
Kan River, 117, 119, 122, 129
Kang Hsi, 149
Kang Yu-wei, 17-21, 34, 35, 37, 38, 44, 58, 273
Kansu, 159, 248
Kautsky, Karl, 47
K'e Chung-ping, 230-231, 235
Kian, 114, 115, 116, 117, 122, 123, 124
Kiangsi, 27, 29, 85, 87n., 99, 101, 106, 108, 109, 110, 111, 112, 113, 114, 119, 122, 124, 129, 131, 135, 139, 140, 143, 147, 151, 155, 165, 170, 191, 204, 250, 269
Kiangsi Soviets, 134, 141, 152, 159, 168, 170, 179, 188, 190, 207
Kiangsu, 243
Kidd, Benjamin, 37-38
Kienning, 116, 118, 129
Kluck, Alexander von, 48
Ko Lao Hui ("Society of Elder Brothers"), 30, 31, 101
Ku Chu-tung, 170
Ku Yuan, 236-237
Kuling, 267
Kung, H. H., 264
Kung-ch'an-tang, 16
Kung Pin-pang, 116
Kung Ping-fan, 119
Kunming, 55, 67n., 144, 145, 146, 217, 243
Kuo Hua-tsung, 119, 120
Kuo Mo-jo, 243
Kuomintang, 16, 23, 42, 43, 47, 48, 51n., 57, 67n., 68, 72, 73, 75, 76, 77, 80, 81, 82, 83, 84, 85, 87, 88, 89, 90, 91, 94n., 96, 97, 98, 99, 100, 105, 106, 108, 110, 112, 114, 115, 116, 117, 121, 122, 123, 124, 126, 129, 130, 131, 132, 133, 135, 140, 141, 146, 147, 148, 149, 150, 152, 154, 155, 156, 158, 159, 160, 161, 166, 177, 178, 179, 181, 184, 188, 190, 192, 193, 194-199, 200,

201, 204, 206, 207, 208, 216, 217, 218, 226, 228, 233, 267, 273, 277; First National Congress of, 77, 79, 88; Communist agreement with, 167-169; defeat of forces of, 113, 241-262

Kutien, 112

Kwang Hsu, 20, 35

Kwangchang, 122, 123, 139

Kwangsi, 6, 8, 169, 248

Kwangtung, 4, 5, 6, 9, 11, 21, 30, 32, 75, 79, 85, 87n., 99, 122, 129, 162, 248, 250

Kwantung River, 33

Kweichow, 139, 141, 142, 143, 144, 145, 147, 248

Kweilin, 169, 248

Kweiyang, 144, 145, 248

Lanchow, 173, 248

Land titles, destruction of, 14

Lao pai hsing, 211

Lao Tzu, 216

Latinxua, 160-161

Lawrence, T. E., 274-275

League to Renovate Hunan, The, 63

Lenin, Nikolai, 22, 45, 52, 67, 77, 81, 89, 126, 134, 184, 235, 239, 257, 259, 260, 263

Leninism, 19, 67, 180

Li Han-ching, 72

Leyte, 201

Li Hsin-cheng, 11, 14, 15-16

Li Kung-po, 243

Li Li-san, 74, 98, 111, 112, 114, 128, 144-145, 160

Li Po, 271

Li Ta, 72

Li Ta-chao, 54, 67, 68, 70, 71, 72

Li Teh, 131, 136, 139, 145, 270

Li Tzu-ching, 166

Li Yuan-hung, 43

Liang A-fah, 5-6

Liang Chih-chao, 35, 37-38, 39-40, 45, 48, 58, 273, 278

Liberation Daily, 197, 221

Lienta University, 243

Lientang, 124

Lichuan, 129

Lilin, 28, 29, 41, 42, 89, 93, 100

Lin Piao, 139, 151, 152, 160, 200, 244

Lin Yu-tang, 3

Lincoln, Abraham, 35

Liu Ho-ting, 119

Liu Pang, 61

Liu Wei-han (*see* Lo Man)

Liuyang, 28, 29, 41, 93, 95, 100, 101

Lloyd George, David, 50

Lo An, 129, 130

Lo Ling, 115, 117

Lo Man, 49, 74, 98

Lo Min, 134

Lolos, 147, 150, 152, 248

"Long March, The," 226-227

London Missionary Society, 5

Long March, 137, 138-156, 157, 158, 160, 193, 215, 216, 226, 227

Lu Huan, 248

Lu Hsun, 172, 184, 239-240

Lu Hsun Academy, 235

Lu Ti-ping, 114

Luce, Henry, 253

Lung Yun, 169

Lungkow, 207

"Lure enemy deep penetration," 114, 128

Luther, Martin, 272-273, 274, 275

Lutingch'iao, 148, 149, 150

Ma An-shan Pass, 151

Ma Hung-kuei, 248

MAGIC, 207

Mahan, Admiral, 276

Mailla, Father de, 7

Malin, 73

Manchukuo, 162

Manchuria, 27, 124, 126, 129, 160, 163, 201, 208, 243, 244

Manchus, 3, 4, 6, 9, 11, 12, 13, 14, 15, 16, 17, 18, 20-21, 25, 27, 30, 35, 43, 44, 51, 166, 241, 242, 246-247, 267, 269

Mantzus, 153, 154

Manuilsky, Dmitri, 135

Mao Jen-sheng, 25, 26, 27, 33, 50

Mao Pin-wen, 116, 123

Mao Tse-hung, 25

Mao Tse-t'an, 25, 102
Mao Tse-tung, Mme. (first wife of Mao), 56, 60, 143, 225
Mao Tse-tung, Mme. (second wife of Mao), 143, 214, 215
Mao Tun, 166
Marshall, George, 207, 243
Marshall, Humphrey, 11, 12-13
Marx, Karl, 37, 38, 40, 46, 67, 184, 265
Marxism, 19, 32, 37, 67, 69, 71, 74, 76, 180, 253, 270, 273
May Fourth Movement, 64-71, 75, 85, 181
May Thirtieth Movement, 85, 145
Mayakovsky, 235
Mencius, 62, 251, 273
Miaos, 24, 147
Michaux, Henri, 264
Mienninghsien, 148
Miff, Pavel, 71, 87, 144
Mill, John Stuart, 7
Min Pao, 40, 47, 79
Ming dynasty, 7, 9, 18, 166
Molotov, V. V., 258
Montesquieu, Charles de, 17, 35, 39, 278
Mosaic law, 8
Mukden Incident, 124
Muraviev, Nikolai, 13n.

Namyung, 110
Nananfu, 110
Nanchang, 99, 111, 119, 122, 248
Nanfeng, 118, 120, 130
Nankai University, 67n.
Nanking, 11, 14, 15, 66, 86, 87, 88, 97, 134, 135, 161, 164, 167, 168, 177, 209, 218, 243, 244, 247
Napoleon Bonaparte, 35, 44, 174, 191, 211, 275
Nazi-Soviet Pact, 180
Nehru, Jawaharlal, 272
New Deal, 182
New Democracy, The, 58, 68, 173, 179-184, 186, 270
New Fourth Army Incident, 169-170, 190, 200
New Stage, The, 177-179, 184, 219
New Youth, 56, 58, 65, 240

Nietzsche, Friedrich, 59
Nineteen, The, 234
Ningtu, 117

On Liberty, 17
On a Prolonged War, 173-179
Opium War, 3, 186
Ordos Desert, 160
Origin of Species, The, 17
"Our Task in 1945," 201
Owen, Robert, 46

Pai Hsiung-hsi, 249
Pailingmiao, 162
Pao An, 156, 157-158, 159, 161, 166, 168
Pao Hui-sheng, 72
"Patmos," 230
Peach Blossom Fountain, 185, 208
Peking, 7, 9, 11, 12, 15, 17, 19, 21, 30, 44, 50, 52, 53, 55-56, 60, 63, 64-70, 72, 81, 86, 206, 208, 209, 224, 240, 247, 254, 255, 256, 260, 263, 268
Peking Man, 250-251
Peking National University, 53, 54, 63, 64, 65, 67n., 69, 71, 72, 94, 102
Peng Kung-ta, 98
Peng Teh-huei, 108, 111, 139, 143, 152, 159, 168, 171, 208, 213, 215, 218
People's Democratic Republic of China, 255
Peoples' Government, 168
Peoples' Red Army, 168
Peter the Great, 35
Pien hua ("reform"), 39
Pinghsiang, 28, 29
Pinghsinkuan, battle of, 200
Pingkiang, 100
Po Ku, 134, 163
Po Yi, 32
"Poem of Farewell, A," 224-225
Political Daily, The, 83
Positional warfare, 139, 145, 146, 174, 191, 202
Potsdam, 258
Pravda, 71
Principles of Sociology, The, 17

Principles of Western Civilisation, 37

Races of China, 51
Red Star over China, 56n., 72n., 138
Reformers, 17-21, 34, 38, 40, 48 (*see also* Reform party)
Reform party, 35, 37, 44, 50, 273 (*see also* Reformers)
Revelations of the Heavenly Father, The, 7
"rifle brigades," 101
"Ring of iron," 141
Rousseau, Jean Jacques, 35, 39
Roy, Manabendra Nath, 87, 96, 98

Saishangah, 9
Sankolinsin, General, 11
Seven Pillars of Wisdom, 274
Shanghai, 11, 12, 13, 18, 19, 50, 53, 60, 62, 66, 71, 76, 77, 80, 81, 83, 85, 86, 87, 88, 90, 100, 107, 117, 127, 131, 155, 243, 248, 250, 257
Shankuan Yun-hsiang, 123, 170
Shansi, 165, 247
Shantung, 63, 64, 79, 166
Shao Li-tse, 72
Shao Shan, 25, 30, 33, 34, 50, 76, 81
Shensi, 72, 139, 140, 143, 152, 154, 155, 157, 158, 159, 160, 165, 171, 207, 212, 215, 226, 233, 236, 238, 263, 267, 268, 269
Shih Ta-k'ai, 16, 148
Shih Tseng-tung, 72
Shihchiachuang, 244, 245
Shihpingchieh, battle at, 207
Shjahrir, Soetan, 272
Sian, 61, 166, 247
Sian incident, 72, 161-166, 167, 209
Sikang, 149, 248
Singapore, 201
Singkiang, 248, 260
Sino-Japanese War, 168, 169, 170, 173-178, 183, 185, 192, 200-205, 241, 267
Slogans, military, 103-104, 113-114, 125, 171, 202, 203
Smedley, Agnes, 106, 131

Smith, Adam, 17
Smith, George, 11
"Snow, The," 216, 228-230
Snow, Edgar, 26, 56n., 72n., 139, 224, 250, 270-271
Socialism, 46-47, 86, 180-181, 187; British, 167n., 219
Soong, T. V., 258
Spanish Republic, 217
Spencer, Herbert, 17, 37, 38, 40
Spinoza, Benjamin, 39
Spring and Autumn Annals, The, 191
Spring and Autumn Dynasties, 104, 177
Ssu-ma Chien, 61
Stalin, Joseph, 82, 92, 96, 134, 188, 214, 250, 271; Mao's visit to, 258-260
Stein, Gunther, 167n.
Steinbeck, John, 238
Stoler, Sydor, 94
Strategic Problems of China's Revolutionary Wars, The, 48, 121, 137, 139, 145, 173, 190-194, 256, 273
Su Tsung, 223
Suiyan-Mongolian Autonomy Council, 162
Sun Wu, 104-105, 191
Sun Yat-sen, 16, 21-23, 28, 29, 31, 42, 44, 47, 50, 52, 58, 73, 76, 77, 78, 79, 80, 81, 82, 84, 85, 87n., 88, 91, 100, 110, 180, 182, 186, 198, 213, 257, 263
Sung dynasty, 18
Sung Jang-kung, 177
Sung Lien-chung, 119
Swan Lake, 259
Swatow, 99
Szechuan, 7, 11, 21, 29, 73, 97, 102, 129, 139, 141, 143, 147, 149, 150, 151, 152, 159, 165, 169, 248

Ta Kung Pao, 208, 228
Ta Tung, 19, 20, 31, 38
Ta-wei, 151
Tai Chi-tao, 72
T'ai Shan, 61-62
Taiping Ching, 8n.

Taiping rebellion, 8-16, 17, 21, 29, 37, 77, 134, 148, 232-233, 264, 267, 269
Taiping Tienkuo, 8
Taiyuan, 162, 247
Taku, 15
Tan Tao-yuan, 115-116
T'ang dynasty, 56, 59, 110, 209, 212, 223, 227, 236
Tang Leang-li, 94n., 96n., 97n.
Tang Ping-shan, 84, 94, 95, 97
Tang Sheng-shih, 88
Tang Yen-kai, 70, 88
Taoism, 6, 8n., 10, 19, 32, 55, 58, 110
Tapoteh, battle of, 110-111
Tatu River, 16, 139, 147
Tennessee Valley Authority, 182
"terminus of withdrawal," 114, 117, 120
Three Kingdoms, The, 31
Three Principles of the People, The, 22, 23, 80, 167n., 168, 177, 183
Tibet, 16, 141, 145, 146, 154, 156
Tien ("heaven"), 58
Tien An Men ("Gate of Heavenly Peace"), 65, 275
Tien Ch'ien, 227, 235
Tien Teh (*see* Hung Hsu-ch'uan)
Tientsin, 50, 53, 60, 65, 206, 247
Tolstoy, Leo, 214
Toupi, 116
Tragedy of the Chinese Revolution, The, 93n., 95n.
Trimetrical Classic, 7, 30
Truman, Harry S., 214
Tsai Ao, 47
Tsai Ho-sheng, 98
Tsai Ting-kai, 117, 120, 128, 131
Tsai Yuan-pei, 50, 56, 59, 65-66, 69
Tsao Ju-lin, 65
Tsao Yu, 250
Ts'en Ts'an, 56, 223-225
Tseng Kuo-fan, 15, 16, 267
Tsinghua University, 67n.
Tsingtao, 248
Tso Chuan, 266
Tsou Lu, 87n.
Tsunyi, 144-147, 158, 194, 204

Tu Fu, 166, 223
T'u-hao, 91, 93
Tuan Chih-jui, 62
Tung Men Hui, 28
Tung Ting Lake, 51, 62
Tungchow, 116, 146
Tungku, 108, 110, 111, 112, 114, 115, 116, 120, 121, 122, 123, 124
Tungpei, 162, 164, 165
Turgenev, Ivan, 36
TVA, 182
Twenty-One Demands on China, 64, 65

Voitinsky, Grigori, 73

Wang Chin-yu, 119, 120
Wang, Tsi C., 59n.
Wales, Nym, 129-130, 163
Walk in the Sun, A, 239
Wang Chia-lieh, 144
Wang Ching-wei, 29, 40, 80, 81, 82, 83, 84, 86, 87n., 88, 94, 96, 186, 188
Wang Jo-fei, 205, 208
Wang Tso, 102, 108
War and Peace, 214
Ward, Frederick Townsend, 15
Washington, George, 35
Wealth of Nations, 17
Wedemeyer, A. C., 206
Wei Li-huang, 168, 200
Weihaiwei, 207
Wellington, Arthur Wellesley, Duke of, 35
Wen, Duke, 264
Wen Yi-tuo, 57, 67n., 217, 235, 243
Whampoa Military Academy, 80, 83, 84, 170
White-Haired Woman, The, 231-233
White Lotus society, 6
Whittlesey Hall, 201
Wind Sand Poems, 154, 225, 230
Workers' and Peasants' Army, 168
Workers' and Peasants' Government, 168
Wu Chih-hui, 257
Wu Pei-fu, 63, 73
Wu River, 142

Wu San-kuei, 166
Wuchang, 11, 247
Wuhan, 43, 85, 86, 88, 91, 92, 93, 94, 95, 97, 101

Yang Chen-chi, 46, 50, 53, 54, 55
Yang Hsiu-ch'ing, 14-15
Yang K'ai-hui (*see* Mao Tse-tung, Mme., first wife of Mao)
Yang-k'o, 209, 234, 256
Yang Shan-k'un, 163-164, 209, 212, 216
Yangtse River, 11, 12, 14, 21, 50, 85, 87, 98, 126, 141, 145, 147, 249, 254
Yeh Chien-ying, 163
Yeh Ming-shen, 11
Yeh Ting, 99, 105, 170, 208
Yellow Flower Mound, 42
Yellow River, 244
"Yellow River Cantata," 208
Yellow Turbans, 8n.
Yen Fu, 17-21, 37

Yen Hsi-shan, 165
Yen Huei, 61, 275
Yen River, 201
Yenan, 50, 59, 61, 113, 138, 139, 154, 161, 163, 164, 166, 168, 171, 188, 193, 194, 201, 203, 204, 205, 206, 207, 208, 209, 210, 211, 212, 215, 216, 218, 220, 222, 228, 230, 234, 235, 236, 237, 238, 242, 244, 245, 268, 269, 272
Yenan Observation Group, 201, 238
Yin dynasty, 32
Yoffe, Adolf, 78, 88
Youth Movement in China, The, 59n.
Yuan Shih-kai, 44, 47, 48, 51, 54, 58, 75, 105, 241, 242, 269
Yuan Wen-tsai, 102, 108
Yunganchow, 8, 9, 11, 14
Yungfeng, 114, 116, 120
Yunnan, 145, 147, 152, 169, 248
Yutu, 122, 136, 140
Yuying, 140